# Spirit of '67

# Spirit of '67

## *The Cardiac Kids, El Birdos, and the World Series That Captivated America*

Thomas J. Whalen

ROWMAN & LITTLEFIELD
*Lanham • Boulder • New York • London*

Published by Rowman & Littlefield
A wholly owned subsidiary of The Rowman & Littlefield Publishing Group, Inc.
4501 Forbes Boulevard, Suite 200, Lanham, Maryland 20706
www.rowman.com

Unit A, Whitacre Mews, 26-34 Stannary Street, London SE11 4AB



British Library Cataloguing in Publication Information Available

**Library of Congress Cataloging-in-Publication Data Available**

ISBN 978-1-4422-3316-4 (cloth : alk. paper)
ISBN 978-1-4422-3317-1 (electronic)

∞™ The paper used in this publication meets the minimum requirements of American National Standard for Information Sciences—Permanence of Paper for Printed Library Materials, ANSI/NISO Z39.48-1992.

Printed in the United States of America

*For my students*

# Contents

# Preface

NO ONE COULD EVER ACCUSE BOB GIBSON OF BEING SOFT. PITCHING against the Pittsburgh Pirates in a home game on July 15, 1967, the towering St. Louis Cardinals right-hander found himself on the receiving end of a Roberto Clemente line drive up the middle. "[Clemente] hits the inside pitch very well so I tried to get the ball away, on the outside part of the plate," Gibson remembered. "I got it away, but not far enough. I got it over the middle of the plate. Two inches farther away and he would not have hit the ball so hard. He might not have hit it at all." But Clemente—a future Baseball Hall of Famer—solidly connected on the pitch and the ball made a beeline toward the mound, fracturing the fibula bone above Gibson's right ankle.

Gibson collapsed to the ground in agony. "The bone was broken when I got hit," he said. "The break was there, and when I twisted my weight on the leg with the last pitch, two parts of the bone popped loose." Cardinals trainer Doc Bauman rushed to his side, but Gibson refused to be taken out of the ballgame. "Just put a little tape on it, Doc," Gibson instructed. Returning to the mound, Gibson somehow pitched to three more Pittsburgh batters before his right leg gave out completely and he had to leave the contest. "I felt something snap and I tumbled to the ground," he said.

Years later teammate Dal Maxvill was still trying to process what he had witnessed. "That was the most extraordinary thing I ever saw in baseball—Gibby pitching to those batters with a broken leg," the Cardinals shortstop told author Roger Angell. "Everyone who was there that day remembered it afterward, for always, and every young pitcher who came onto our club while Gibson was still with us was told about it. We didn't have too many pitchers turning up with upset stomachs or hangnails on our team after that."

The entire 1967 baseball season was not for the faint of heart. For the year witnessed one of the most extraordinary pennant races in history and a World Series that pitted two proud old franchises with embarrassing records on race and integration overcome their checkered pasts to deliver a great Fall Classic.

The St. Louis Cardinals and Boston Red Sox truly embodied the spirit of '67. The following pages tell their story and the uniquely special times in which they lived.

# Acknowledgments

As a former high school and college cross-country runner, I can attest from personal experience that writing a book is an awful lot like surviving a long-distance race. There is a fair amount of aches and pains along the way, but the end result is hugely satisfying.

Of course, I had plenty of help in achieving my goal, starting with my wise and supportive book editor Jon Sisk. Jon smoothly guided me through the entire publishing process while keeping me abreast of the latest baseball news and player transactions. He has been a joy to work with.

Former *Harvard Crimson* outfielder Elizabeth Crowley reviewed several chapters of my first draft and provided invaluable advice on how to improve the final manuscript. She is a true All-Star both as an editor and as a friend.

Old high school chums Chris Callely and Don Clemenzi boosted my spirits at critical points along the way. I am forever in their debt. Ditto for fellow seamheads Chris Fahy and Andy Andres. Together we teach an interdisciplinary baseball course at Boston University (BU) and love every second of it. They help keep my love for the game alive.

BU Dean Natalie J. McKnight graciously granted me a sabbatical leave from my teaching to complete the book. Although a diehard Pittsburgh Pirates fan, Natalie saw the value of this project from the beginning. I can't thank her enough. Additional debts of gratitude are owed to Sarah Coffin and the late great Dick Bresciani of the Red Sox who opened the team's archives to me. The staff of the Baseball Hall of Fame was equally helpful.

Others for whose strong support I'd like to thank are the following: Steve and Jodi Blumenkrantz, Gayle Clemenzi, Dan and Mary Hammond, Tom Testa, Bobby Connors, Joseph and Kristin King, Scott Ferrera, Joseph and Theresa Dever, Barbara Storella, Illana Rosen, Fred Hammond, Neil Leavitt, Pat and Hillori Connors, Laureen Fitzgerald, Bill and Nancy Cook, Katherine Hammond, Greg Morose, Ross Madore, Alyse Bithavas-Glac, Jessica Angotti, Joe Breiner, Kira Jastive, Mary Tunney, John Lyons, Tracey Knickerson, Stacy Godnick, and Bob Oresick.

Finally, former student Makinna Akers deserves a special shout out. A standout pitcher with the BU Terriers, Makinna selflessly volunteered her time and talents as a research assistant over the past three years. I wish her well in her future career as a professional athletic trainer.

# Chapter One

# 1967

In the December 1967 issue of the satirical humor magazine *Mad*, a parody of the popular sci-fi television series *Star Trek* appeared on its pages. The piece featured a certain pointy-eared science officer ("Mr. Spook") notifying his dashing square-jawed commander ("Captain Kook") that their space vessel (the "Star Ship Booby Prize") was hopelessly caught in a time warp. The anomaly was taking them back to "the ***Pre-Historic Ages*** . . . when Man was **savage** and **bloodthirsty** and **cruel**!" "You mean . . . ," Kook asks. "**Yes**—we're headed for **1967**!!" Spook answers.

Nineteen sixty-seven was an *annus horribilis*. War, racial tensions, urban riots, massive protests, and countercultural upheaval all marked this seminal point in American history. At the center of the maelstrom stood Lyndon Baines Johnson. This "accidental president," who had come to power in the aftermath of John F. Kennedy's assassination four years earlier, was at a political crossroads. Cloaking himself in the mantle of the martyred Kennedy, Johnson began his presidency with impressive legislative accomplishments such as the Civil Rights Act, Head Start, the Voting Rights Act, Medicare, Job Corps, Medicaid, Upward Bound, and federal aid for higher education. The tall, jug-eared Democrat from the Texas Hill Country claimed he wanted to create a "Great Society" where poverty and racial injustice would be eradicated and social and economic opportunity existed for all. "It is a place where men are more concerned with the quality of their goals than the quantity of their goods," he said. "But most of all, the Great Society is not a safe harbor, a resting place,

1967 Antiwar Protest in Washington, D.C. PHOTOGRAPH BY WARREN K. LEFFLER, COURTESY OF THE LIBRARY OF CONGRESS PRINTS AND PHOTOGRAPHS ONLINE CATALOG, U.S. NEWS & WORLD REPORT MAGAZINE PHOTOGRAPH COLLECTION

a final objective, a finished work. It is a challenge constantly renewed, beckoning us toward a destiny where the meaning of our lives matches the marvelous products of our labor."

Yet Johnson, having won the presidency in his own right with a historic landslide victory over Republican nominee Barry Goldwater in 1964, hit a major political rut in 1967. Public support for his ambitious domestic reform program was on the wane, as evidenced by the large number of congressional seats Republicans had gained during the 1966 midterm elections. The Democrats still retained majority control in the House of Representatives and the Senate, but the electoral results were going to make it "exceedingly difficult for Johnson to muster a majority for his [progressive] agenda," noted Special Assistant to the President Joseph Califano. Refusing to openly acknowledge the new political reality, Johnson characteristically attempted to put his best spin on the situation. "As a good American," he said, "I think we are all glad to see a healthy and competent existence of a two party system." No one believed him. For the crux of Johnson political troubles lay not in the number of Republicans elected to high office but in a conflict-ridden land 8,000 miles away—South Vietnam.

Under the inept and corrupt leadership of a series of United States–backed regimes, the small Southeast Asia country had been unsuccessfully waging a decade-long war against North Vietnamese communists, who were conducting large-scale guerilla operations in the south alongside local rebel groups and sympathizers. As the tide of battle worsened, the former French colony appeared in danger of collapse, a situation the president found unacceptable. For Johnson was a firm adherent of the domino theory—the popular Cold War belief that if any society fell to the Marxist-Leninist allies of the Soviet Union or Red China, then all countries bordering it would suffer the same fate. Playing out this dire scenario, the security of the entire free world would be put at risk. "You see," Johnson later told his biographer Doris Kearns Goodwin, "I was sure as any man could be that once we showed how we weak we were, Moscow and Peking would move in a flash to exploit our weakness. They might move independently or they might move together. But move they would—whether through nuclear blackmail, through subversion, with regular armed forces or in some other manner. As nearly as anyone can be certain of anything. I knew they couldn't resist the opportunity to expand their control over the vacuum of power we would leave behind us. And so would begin World War III."

To prevent such a cataclysm, LBJ felt the United States had to take a firm stand in South Vietnam. So he poured hundreds of thousands of American combat troops into the country while ordering a massive bombing campaign ("Rolling Thunder") of the North. But the communist infiltration of the South continued. By 1967, the president's generals were lobbying him to use even greater military force, which meant more boots on the ground and intensified air attacks on enemy strategic targets. But Defense Secretary Robert McNamara, who had developed strong reservations about America's widening role in Vietnam, urged restraint. "There is, in my opinion, a very real question whether under these circumstances it will be possible to maintain our efforts in South Vietnam for the time necessary to accomplish our objectives there," he

President Lyndon B. Johnson visits Cam Ranh Bay, South Vietnam in the fall of 1966. LBJ LIBRARY PHOTO BY YOICHI OKAMOTO

argued. Seeking a diplomatic solution, McNamara called for a unilateral bombing halt. "The bombing halt would have dual objectives," he claimed. "We would hope for a response from Hanoi, by some parallel reduction in its offensive activity by a movement toward [peace] talks or both. At a minimum, the lack of any kind of response from Hanoi would demonstrate it is North Vietnam and not the United States that is blocking a peaceful settlement."

Johnson, who had campaigned as a peace candidate in 1964, rejected the advice of both sides. On the one hand, he believed any cessation of the bombing would convey to the communists a message of America's "weakening will" in the ongoing war effort. On the other, he feared expanding the military footprint would be too provocative. "I thought," Johnson later wrote in his memoirs, "we should continue to hit significant targets but I insisted we weigh heavily in each case whether U.S. losses might be excessive and whether any strike might increase the risk of Peking or Moscow becoming more involved. I wanted to remove as much drama as possible from our bombing effort while doing what had to be done." Put another way, LBJ was trying to steer a middle course when it came to Vietnam policy.

Unfortunately, this temporizing approach satisfied no one, least of all the thousands of Americans who had taken to the streets across the country voicing their opposition to the war. The protesters—many young and college-educated—had reached the conclusion the war was immoral, needlessly claiming the lives of Vietnamese civilians and American soldiers alike. "Hey, Hey, LBJ, How Many Kids Did You Kill Today?" became a popular chant at antiwar rallies. The biggest occurred in late October at the Pentagon in Washington, D.C. A crowd estimated to be over 100,000 strong marched on the fabled symbol of US military might, burning draft cards and facing off against federal marshals and heavily armed soldiers guarding the building. "We are here not for a confrontation with the privates and corporals and sergeants, but for a confrontation with our Government," claimed one participant wielding a bullhorn. "We want to come to this building, which is the single greatest center of war in the history of the world, and say, 'Peace, peace, peace.'"

For those observing from inside the Pentagon, the protest had an unpredictable, if surreal quality about it. "Here it is," remembered assistant defense secretary Leslie Gelb, "a huge mob. . . . You watch for a while in a kind of amazement and horror. You didn't know what they were going to do, whether there would be shooting." What Gelb and his fellow Pentagon workers ended up getting was a front-row seat to mayhem. "We saw at first individuals in the front lines [of the demonstration] being dragged behind the troop lines and carried away," wrote Margie Stamberg of the *Washington Free Press*. "Suddenly, the troops which had been in single rows in front of the crowd formed into a wedge on the right side. . . . Slowly the wedge began to move in on people. With bayonets and rifle butts, they moved first on the girls in the front line, kicking them, jabbing at them again and again with the guns, busting their heads and arms to break the chain of locked arms. The crowd appealed to the paratroopers to back off, to join them, to just act human. They sang the 'Star Spangled Banner' and other songs: but the troops at this point were non-men, the appeals were futile."

Over 650 people were arrested, including best-selling novelist Norman Mailer, who likened the melee to "a harbinger of what will come next . . . if the war doesn't end next year." "Armed authorities usually over-react to civil disorder," the student-run *Harvard Crimson* offered. "But this is no excuse for the behavior of many of the troops this weekend. They should have known that the demonstrators were not lawless thugs, bent on ravaging the insides of the Pentagon." Indeed, one young turtleneck-wearing protester attempted to convey this message by gently placing carnations in the rifle barrels of several of the troops. The moment was famously captured by *Washington Star* photographer Bernie Boston and distributed around the world. Whether such benign acts of protest registered with those in power remained unclear. "I was not terribly sympathetic," Gelb later admitted. "Now, if you ask people who were in the Pentagon but not in uniform, most of them will say, 'Oh, I agreed with the protesters. I was already against the war, but I couldn't say it. . . .' That's all bullshit."

A prominent voice adding gravitas to the swelling chorus of protest was that of famed civil rights leader Dr. Martin Luther King Jr. Earlier that spring, King had publicly denounced America's ongoing involvement in the war as "madness." The South Vietnamese "languish under our bombs and consider us, not their fellow Vietnamese, the real enemy," he told a gathering of concerned antiwar clergymen and lay people at the Riverside Church in New York City. "They know they must be moved on [from their homes and villages] or be destroyed by our bombs." King added that the war was having a corrosive effect on the moral psyche of America's young fighting men, a disproportionate number of who came from black, poor, and disadvantaged backgrounds. "For it occurs to me," he said, "that what we are submitting them to in Vietnam is not simply the brutalizing process that goes on in any war where armies face each other and seek to destroy. We are adding cynicism to the process of death, for they must know after a short period there that none of the things we claim to be fighting for [democracy and freedom] are really involved." He also saw "cruel irony" in that "Negro and white boys" were fighting and dying for a country that was "unable to seat them together at the same schools." King demanded a unilateral withdrawal of all American troops from Vietnam as a necessary precondition for a final peace settlement.

King—a former Nobel Peace Prize winner—had been initially reluctant to speak out from fear of offending the Johnson administration, a longtime political ally in the fight to secure civil rights and antipoverty legislation. But King reached the conclusion that the historic and moral urgency of the moment trumped such concerns. "Now it should be incandescently clear that no one who has any concern for the integrity and life of America today can ignore the present war," he said. "If America's soul becomes totally poisoned, part of the autopsy must read 'Vietnam.' It can never be saved so long as it destroys the deepest hopes of men the world over. . . . This is a calling that takes me beyond national allegiances."

King's impassioned remarks were roundly panned in the press. Labeling them "wasteful" and "self-defeating," a *New York Times* editorial predicted King's political strategy of linking the peace and civil rights movements on this issue would prove "disastrous for both causes." "As an individual, Dr. King has the right and even the moral obligation to explore the ethical implications of the war in Vietnam, but as one of the most respected leaders of the civil rights movement he has an equally weighty obligation to direct that movement's efforts in the most constructive and relevant way [toward addressing racial inequality]. . . . Linking these hard, complex problems will lead not to solutions but to deeper confusion." *Reader's Digest* didn't pull any punches either. "King," the popular family magazine claimed, "has alienated many of the Negro's friends and armed the Negro's foes, in both parties, by creating the impression that the Negro is disloyal. . . . [H]e has taken a tack that many Americans of all races consider irresponsible." Despite the harshness of these attacks, King held his ground. "The war in Vietnam is a much greater injustice to Negroes than anything I could say against that war," he said.

Truth be told, King's dream of a harmonious, racially integrated society appeared to be coming off the rails in 1967. Prompted by persistently high levels of black unemployment, poverty, and discrimination, race riots broke out in several major urban metropolitan areas. Detroit, Michigan, was the worst. Triggered by a police raid on an unlicensed drinking establishment frequented by local African Americans, the Motown riot unfolded over five violent days in late July and claimed the lives of 43 people—33 blacks and 10 whites. "Firebombers and looters struck in commercial districts in almost every area of the city—north, east and west," the *New York Times* reported. "Variety stores and shops of every description were put to the torch over a 14-square-mile-area of the city. Windows were smashed at Saks Fifth Avenue in the shadow of the General Motors headquarters." Looters carried away armfuls of stolen merchandise as the fires spread, resulting in $50 million in property damage and over 7,000 arrests. "It looks like Berlin in 1945," Detroit Mayor Jerome P. Cavanagh said.

Pitched gun battles between rioters and authorities erupted over several city blocks. "If we see anyone move, we shoot and ask questions later," one on-duty National Guardsman said. The mayhem ended when paratroopers from the US Army's 82nd and 101st Airborne Divisions were called in to restore order. "We will not tolerate lawlessness," said Lyndon Johnson in a nationally televised address on the crisis. "We will not endure violence. It matters not by whom it is done, or under what slogan or banner. It will not be tolerated. This nation will do whatever it is necessary to do to suppress and to punish those who engage in it." King could only stand back in horror and dismay. "The turmoil of the ghetto is the externalization of the Negro's inner torment and rage," he declared.

Culturally, things appeared to be teetering on the brink as well. The traditional conservative values and rigid conformity of the 1950s and early 1960s had given way to the "Summer of Love"—a time of bold new experimentation, evolving interpretations of community and alternative lifestyles. Many young Americans—now representing the demographic majority of the nation's population—rejected the staid middle-class mores of their parents and flocked to places like the Haight-Ashbury district of San Francisco, California, a popular haven for street artists, would-be poets, and runaways. These countercultural dropouts or "hippies" as they were more widely known were all about living for the moment and flaunting societal conventions. They were sexually promiscuous, rejected mass consumerism, sported long hair and beards, and preferred tie-dyed T-shirts to three-piece suits. "You want to know what a hippie is," one of these self-identified "flower children" offered. "A hippie is a young person who older people in authority feel is having more fun than they think he should having. That's what a hippie is."

Use of hallucinogenic drugs like LSD became widespread among hippies and other youth as self-proclaimed generational gurus like former Harvard psychology professor Timothy Leary claimed they were pathways to higher forms of consciousness. "Leary was a charming and manipulative hustler," remembered Dr. David Smith, a former LSD user who was later interviewed by author Tom Brokaw for his 2007 best-selling book *Boom! Voices of the Sixties*. "He was a merry medicine man—although a PhD and not a MD—peddling his message and his tabs of LSD from coast to coast, often just a step ahead of the law." The drugs were often consumed to the loud psychedelic sounds of rock bands such as The Rolling Stones, Jefferson Airplane, the Grateful Dead, and, most famously of all, The Beatles.

Since their spectacular American television debut on *The Ed Sullivan Show* in 1964, the British quartet of John Lennon, Paul McCartney, George Harrison, and Ringo Starr had produced one chart-topping hit after another, including "I Want to Hold Your Hand," "Can't Buy Me Love," "A Hard Day's Night," and "Help!" They popularized mop-top hairdos and ankle-high boots while adding the term "Beatlemania" to the English language to describe the intense emotional attachment their young fans had for them. But the group was going through some dramatic changes in 1967. Physically and emotionally exhausted from years of touring around the world, they announced they would become exclusively a studio band, focused on producing albums only. "We'd had enough of performing forever," Lennon later said. "I couldn't imagine any reason that would have made us do any sort of tour again. We were all very tired. It did nothing for us anymore. That was really unfair to the fans, we knew, but we had to think of ourselves."

Their decision led to one of the greatest rock albums ever recorded—*Sgt. Pepper's Lonely Hearts Club Band.* Released in early June, the album flew off the record shelves in America and Europe, prompting the music critic Langdon Winner to observe it "was the closest Western Civilization has come to unity since the Congress of Vienna in 1818." Influenced, in part, by the LSD the Beatles were taking at the time, *Sgt. Pepper's* was filled with trippy numbers like Lennon's "Lucy in the Sky with Diamonds," which appeared to be describing an acid trip. "Picture yourself in a boat on a river," the song memorably began. "With tangerine trees and Marmalade skies." Unsurprisingly, drug maven Timothy Leary was filled with rapturous admiration. "I declare the Beatles are mutants," he said. "Prototypes of evolutionary agents, sent by God, endowed with a mysterious power to create a new human species, a young race of laughing freemen."

The Beatles didn't feel like evolutionary agents. Burned out by fame and devastated by the suicide of their longtime business manager Brian Epstein, they sought spiritual comfort and guidance from the Maharishi Mahesh Yogi, a publicity savvy Indian seer who traveled throughout the West spreading his faith in transcendental meditation. "I teach a simple system . . . that gives people the insight into life to begin enjoying all peace and happiness," the Maharishi said. Meeting with him first in London and later in India, the Beatles for a time became the Maharishi's devoted followers until the holy man reportedly made unwanted sexual advances on one of their friends. "We made a mistake," McCartney admitted afterward. "We thought there was more to him than there was. He's human. We thought at first he wasn't."

The Beatles' runaway success inspired a wildly popular American copycat act—The Monkees. Conceived by up-and-coming film producers Bob Rafelson and Bert Schneider, who went on to make such cinematic classics as *Easy Rider* and *Five Easy Pieces*, *The Monkees* debuted in 1966 as a network television sitcom about four young aspiring musicians—Michael Nesmith, Peter Tork, Micky Dolenz, and Davy Jones—trying to fulfill their dreams of rock stardom. During their comic misadventures, this "Prefab Four" overcame such varied obstacles as prying landlords, organized crime bosses, foreign spies, mad scientists, overweening magazine journalists, and even the occasional extraterrestrial. But the highlight of each episode was a Monkees' song, which invariably became a Top 20 hit. While no one confused "Last Train to Clarksville," "Pleasant Valley Sunday," or "I'm a Believer" with anything in the Lennon-McCartney songbook, these catchy pop tunes nevertheless struck a pleasing chord among younger fans, who might have been confused by the adult drug references on the *Sgt. Pepper's* album. As one former Beatles enthusiast put it, "You saw the Monkees on TV and you saw their personalities; the Monkees included me in their clubhouse; I could enter their world. The Beatles world was too hard to figure out. You didn't get to hear the Beatles talk; they stopped interacting with you."

An instant ratings hit, *The Monkees* won an Emmy Award in 1967 for Outstanding Comedy Series. "Television is a vast wasteland," Nesmith told a reporter not long afterward. "So we went in and said, let's waste it. Even so, I think what we do is pretty important for the kids because it takes a little edge off the pain of having to grow up. From the way they react to us, it's obvious that they have something to let out, and we're the outlet."

On the big screen, films like *The Graduate* provided a more sophisticated kind of safety valve. Directed by 33-year-old auteur Mike Nichols and starring newcomer Dustin Hoffman—a former medical school dropout turned stage and big screen actor—this satirical comedy of manners depicts a disaffected recent college graduate named Benjamin Braddock trying to find meaning in his sheltered Californian upper-middle-class life. After conducting a joyless affair with the wife of his father's business partner—the alcoholic Mrs. Robinson, as played by the sullenly wondrous Anne Bancroft—Braddock comes to the realization it is her daughter Elaine he really loves. The film ends with Braddock melodramatically whisking Elaine away from her hastily arranged church wedding to another man aboard a crowded city bus with an uncertain destination.

Hoffman—coming off some success as an off-Broadway performer—was initially reluctant to audition for the role. "I'm not right for this part, sir," he told Nichols, a fellow Jew. "This [Braddock's part] is a Gentile. This is a Wasp. This is Robert Redford." Nichols would not be dissuaded, however. "Maybe he's Jewish *inside*," he responded. Although the screen test didn't go particularly well, Nichols knew he had his Benjamin Braddock. "I had come all the way from seeing the character as a super-goy to being John Marcher in 'The Beast in the Jungle,'" Nichols later revealed in a *Vanity Fair* piece by Sam Kashner. "He had to be the dark, ungainly artist. He couldn't be a blond, blue-eyed person, because then why is he having trouble in the country of the blond, blue-eyed people? It took me a long time to figure that out—it's not in the material at all. And once I figured that out, and found Dustin, it began to form itself around that idea."

Especially popular among the under-30 set, *The Graduate* became a top-grossing film, earning seven Academy Award nominations, including Best Picture and Best Director, which Nichols won. "It is funny, not because of sight gags and punch lines and other tired rubbish, but because it has a point of view," wrote movie critic Roger Ebert of the *Chicago Sun-Times*. "That is to say, it is against something. Comedy is naturally subversive." Lyndon Johnson, though, counted himself among the many older viewers who didn't get the punch line. "How the hell can that creepy guy be a hero to you," he asked 24-year-old White House intern and future Pulitzer Prize–winning historian Doris Kearns Goodwin following a special screening of the film at his Texas ranch. "All I needed was to see ten minutes of that guy, floating like a big lump in a pool, moving like an elephant in that woman's bed, riding up and down the California coast polluting the atmosphere, to know that I wouldn't trust him for one minute with anything that really mattered to me." No doubt Benjamin Braddock would have responded with one of his patented sardonic smiles.

Sports were not immune from the rebellious new spirit of the times. In late April, heavyweight boxing champion Muhammad Ali—a convert to the Nation of Islam—refused induction into the US Army on conscientious religious grounds. "Why should they ask me to put on a uniform and go 10,000 miles from home and drop bombs and bullets on brown people in Vietnam while so-called Negro people in Louisville are treated like dogs and denied simple human rights?" Ali argued. Fellow blacks like outspoken NBA superstar center Bill Russell of the Boston Celtics were largely in sympathy with this principled stance. "I envy Muhammad Ali," Russell said. "He has something I have never been able to attain and something very few people I know possess. He has an absolute and sincere faith." White America disagreed. To them Ali was using his religion as an excuse to shirk his patriotic duty. "My son's in Viet Nam, and you no better'n than he is," an elderly woman chided Ali shortly after he made his controversial announcement. "He's there fighin' and you here safe. I hope you rot in jail. I hope they throw away the key." Ali was convicted of draft evasion and given a maximum five-year prison sentence along with a $10,000 fine. He also had his heavyweight title stripped away by the World Boxing Authority. Still, he held fast to his convictions. "I ain't got no quarrel with those Vietcong," Ali said. Although he ultimately served no jail time as his conviction was eventually overturned on appeal before the US Supreme Court, Ali did miss out on what should have been the prime years of his boxing career. Indeed, he was barred from stepping into a ring again until 1970 and did not earn back his heavyweight title until 1974, when he knocked out George Foreman in the epic "Rumble in the Jungle" showdown in Kinshasa, Zaire. By then, Ali had lost much of his former speed, grace, and athleticism. But he didn't complain. "Everything changes," he said. "Governments change, kings fall, people change. I've changed."

Lew Alcindor was solid proof of that. In 1967 the formerly reticent star center of UCLA's powerhouse college basketball team took high-profile stands on a wide array of issues, none more near and dear to his heart than racial injustice. Feeling that African American athletes had been traditionally exploited by an uncaring and unscrupulous white sporting establishment, Alcindor, 20, joined a boycott movement of the upcoming 1968 Summer Olympic Games. Organized by a radical young sociology professor from San Jose State College named Harry Edwards, the movement had specifically sought out likely Olympic participants like Alcindor, who was expected to lead the USA basketball team to a gold medal. Alcindor was enthusiastically supportive. "If white America was going to treat blacks poorly, then white America could win the Olympics on its own," he later said. "We [elite black athletes] had all felt the effects of racial prejudice, from individual hurtful remarks to difficulties getting decent housing or good jobs, and while some of us were obtaining the privileges that athletic celebrity will bring, none of us had forgotten where he came from." Alcindor offered other practical reasons as well. "Playing in the Olympics would have meant losing a quarter's worth of classes and not graduating from UCLA on time, and I had no intention of disrupting my education so that a country that was abusing my people could be made to shine for the world."

Like Ali's refusal to serve in the military, Alcindor's stance earned him widespread condemnation and loads of hate mail. But he let none of this bother him. The future Kareem Abdul-Jabbar and all-time NBA scoring champ saw himself as having a special responsibility to the black community as a role model. "When I was a kid," he told Phil Pepe of *Sport* magazine, "Jackie Robinson and Joe Louis were Gods. It's important that we start looking out for ourselves because too many times black people are being looked after paternally or are being downgraded and we want to end all that. We know what's best for us. You can tell me what to think, but I know what's best for me."

Whether Major League Baseball knew what was best for itself was a highly debatable proposition. Once the country's unchallenged National Pastime, the sport was exhibiting signs of decline by 1967. Although the National and American Leagues had seen significant attendance bumps over the previous decade, the underlying cause was mainly due to the increase in the total number of franchises. A 16-team business arrangement primarily centered in the eastern half of the country since the beginning of the 20th century, MLB had added four new ball clubs by the early 1960s. But in placing teams in promising western markets such as Houston, Texas, where locals flocked to see an underperforming NL squad play in the enclosed, architecturally arresting Astrodome, MLB was watering down the game's overall talent pool. Players who had no business being in the majors were being passed off as big leaguers for the sole purpose of filling out team rosters. As one veteran pitcher playing for the execrable New York Mets expansion team put it, "The Mets is a very good thing. They give everybody a job. Just like the WPA." The consequences became all too obvious—overall quality of play suffered, games took longer to complete, and fans grew restless and bored. "All the old certainties were gone," sports columnist and author George Vescey has written. Further diminishing baseball's appeal was the fact that the sport now had to compete with a surging National Football League, which had been founded in a Canton, Ohio, auto dealer's showroom in 1920. Faster-paced, visually more compelling on television, and extremely violent, the NFL seemed to be better in tune with the turbulent direction the country was heading.

Stand-up comedian George Carlin brilliantly captured this contrast in his instantly classic "Baseball-Football" routine. "In football," Carlin said, "the object is for the quarterback, also known as the field general, to be on target with his aerial assault, riddling the defense by hitting his receivers with deadly accuracy in spite of the blitz, even if he has to use shotgun. With short bullet passes and long bombs, he marches his troops into enemy territory, balancing this aerial assault with a sustained ground attack that punches holes in the forward wall of the enemy's defensive line.

"In baseball the object is to go home! And to be safe!—I hope I'm safe at home!"

Where Carlin saw humor, Marvin J. Miller felt outrage. Hired as Executive Director of the Major League Players Association in 1966, Miller—a seasoned labor organizer—believed the players had historically been given the economic equivalent of the shaft by baseball's ruling magnates. "This is an important industry," Miller remembered telling his new charges in Fay Vincent's 2010 book *It's What Inside the Lines That Counts:*

*Baseball Stars of the 1970s and 1980s Talk About the Game They Loved.* "[Owners] make a lot of money. Your salaries—by this time I had done enough research to know—are a far tinier proportion of what they take in than people who work in a factory." Miller pointed out that since the sport was "a labor-intensive industry," the vast majority of the operating costs were contained in the players' salaries themselves. "And yet," he said, "you don't come anywhere near having the proportion of the revenue that an ordinary worker has, a steel worker has, et cetera."

The revelation raised more than a few hackles. The players had always been told by their teams that they were playing a child's game and should consider themselves lucky to be receiving any kind of financial remuneration. Now Miller was informing them that this was hogwash. "Remember, we're talking now in the year 1966," Miller said. "Major League Baseball's first minimum salary was established nineteen years before that, 1947. It was $5,000 a year in the major leagues. Nineteen years later, when I'm coming through. . . . It's $6,000 a year. In nineteen years, it went up by $1,000. This covered periods of some of the most horrendous inflation the United States had ever seen, and it wasn't just the minimum salary. It ran all the way up [to elite players and what they made]." To add further insult to injury, baseball owners had also gotten into the habit of falsely claiming they were turning no profit. "I think most people don't examine the meaning of the word *exploitation*," Miller said. "I think if you ask most people they would say to be exploited is to have a low wage. Whereas the real meaning of it is to have a tremendous discrepancy between what your services are worth and what you are paid."

The players were clearly being taken advantage of and Miller aimed to do something about it in 1967. He successfully pushed MLB for a major increase in the minimum player salary in a new collective bargaining agreement, the first the sport had ever seen. Henceforward, the salary base for major leaguers would start at $10,000 a season. There were other significant concessions Miller secured in addition—spring training and meal money allowances were increased and teams were limited to the amount of money they could dock from a player's paycheck. Most importantly, Miller got the owners to agree to a formal grievance procedure. "At last [the players] had a mechanism which they could use to fight violations of their contractual rights," Miller said. "If you exercise this right. I said to each and every club . . . I will provide all the necessary help to process your grievances."

Miller had pulled off a minor miracle. His leadership, as historian Krister Swanson has correctly pointed out, "allowed the MLBPA to establish a beachhead for unionization in the management-dominated world of Major League Baseball." There was no turning back. "From their new beachhead," Swanson continued, "Miller and the MLBPA continued their quest for further gains in salary, pension, shop-floor control and the freedom of contract."

While this ongoing labor-management battle would threaten to tear the game apart in the coming years, it did take a back seat to the exciting events on the field in 1967. And for this, baseball had, in part, the histories of two colorful ball clubs to thank.

# Chapter Two

# Dizzy, El Cheapo, and Stan the Man

For a franchise that would come to be regarded as the flagship of the National League, the St. Louis Cardinals had very modest beginnings. Incorporated in 1892 when the NL temporarily expanded to twelve teams, the ball club had previously been a member of the American Association, a rival circuit that went out of business in 1891. Operating under the ownership of Christian Von der Ahe—a wealthy German immigrant who ran a popular local saloon—the team won four straight AA pennants in the 1880s. "Loving the spotlight," historian Geoffrey C. Ward noted, "[Von der Ahe] insisted on personally leading his team to the railroad depot every time they left town, sometimes marched the cash receipts to the bank in a wheelbarrow, and commissioned a life-size statue of himself to greet patrons as they filed into his park." But that heady early success didn't carry over to the new league. The team dropped to last place and that frustrated Von der Ahe, a petty martinet who referred to himself as "Der Boss President." He expected results and when he didn't get any, he publicly heaped scorn on his players, managers and even fellow owners, whom he likened to "porch-climbers and sandbaggers."

Running out of people to blame and facing personal bankruptcy, Von der Ahe was forced to relinquish control of the club at the beginning of the 1899 season. The new owners—brothers Frank and Stanley Robison—restocked the team with players from the Cleveland Spiders, the other NL franchise they operated. Under existing league rules at the time, this peculiar business arrangement was completely permissible and allowed St. Louis to add several Cleveland stars, most notably future Hall of Famer Jesse Burkett. A two-time .400 hitter and fierce competitor, Burkett earned the nickname "The Crab" for his combative attitude toward opponents and umpires. "You've got to be a battler," he argued. "If you don't, they'll walk all over you." The Robison brothers shut down the Spiders after the 1899 season to focus their efforts on the Cardinals, so named because of the vibrant scarlet trim the team adopted for their uniforms.

The maneuver did nothing to improve the Cards prospects, however. The club remained near the bottom of the NL standings, clearing the .500 mark only three times over the next 12 years. Making matters worse, the Cardinals now had to compete for fan dollars and attention with the Browns, a charter American League franchise that had moved to St. Louis from Milwaukee, Wisconsin, in 1902. While hardly an elite ball club, the Browns were nevertheless more competitive than the Cards in their early years, finishing a close second in their inaugural St. Louis season. They also possessed a certifiable drawing card in George "Rube" Waddell, a former standout with Connie Mack's Philadelphia Athletics. Although past his prime in St. Louis, the hard-drinking and hard-throwing left-hander had enough left in his arm to win 19 games in 1908 and lift the Browns to within 6 1/2 games of the AL pennant. "He had more stuff than any pitcher I ever saw," Mack said.

Poor health compelled Frank Robison to step away from the game in 1906, leaving his brother Stanley in sole control of the Cardinals. But when Robison, a lifelong bachelor, suddenly passed away in 1911, ownership of the team fell to his niece, Helene Hathaway Robison Britton. Highly intelligent, energetic, and progressive-minded, Britton had grown up a baseball fan at a time when the sport—like most other American institutions—was considered a males-only preserve. To her credit, Britton did not let such attitudes discourage her. "I don't think that because I am woman I will be handicapped in managing a baseball team," she said. Yet mounting debts and a messy public divorce from her husband Schuyler Britton, a Cleveland native whose court documents revealed as "addicted to habitual drunkenness," convinced Britton to sell the team to a syndicate headed by club attorney James C. Jones in 1916. The purchase price was $350,000. "She knew Jones well and even trusted a member of his firm to handle her affairs," notes Britton's biographer Joan M. Thomas. Although her time as owner was brief, Britton was the first woman to crack baseball's glass ceiling, blazing a trail for others to follow such as the late Joan Whitney Payson of the New York Mets and Sue Burns of the San Francisco Giants. "Being a woman owner of a baseball club was difficult, of course, at first," Britton later said. "It was all so new to me, you know, even though I had heard and talked baseball all my life and had watched so many games. I loved it though, and regretted selling it: I had been holding it for my son."

One of Jones's first moves was to hire Wesley Branch Rickey as the team's new president. A former catcher with the Browns and Yankees, Rickey had been raised by devout Methodist parents in rural Ohio at the end of the 19th century. He moved on to Ohio Wesleyan, where he received a bachelor of arts degree and starred on the football and baseball squads. The school's athletic facilities and equipment left much to be desired, however. "There was an old gymnasium that was too small for basketball [and] a couple of showers where the water was usually cold," Rickey remembered. "We usually bought our own shoes and had cleats nailed on by the shoemaker. Before the football season, we let our hair grow so our heads would have protection without head guards in the old center rushes. Five yards in three downs meant mass plays, and everyone piled up."

Rickey, who also earned a law degree from the University of Michigan, did not leave much of an impression when he made it to the majors. He played in only 120 games stretched across four seasons and batted a forgettable .239. Nor did he endear himself to his managers when he steadfastly refused to play on Sundays for personal religious reasons. "[M]y people are all Methodists," Rickey explained. "Sundays to me has always been a day apart. I can't help it. It was bred in me. You might also call it a prejudice. So I won't play Sunday ball. I made them put it in my contract that I wouldn't have to. Instead I go to church." Rickey did possess an exceptional baseball mind and that led to top front-office postings, including the Cardinals, which he ran from 1919 to 1942. The club was in desperate financial shape when he took over. It had trouble paying its bills and was forced by necessity to sell its longtime home ballpark—Robison Field—to generate needed revenue. Henceforward, the team rented out Sportsman's Park, the Browns' renovated home ballpark on Dodier Street and Grand Avenue in north St. Louis which they would both share together for the next three decades. "We didn't even have the money to send the team south for spring training, so we trained at home," Rickey said. "We even wore the same uniforms at home and on the road. They were really ragged." Worse, Rickey soon discovered he was at a competitive disadvantage when trying to identify and sign quality prospects. "Other clubs could outbid," he explained. "They had money. They had superior scouting machinery. In short, we had to take what was left or nothing at all."

To fix the situation, Rickey hit upon a bold new approach that would revolutionize the way major league ball clubs conducted business. He created a vast farm system of affiliated minor league franchises whose main purpose was to provide a steady stream of low-cost talent to the parent club. "To gather the raw material," New York sports columnist Red Smith wrote, "[Rickey] set up tryout camps for free agents. These three-day workouts were conducted in various parts of the country, and kids without ties to professional ball were invited to the camp nearest their homes to display their talents to a jury of scouts."

Old-fashioned rivals like John McGraw of the New York Giants dismissed the whole farm system concept as "the stupidest idea in baseball." But Rickey and new Cardinals majority owner Sam Breadon—a wealthy local auto dealer who assumed principal team ownership in 1920—had the last laugh. They restocked the club with fresh young talent such as Chick Hafey, Les Bell, Spec Toporcer, and Flint Rhem. Hafey, Bell, and Toporcer all became .300 hitters while the right-handed Rhem won 20 games. "There is quality in quantity," Rickey said. The Cardinals proved it in 1926 when they won 89 games and captured their first NL pennant by two games over the Cincinnati Reds. "We felt confident from the beginning," said player-manager Roger Hornsby, a .358 lifetime hitter. Hornsby was an idiosyncratic perfectionist who expected everyone to possess the same kind of drive and devotion that he put into the game. "People ask me what I do in winter when there's no baseball," he said. "I'll tell you what I do. I stare out the window and wait for spring." So dialed in was Hornsby that he denied himself the kind of simple pleasures most took for granted. "He didn't go to the movies for fear his eyes might be strained," noted Jimmy Powers, the longtime columnist and sports editor of the *New York Daily News*. "He read few newspapers or books and never read on a moving train. He watched his diet carefully and slept 10 to 12 hours every night. He trained diligently and didn't drink or smoke." Hornsby never even bothered to take time off to attend his mother's funeral after the Cards wrapped up their pennant. "I've got a job to do here," he told reporters.

Hypersensitive to any form of criticism, Hornsby was not afraid to direct his tart tongue at his bosses, and that included Rickey, who claimed the surly, uncompromising Texan had once used "vile and unspeakable language" toward him. Still, Hornsby's superlative showing in 1926 (.317 average, 93 RBIs) gave Rickey scant reason to complain. Neither did the Redbirds performance in the World Series against the New York Yankees, winners of 91 games behind a "Murderers Row" lineup that included Babe Ruth and Lou Gehrig. Although decided underdogs, the Cardinals beat the Yankees in seven games. "We figured the Yankees were only human and that we wouldn't be playing the series if we didn't have a chance to win," Hornsby said. Six-time NL strikeout leader and incorrigible alcoholic Grover Cleveland Alexander—who Rickey had snatched off waivers from the Chicago Cubs in midsummer—proved the difference. "Hell, I'd rather him pitch a crucial game for me drunk than anyone I've known sober," Hornsby said. The aging right-hander had tossed victories in the second and sixth games and didn't expect to see any action in the seventh game held at Yankee Stadium. That is, until Cardinals starter Jesse "Pop" Haines ran into trouble and loaded the bases with two outs in the bottom of the seventh inning with a 3–2 lead.

"So I walked into that without even taking off my sweater," Alexander recalled. "I was cold but if Hornsby needed me, I was ready to pitch. That's what they were paying me for." The Yankees batter was rookie Tony Lazzeri, who had hit 18 homers during the regular season. After running the count to 1–1, Alexander threw him a fastball that Lazzeri just missed hitting out of the ballpark. "The Yankees were on top of the dugout steps to run and meet Lazzeri at home plate," Hornsby said. "And I was going to be the biggest bum in the history of the World Series [for bringing in Alexander]. I knew it, too. But just before the ball went into the left field stands, where it was supposed to go, we got a break. The wind pushed the ball a little more to the left. Enough left to make the drive foul by about ten inches." Having narrowly earned a reprieve from Mother Nature, Alexander decided to go with a curve for his next pitch. It worked to perfection. "Lazzeri swung where that curve started but not where it finished," he said. "The ball got a hunk of the corner and then finished outside." Alexander got the inning-ending strikeout and then held the Yankees scoreless the rest of the way. "I think it's one of the most dramatic things in all of baseball history, because it was Grover Cleveland Alexander who was involved," contended teammate Les Bell. "Anytime you have a really great athlete who's at the twilight of a long career come in and rise to the challenge, it's truly something to see and to remember."

For Hornsby, the championship marked the high-water mark of his baseball life, but unknown to him his days as a Cardinal were numbered. He and Sam Breadon had earlier clashed over the Cards owner's insistence the team play meaningless exhibition games in the middle of the pennant race to help fill club coffers. "We had a small squad, with no reserves to play those exhibitions," Hornsby insisted. "I told [Breadon] what I thought of exhibition games and people who book them to take away the days of rest that ballplayers needed." Breadon did not take kindly to Hornsby's opposition. "He was flushed and angry when he left the clubhouse," Hornsby remembered. "I believe he made up his mind then and there that, come pennant or last place, Hornsby wouldn't be with the Cardinals the next season." He wasn't. Over Branch Rickey's objections, Breadon dealt his insolent star to the New York Giants for second baseman Frankie Frisch. "Had I been in sole charge, Hornsby never would have left St. Louis," Rickey maintained. "Depriving the Cardinals of a known quantity of greatness in batting and competitive spirit wasn't right. Whether Frisch was good or better, personal affront is never enough to justify a move of such magnitude."

Hornsby's departure did little to hamper the team's success moving forward. The Cardinals won pennants in 1928, 1930, 1931, and 1934, thanks to the club's booming farm system and Rickey's uncanny ability to acquire the right kind of player in trades. Leo "The Lip" Durocher was one such example. Rickey picked him up in the middle of the 1933 season. A slick fielding shortstop with limited hitting ability (Babe Ruth dubbed him "the All-American Out"), Durocher made up for his lack of offense with a brash winning attitude that often got under the skins of opponents. When he once threw out Ty Cobb on a wide-ranging grounder to third, the mercurial Baseball Hall of Famer growled Durocher was a "lucky busher" for fielding the ball so far out of position. "Well I was playing you for a better hitter than you are," Durocher cheekily told Cobb, the holder of baseball's highest career batting average (.367). "He knew how to find the raw spot and stick in the knife," posited writer Richard Scheinin. While many were put off by Durocher's sharp tongue and alleged criminality—he was rumored to have stolen Babe Ruth's watch and one of Lou Gehrig's championship rings while playing for the Yankees—Rickey was not. "I made this trade because I have the firm belief that with you at shortstop we can win a lot of pennants," Rickey informed Durocher in their first meeting. "You can do a lot for us. You can spark this team. You can help us win pennants. That's all I care about."

Durocher had an integral role in the Cardinals' 1934 pennant run, playing superb defense and driving in 70 runs. But the heart and soul of the team, which was reportedly given the colorful nickname "Gas House Gang" by Durocher, was pitcher Jay Hanna "Dizzy" Dean. A free-spirited sharecropper's son from Arkansas, Dean was the talk of baseball, winning 30 games while leading the league in strikeouts (195), shutouts (7), and overall winning percentage (.811). He would add two more victories in the World Series against the Detroit Tigers, including an 11–0 shutout in the seventh and deciding game. "I felt great out there this afternoon," Dean exulted. "Had a lot of fun. Let them get a couple of hits, and then, I decided to stop foolin' around and get those strikes past 'em." Dean knew he was good and wasn't shy about letting others know. When his younger brother Paul—a fellow starter and 19-game winner on the 1934 squad—tossed a no-hitter in the second game of a doubleheader against the Dodgers, Dean was nonplussed. He said if he had known Paul was

The colorful and unconventional leader of the Gas House Gang Dizzy Dean. BASEBALL HALL OF FAME PHOTO ARCHIVE

going to throw one, "I'd a throwed one, too" in the first game, a 1–0 win. Such cockiness extended well beyond the clubhouse. In the aftermath of his first major league victory over the Pittsburgh Pirates in 1930, Dean made a point to visit Rickey in his office and inform him he was going to be the sport's best drawing card since Babe Ruth. "That—country jake!" Rickey exploded afterward. "Judas priest, if there were one more like him in baseball, I'd get out of the game!" Dean would later suffer arm trouble and be traded to the Chicago Cubs in 1938. By the early 1940s, he was back with the Cardinals calling their games on the radio. He left a lasting, if perplexing, impression on Rickey. "I'm a man of some intelligence," the general manager once told his family. "I've had some education, passed the bar, practiced law. I've been a teacher and I deal with men of substance, statesmen, business leaders, the clergy. Then why—why do I spend my time arguing with Dizzy Dean?"

The Cards returned to championship form with a mostly new cast during the wartime season of 1942. Sparked by rookie outfield sensation Stan Musial—a converted pitcher from a small Pennsylvania steel mill town—the team overcame a 10-game deficit to the Brooklyn Dodgers in early August to take the pennant with a franchise-record 106 victories. Musial batted a club-best .315 with 32 doubles, 10 triples, and 10 homers. "Once Musial timed your fastball," Hall of Fame pitcher Warren Spahn said, "your infielders were in jeopardy." Indeed, the hard-hitting Polish immigrant's son was nicknamed "Stan the Man" by Dodgers fans for the impressive hitting exhibitions he'd put on at Brooklyn's Ebbets Field, where he enjoyed a lofty .360 career average. "Here comes the man," they would chant as he strode purposely in from the on-deck circle to face the latest Dodgers victim on the mound. Said Musial: "I consciously memorized the speed at which every pitcher in the league threw his fastball, curve, and slider; then, I'd pick up the speed of the ball in the first 30 feet of its flight and knew how it would move once it crossed the plate."

Aside from Musial, the Cardinals received solid offensive contributions from shortstop Marty Marion (.276 average, 38 doubles) and outfielders Enos "Country" Slaughter and Terry Moore, who hit .318 and .288, respectively. Slaughter—known for his aggressive style on the base paths and in the outfield—would eventually appear in parts of 19 big league seasons with three other teams, average .300, and earn induction into the Hall of Fame in 1985. He "would run through a brick wall, if necessary, to make a catch, or slide into a pit of ground glass to score a run," *New York Times* sports columnist Arthur Daley wrote. On the hill the Cards received 20-win seasons from veteran right-handers Mort Cooper and Johnny Beazley. But the team's principal catalyst remained Musial, who apart from being a model of rectitude on the diamond, was also one away, too. "You could make a study of Musial's life and learn how to be a decent person," Rickey once said. "He did not have a shred of ego or temperament. He was always serene, no matter the situation. How he was able to maintain this serenity, this calm and be at all times the most self-confident, highly concentrated, and zealous competitor that he also was, is surely worth reflecting upon."

Facing the Yankees of Joe DiMaggio, Bill Dickey, and Phil Rizzuto in the Fall Classic, the Cardinals surprised most baseball observers by dispatching them in five games. "The Yankees had been in a lot of World Series and they were a little bit cocky, though any ballclub that had won as many pennants as they had had a right to be," recalled Redbirds pitcher Max Lanier, a 13-game winner that season. The turning point was the first contest when the Cardinals stormed back from a 7–0 deficit in the bottom of the ninth inning to almost tie the game. "Well, that rally made us feel better, even though we lost the game," Lanier said. "It showed we could throw a scare into the Yankees. And then we did more than scare them. We beat them four straight. I think that was one of the biggest World Series upsets ever."

The victory marked the end of an era for the Cardinals. Rickey left the organization shortly afterward to accept an offer to run the Brooklyn Dodgers. "I would rather dig ditches for a few cents an hour than to work for [Breadon] any longer than my contract requires," he had told intimates. The behind-the-scenes breach between Rickey and the Cardinals owner had been growing for some time. Breadon resented the fact that Rickey had been receiving the lion's share of the credit for the team's success in the press. Moreover, Breadon was no longer happy paying the relatively high salary ($90,000) that Rickey had commanded

An indispensable man—Branch Rickey literally brought the Cardinals from rags to riches during his front office tenure. BASEBALL HALL OF FAME PHOTO ARCHIVE

as director of the team's baseball operations. "The truth is," wrote journalist Frederick G. Lieb, "that while the two men were closely associated in business, there were many things on which they never saw eye to eye. Breadon recognized Rickey's talents and what they did for the Cardinals, but Sam wasn't a man who can sit back and play second fiddle in his own organization. Too often the Rickey wits clashed with Breadon's business acumen. The time simply came when Sam and Branch no longer could live happily in the same ball park."

Most Cardinals—believing the penurious Rickey routinely shortchanged them when they negotiated their contracts—shed no tears over his departure. Indeed, Rickey's nickname was tellingly "El Cheapo." "Mr. Rickey likes ballplayers," Enos Slaughter said. "And he likes money. What he don't like is the two of them getting together." Players preferred dealing with Breadon. "Mr. Breadon was a businessman," Marty Marion explained. "He loved baseball, and he always liked me. I used to give him trouble, contract-wise. But unlike Rickey, he didn't send you two pages of silver-toned oratory telling you how lousy you were and give you a cut for not being able to hit 25 home runs rather than hit .300. Mr. Breadon would just send you a contract, and he'd always say, 'Dear Marty, Please sign the contract and return it. See you in spring training.' That was about it. I'd always write him back, 'Dear Mr. Breadon, I'm not signing for that.'"

Despite Rickey's exit, the Cardinals continued to be a juggernaut, winning three pennants and two World Series over the next four seasons. Stan Musial was at the top of his game. Apart from the 1945 season, when he was away in the service, Musial batted .345 or better each year with an average of 215 hits. "That Musial!" Boston Braves manager Casey Stengel exclaimed. "You're going to wake up one day and discover that he is the best player in the big leagues, I'm not sure he isn't already." Such was the dominance of the Cardinals, however, that they didn't need a strong offensive showing by Musial to win when they met the Boston Red Sox in the 1946 World Series. Entering the Series as the decided underdogs to the Ted Williams–led Sox, the Cardinals rode the hot pitching arm of lefty Harry "The Cat" Brecheen, a 31-year-old Oklahoman who had won 15 games during the regular season. Brecheen twirled his way to three victories, the first southpaw in Fall Classic history to do so. "Let me tell you something," Williams told writer Henry Berry in 1975. "Brecheen was great in that Series, had the ball doing just what he wanted. . . . He was *the* pitcher in that Series. Goddamn it, I hate to admit it, but he was beautiful to watch." Brecheen was also the winning pitcher of record in the seventh and deciding game, a 4–3 nailbiter over Boston which is best remembered today for Enos Slaughter's "Mad Dash" home with two outs in the eighth inning. The speedy Cardinals outfielder, who had earlier singled, scored all the way from first base on a teammate's double to left-center when Boston shortstop Johnny Pesky fatally "hesitated" making a routine relay throw to the plate. The run broke a 3–3 tie and provided the Redbirds the winning margin of victory. "I'm the goat," a distraught Pesky said after the game. "I never expected [Slaughter would] try to score. I couldn't hear anybody hollering at me above the noise of the crowd. I gave Slaughter at least six strides with the delay. I know I could have nailed him if I had suspected he would try for the plate. I'm the 'goat.' Make no mistake about that."

The Cardinals did not repeat in 1947, finishing second with an 89–75 mark. A poor start and injuries to key regulars such as Musial made the season one to forget. But the Cardinals still managed to make national headlines. For 1947 was the year Jackie Robinson integrated major league baseball with the Brooklyn Dodgers and many Cardinal players, especially southerners Enos Slaughter, Terry Moore, and Marty Marion, objected to his presence in the Brooklyn lineup. Put another way, they did not want to be on the same field as a black. To demonstrate their unhappiness, they organized a planned team walkout when the Cards were scheduled to play the Dodgers in May. "I heard talk," Stan Musial later confessed to author Roger Kahn. "It was rough and racial and I can tell you a few things about that," he said. "First of all, everybody has racial feelings. We don't admit it. We aren't proud of it. But it's there. And this is big league baseball, not English tea, and ballplayers make noise. So I heard the words and I knew there was some feeling behind the words, but I didn't take it seriously. That was baseball." NL president Ford Frick did take the threatened players' strike seriously. He issued the following statement to the Cardinals squad: "If you do strike, you will be suspended from the League. You will find the friends you think you have in the press box will not support you. You will be outcasts. I do not care if half the league strikes. Those who do will encounter quick retribution. All will be suspended and I don't care if it wrecks the National League for five years. This the United States of America and one citizen has as much right to play as another. You will find if you go through with your intention that you will have been guilty of complete madness." Frick's strong message had the desired effect. The dissident Cardinals backed down. "None of us was making a lot of money," Moore later said. "A suspension without pay would mean some fellers would lose their homes or the family farm. That killed the strike movement right there." Robinson breathed a long sigh of relief. "If successful, the plan could have had a chain reaction throughout the baseball world—with other players agreeing to unite in a strong bid to keep baseball white," he said.

St. Louis had long wrestled with the subject of race. Dating back to the years before the Civil War, the former French settlement along the twisting banks of the Mississippi River was part of the larger slave state of Missouri. Blacks were forbidden under then existing city laws to read or write or congregate in houses of worship without the presence of a white person. Nor were they permitted to testify against a white person in a court of law. Slave auctions were a common sight. Former bondsman William Wells Brown—the first published African American novelist—once said he could never get out of his head the memory of a married couple being sold at one of these events. "The man was first up, and sold to the highest bidder," he wrote. "The wife was next ordered to ascend the platform. I was present. She slowly obeyed the order. The auctioneer commenced, and soon several hundred dollars were bid. My eyes were intensely fixed on the face of the woman, whose cheeks were wet with tears. But a conversation between the slave and his new master attracted my attention. I drew near them to listen. The slave was begging his new master to purchase his wife. . . . The new master replied that he did not want her but if she sold cheap he would purchase her. I watched the countenance of the man while the different persons were bidding on his wife. When his new master bid on his wife you could see the smile upon his countenance, and the tears stop; but as soon as another would bid, you could see the countenance and the tears start afresh."

With the abolition of slavery after 1865, conditions improved for the local African American community. But racial injustice and discrimination persisted. Blacks were simply not accorded the same economic opportunities or legal rights as whites. The racial divide was fed, in no small measure, by white fears about blacks competing for their jobs and moving into their neighborhoods to drive down local property values. As a result, "realtors, developers, and white property owners erected elaborate obstacles to black property ownership and occupancy," notes historian Colin Gordon. "The net effect was not just spatial segregation of metropolitan St. Louis by race and class, but also a cascade of disinvestment and disadvantage in the City's [predominantly black] northside residential neighborhoods, an uneven and fragmented pattern of residential development and land-use zoning, and a yawning racial gap in wealth." The pattern was well established by 1967 and has continued into the 21st century.

The Cardinals' failure to adapt to the changing times was a major factor in the team's inability to raise another championship banner in the late 1940s. As Musial later explained to writer Peter Golenbock, "We finished second in '47, '48, and '49. We weren't far behind, but the Dodgers signed Robinson, [Roy] Campanella, and [Don] Newcombe, three of the best black ballplayers at the time, and that made the difference as far as winning the pennant. If the Dodgers hadn't signed them . . ." Management's stubborn insistence on keeping the club lily-white remained team policy until August Anheuser "Gussie" Busch Jr. purchased the club for $3.75 million in 1953. Busch was the president and CEO of the St. Louis–based Anheuser-Busch Brewing Company and notably progressive on the subject of race. "Hell, we sell beer to everybody," he once said. Busch grasped the importance of signing and developing African American ballplayers. Since Robinson's historic breakthrough season in 1947, only two all-white teams had been able to win NL pennants—the 1948 Boston Braves and the 1950 Philadelphia Phillies. From a competitive standpoint then, it made perfect sense to integrate. And the

Cardinals did under Busch, beginning with Tom Alston, a 25-year-old Navy veteran who debuted at first base for the team in 1954. "I have been hoping that it would happen, hoping and waiting, and now it's a wonderful feeling to know the dream has come true," Alston said. While Alston never quite panned out as expected due to a debilitating mental disorder—hitting only .244 in 91 games—Busch was not discouraged. In the years ahead, his regime would double-down and acquire a number of top caliber African American players—performers such as Bill White, Bob Gibson, Curt Flood, and Lou Brock. "Mr. Busch knew the Cardinals had to have blacks," second baseman Red Schoendienst said.

Success had always seemed to follow Busch around. The scion of a famous German-American brewing family, Gussie understood how to inspire loyalty in his employees with his brash, endearing personality and self-deprecating sense of humor. "All right, you guys," he informed them on one particularly sticky occasion. "Let me blow my stack. Then you can blow yours." Married four times, Busch had a notorious wandering eye and a penchant for partying after hours. "Gussie Busch was my kind of guy, what I call a booze-and-broads man," longtime Cardinals broadcaster Harry Caray said. "He liked to have a drink, appreciate the qualities of a beautiful woman, tell a few stories, and play a few hands of cards. No pretense. No bull. Gussie [was] a basic, down-to-earth person."

Busch also was an incredibly hard worker with a P. T. Barnum–like gift for self-promotion. He is credited with creating one of the most iconic brands in American corporate advertising—an old-fashioned beer wagon drawn by a team of Clydesdale horses—to sell his product. Not coincidentally, Anheuser-Busch became the largest brewery in the world under his stewardship. Owing to his own restless nature, however, Busch wasn't satisfied with just peddling beer. A former rodeo competitor, he was drawn to the roar of the crowd and the popular attention that only owning a major league baseball club could offer. "Not many people wrote to me when I was just a brewery president," he liked to say. Although he possessed limited knowledge of the game, Busch was confident his success in the brewery business would carry over. "My ambition is, whether hell or high water, to get a baseball championship team for St. Louis before I die," he said. But as author and historian David Halberstam points out, "[w]hat worked in the world of beer—hiring, if need be, the best men available—did not work in baseball."

Busch learned this lesson the hard way as he burned through several front office executives and field managers in his first years. Eddie Stanky was a prime example. On paper, "the Brat"—as the former All-Star second baseman was called during his playing days with the Dodgers and Giants—seemed ideal to manage the Cardinals when Busch retained him in 1953. Stanky had been a sparkplug on three World Series teams and Leo Durocher had once paid him the ultimate compliment when he said, "He can't hit, can't run, can't field . . . all the little SOB can do is win." Stanky's slender 5'8", 170-pound stature also belied a certain steeliness that manifested itself in 1947, when he famously came to the defense of rookie Brooklyn teammate Jackie Robinson in a game against Philadelphia. The Phillies bench had been riding Robinson hard all contest, hurling crude racial insults his way. Stanky had finally heard enough. "You're all a bunch of cowards," he yelled back. "What kind of men are you anyway? You're all yellow! Why the hell don't you pick on someone who can fight back! You know Robinson can't fight back—knock it off and just play ball!" Unfortunately, this confrontational approach did not work with the Cardinals. "We had a lot of guys who didn't take to Stanky," infielder and future Milwaukee Brewers manager Alex Grammas said. "He was the kind of guy who was all business." The team grew progressively worse under his watch, finishing 25 games out in 1954—Stanky's last full season in the dugout.

One less thing Gussie Busch had to worry about, though, was competing with the Browns for local support. The American League franchise pulled up stakes in St. Louis after the 1953 season and moved to Baltimore, Maryland, where they became the Orioles. "I wasn't going to run Gussie Busch out of town," undercapitalized Browns owner Bill Veeck said. Veeck, who had lost his right leg while serving with a US Marines artillery unit in the South Pacific during the second World War, had made a major push to remain in St. Louis after he bought the franchise in 1951. Although the team was a perennial loser in the standings—it never broke 70 wins under his ownership—Veeck had frantically tried to drum up popular interest through a number of colorful promotions, including

"Grandstand Managers Day." "The way it worked [regular paying customers behind home plate] as they entered [the park] were given large white signs with YES printed in green on one side, and NO printed in red on the other," Veeck later recounted. These fans would then get the opportunity to vote on whether the team should bunt, steal, or warm up a reliever when Browns coach Bob Fishel, who was positioned behind the St. Louis dugout, held up a sign pertaining to the specific situation on the field. Fishel would then relay the crowd's choice to team manager Zack Taylor, who was improbably sitting in a rocking chair smoking a pipe. "The fans were brilliant," Veeck said. "We won the game 5–3 to end a four-game losing streak. I retired all my amateur managers with honors, went back to my professional and lost five of the next six games."

Bizarre as this promotion may have been, it still did not hold a candle to the more celebrated Eddie Gaedel stunt. On August 19, 1951, Veeck arranged to have Gaedel—a 3'7" former circus performer—pinch hit in the second game of a Sunday doubleheader against the Detroit Tigers. "Eddie," Veeck jokingly informed him, "I'm going to be up on the roof with a high-powered rifle watching every move you make. If you so much as look like you're going to swing, I'm going to shoot you dead." Gaedel, who was sporting "1/8" as his uniform number, did as he was told. He received a walk on four consecutive pitches. "Eddie trotted down to first base to the happy tune of snapping cameras," Veeck said. "He waited for the runner, one foot holding to the bag like a pro, and he patted [pinch runner Jim Delsing] on the butt in good professional exhortation before he surrendered the base. He shook hands with our first base coach and he waved to the cheering throng." For the 26-year-old Gaedel, who would later appear as a Martian in yet another famous Veeck ballpark promotion in 1959, the at-bat represented the high point of his life. "For a minute, I felt like Babe Ruth," he said.

The Cardinals continued to struggle in the standings throughout the 1950s and early 1960s. The lone exception was 1957 when the team won 89 games and remained in the pennant hunt most of the season, thanks to Stan Musial's last great statistical year. Now 36 and slow afoot, Stan the Man had to be moved from the outfield to first base for defensive purposes. Though he preferred his old position, he didn't let the switch affect his hitting. Musial won his seventh and final NL batting crown with a .351 average while leading the league with a .423 on-base percentage. He was also named *Sports Illustrated*'s Sportsman of the Year. "In his 17 years with St. Louis," Paul O'Neil wrote for the magazine's cover story, "quiet, handsome Musial has proved himself—with Ruth, Cobb, Hornsby, Wagner and Speaker—one of the genuinely great hitters in the history of baseball." O'Neil went on to praise Musial for being "most durable," citing his streak of playing in a NL-record 895 consecutive games from 1952 to August 22 of that year. "We were a tough bunch of guys back then," Musial later said. "We played hurt a lot. We had a game to play, and when you hit the field you forgot a while about this or that hurting you. You get a bruise, you pour a little iodine on it and keep on playing. You get a sprain, either you or the team doctor would tape it up real tight and you'd head back out in the field. I used to think of all the fans that paid their hard earned money to come see me play. They didn't buy tickets to see me sitting on the bench."

St. Louis fans almost didn't get the chance to see Musial play at all. Newly hired Cardinals GM Frank Lane—known as "Trader Frank" for his proclivity of swapping players like bubblegum cards when he headed the White Sox and Orioles—had tried to deal Musial to the Phillies straight up for All-Star pitcher Robin Roberts. Musial was horrified by the idea. "I'm not going to go," he told Red Schoendienst, his best friend on the team. Luckily for all parties concerned, Gussie Busch pulled the plug on the trade. St. Louisans would have run Lane out of town on a rail and Musial would have ended his Hall of Fame Cardinals career on an inglorious note. "Mr. Busch wanted to have some control over what went on," said Bing Devine, Lane's assistant at the time. "If you wanted to make a player deal, Mr. Busch wanted you to talk to him first. Frank didn't like that. Frank's philosophy was: 'You want me to operate the club? Okay, I'm going to operate it, but don't try tell to me what to do.' After a couple of years, Frank began to find out with Mr. Busch it never worked like that." Lane was gone from St. Louis by the end of the 1958 season.

Devine was bumped up to GM and the team slowly began to show signs of progress. Top pitching prospect Bob Gibson developed into a top flight right-handed starter while other youngsters such as Curt Flood, Tim McCarver, Mike Shannon, Bill White, and Julian Javier became effective regulars. They complemented a veteran lineup led by power-hitting third baseman Ken Boyer. "There were unmistakable signs that a new day was at hand for the Cardinals," Gibson later said. Fresh blood was also brought into the dugout with the hiring of Johnny Keane as skipper in 1961. A successful minor league manager who had never played in the majors, Keane related well to the younger players on the roster, who appreciated his patience and overall evenhandedness. "These fellows are well paid," Keane told *Sports Illustrated*. "They live on a high level, and they try to meet their responsibilities in the public eye. They're not going to be treated like animals." Incorrigible veterans like pitcher Maury McDermott were another matter. McDermott liked to step out on the town between his starts and generally raise hell. This got him into hot water with the Keane. "Maury," the manager lectured him in 1961, "you came to spring this year without even cab fare and the Cardinals gave you a contract. And to show your appreciation, all you've done is fuck around all year." A not-contrite McDermott responded by saying if this was how Keane truly felt, he would take off his uniform and part ways with the team. "That's exactly what you'll do," Keane said. "You're released."

While the team got better, Gussie Busch expressed dissatisfaction. He thought Devine was not doing enough to build a winner. So in 1962 he brought back a familiar old face to the Cardinal fold—Branch Rickey. Hired on as a special advisor, Rickey was given unspecified authority to make changes. Busch didn't seem to mind that Rickey was a less than spry 81. Rickey's record since leaving the organization 20 years earlier seemed ample justification for the move. As president and CEO of the Brooklyn Dodgers, Rickey had produced two NL pennant winners while keeping his team consistently in contention from 1946 to 1950. More impressively, he had signed Jackie Robinson in 1947 to break baseball's color barrier. But toward the end of his Brooklyn run, Rickey had come into conflict with Walter O'Malley, a former club lawyer who had managed to gain majority control of the team's stock. "He is *the* most devious man I've ever met," Rickey said. O'Malley believed Rickey had been financially mismanaging the Dodgers for years and arranged a buyout of Rickey's club holdings. O'Malley was not prepared for the price tag, however, which came to over $1 million. "From this day forward," the frustrated new Dodgers team president told his employees, "anyone from the Brooklyn front offices who mentions the name of Branch Rickey will be fined one dollar on the spot." A substantially richer Rickey moved on to run the hapless Pittsburgh Pirates where he replenished the team's farm system and acquired such future stars as Roberto Clemente. His painstaking efforts would eventually result in the Pirates becoming World Series champions in 1960.

Rickey did not hit it off with Devine in St. Louis. Devine was understandably weary of Rickey's intrusion on his front office turf. "I liked to protect my area," Devine explained. Rickey was equally defensive of his own prerogatives. "I'm here to make the final decisions on this ball club," Rickey bluntly told Devine during one awkward early encounter. Devine did consider resigning, but thought better of it. He was not a quitter and, besides, he was confident his personnel decisions would stand up to scrutiny. This was especially true when it came to the fate of Stan Musial. Entering the 1963 season, Musial was 42 and Rickey felt it was time for the team to cut the cord and replace him, preferably with someone younger and more athletic. "He is still a grand hitter but not at all the hitter of former days," Rickey argued. Devine thought otherwise and with the support of Johnny Keane successfully lobbied Gussie Busch to keep Musial on for one last season. "So he played in '63 and hit .255 with 12 homers, splitting time in left field with [25-year-old reserve] Charlie James," Devine said.

Musial almost got to play in another World Series. With Devine's methodical rebuild over the previous years finally showing results, the Cardinals won 93 games-their most since 1949-and kept within striking distance of eventual pennant winner Los Angeles most of the summer. Devine, who would be named *The Sporting News* 1963 Executive of the Year, had aided his team's cause by shoring up the infield with the acquisition of veteran shortstop Dick Groat from the Pirates. But the deal had been a tough sell to ownership as it involved giving up two promising younger players (pitcher Don Cardwell and infielder Julio Gotay)—a trading practice Rickey had long frowned upon. "I'm a young ballplayer man," Rickey told Devine. Devine eventually wore down Busch and Groat responded with a .319 average and 43 doubles. "All in all it had not been a bad year even if it did come to a disappointing conclusion," said Bob Gibson, who won 18. "It gave us good reason to look forward with hope and confidence in 1964."

That hope and confidence appeared misplaced when the team limped out to a 47–48 start the next season, despite stellar performances by Gibson and team captain Ken Boyer, who drove in a league-leading 119 runs that summer to become the NL's Most Valuable Player. "[Boyer] was the boss of our field," catcher Tim McCarver later said. "He was the guy everyone looked up to. He was the guy who really filled that role, if that role needed to be filled." With the club seemingly out of contention, Busch began planning ahead for the 1965 season. Tops on his to-do list was sacking Bing Devine, a move Rickey had been pressuring him to do for some time. Busch performed the deed in early August, much to Devine's consternation. "If you weren't a grown man you might cry," Devine said. Devine did manage to swing one last major trade. He acquired underachieving speedster Lou Brock from the Chicago Cubs to play left field. And while Brock responded with a spectacular year-hitting well over .300 and terrorizing opponents' infield defenses with his stolen base ability—the move came too late to save Devine's job.

Former Rickey business associate and Navy pilot Bob Howsam was tapped to replace him, but the team purge was not over. Busch also wanted to fire Johnny Keane in favor of one-time Gas House Gang member Leo Durocher at season's end. Durocher, who had not held a full-time managerial post in the majors since stepping down from the New York Giants in 1956, was initially skeptical. "How do you think Johnny Keane is going to feel when he hears about this?" he asked Busch. "Because you're not out of it yet, Gus. You're only seven and half games out, you could win this thing yet. Anything can happen in this game." Still and all, the lure of a sizable paycheck made Durocher come around to Busch's entreaties. "You're the manager of the ball club," Busch told him in a private handshake deal. Then, as Durocher had suspected, the Cardinals started winning. They stormed back into the pennant race and beat out the Phillies—who had entered September with a substantial lead—on the last day of the season. "The upshot was that in two months we went from fifth place to first in the National League," said first baseman Bill White, who batted .303 with 102 runs driven in.

Busch was forced to rescind his job offer. After all, it would have been a public relations nightmare for him to remove Keane, the skipper who had just guided the Cards to their first pennant in 18 years. "I could understand the fix he was in," Durocher sympathized. Ironically, the miracle finish had been accomplished entirely by players that Devine had either signed, developed or traded for as GM. This fact was not lost on any of the Cardinals. When the ball club went on to defeat the Yankees in seven games in the World Series, Ken Boyer emotionally drove this point home during the extended celebration that followed. "We won this title for Bing Devine," he said. "Bing put this thing all together. And Bing is the reason we're all here."

The thrill of victory had barely sunk in, however, before Johnny Keane announced he would not be returning to the St. Louis bench the next season. The shocking disclosure was made at a press conference originally set up by Gussie Busch to proclaim Keane's rehiring. But Keane had other ideas. Perturbed to learn that Busch had intended to sack him, Keane told the assembled media he was resigning his position effective immediately and going back home to fish. "I told Mr. Busch not to make any [contract] offer," he said. What Keane failed to mention was that he had already lined up a new managerial job—replacing the recently pink-slipped Yogi Berra of the Yankees. Cardinal players were dumbstruck, but not necessarily surprised by the bizarre turn of events. They too had heard about Busch's intention to replace Keane with Durocher. "John had to take care of himself," Bill White later explained. "If we hadn't won, Johnny would have been fired."

For Keane—a Cardinal organization employee for over three decades—the move turned out to be colossal error in judgment. "Literally, I watched Johnny Keane age 20 years in the year and a little he managed the Yankees," New York pitcher Jim Bouton later wrote. "[He] was the perfect example of the wrong man for the wrong team at the wrong time." Indeed, Keane's no-nonsense approach was better suited for impressionable younger players on an up and coming ball club than the sullen, fading veterans of the Yankees in the mid-1960s. "[He] belonged in the St. Louis environment," Bing Devine maintained. Keane was thus doomed to fail and he did in 1965, leading the Yankees to a sixth-place finish, their worst showing in 40 seasons. "The year was a disaster," Bouton concluded.

Keane would be gone the following spring after the Yankees stumbled out to a 4–16 start. His overall record in the Big Apple was a forgettable 85–101. "He never got to know the Yankees," wrote Arthur Daley of the *New York Times*. "Nor did they get to know him. Unlike the Cardinals, whom he had watched advance from the minors, the [once mighty] Bombers were strangers of almost demi-god status." Tragically, Keane never got a chance to redeem his tarnished managerial reputation. He passed away from a sudden heart attack at 55 on January 6, 1967, exactly 27 months after his abrupt exit from St. Louis. "[Keane] never took anything from anybody," Bob Gibson said. "If he thought he was right and you were wrong about a certain thing, he was not going to tell you different, no matter who you happened to be." Gussie Busch had discovered this truth too late.

To earn back the good graces of the fans, who were dispirited by Keane's departure, Busch decided to name 41-year-old Red Schoendienst as the Cards' new field manager. The move made perfect sense. Though he lacked managerial experience, Schoendienst had been a beloved former player and a major contributor on the 1946 championship squad. He also had been a member of Keane's coaching staff, which made it easier for the other Cardinals to accept him. "There was no lingering resentment over Johnny Keane's leaving because Red was so popular with everybody on the ballclub," noted Carl Warwick, a part-time outfielder who batted .259 in 1964. "If they'd gone out and hired someone from outside who no one knew, they might [not] have felt that way, but with Red there, you couldn't not help but love Red. You knew he was going to be on your side all the time." The good karma, however, did not translate into many victories. The Cardinals dropped all the way to seventh place in 1965 with an 80–81 record. Declining productivity from veterans such as Groat, Boyer, and White mostly accounted for the disappointing finish.

The 1966 season was hardly any better. The Cardinals improved to 83 wins with a dominant pitching staff consisting of Gibson, Al Jackson, Ray Washburn, Larry Jaster, and Nelson Briles. Together they combined for the second-best team ERA (3.11) in the NL. But the club ended up in sixth place with a poor hitting attack that struggled to adapt to the larger confines of Busch Memorial Stadium, the gleaming new multi-purpose athletic facility the club had moved into that May. Built at a cost of $24 million and shared with the National Football League's Cardinals, the circular concrete bowl structure seated 50,000 and was located in the heart of downtown St. Louis, just blocks away from the soon-to-be iconic Gateway Arch that was then under construction. "At the time it seemed like the Taj Mahal," commented pitcher Nelson Briles. "It brought us into the state of the art. We even had air conditioning in the clubhouses. And that was a treat in St. Louis. That air conditioning came down the tunnel leading to the dugout, and in those hot summer months, you could sneak in the tunnel and get a little break."

As appealing as these creature comforts were, the venue was not ideal for playing baseball. Like other "cookie-cutter" ballparks constructed in the late 1960s and 1970s (Pittsburgh's Three Rivers Stadium, Philadelphia's Veterans Stadium, and Cincinnati's Riverfront Stadium spring to mind), Busch had deep power alleys (386 feet) and a cavernous center field (414 feet) that made hitting home runs there challenging for even the most accomplished of sluggers. The team offensive disadvantage was largely offset, though, by the edge the expanded field of play gave to hurlers like Gibson. Indeed, after giving up a league-leading 34 home runs to opponents the previous season, the right-hander allowed only 20 in 1966. "It was a pitcher-friendly park, especially at night," Briles said. "If you were a pitcher who could make the hitters hit the ball from left-center to right-center, it was spacious. The ball didn't seem to travel as well."

In the meantime, the person who had been the most responsible for putting St. Louis on the baseball map quietly passed away on December 9 at 83. Branch Rickey had been in declining health for some time, but his passion for baseball never wavered. Even when Gussie Busch removed him from the Cardinals front office after an insecure Howsam objected to his presence, Rickey still held out hope his vast accumulated knowledge of the game would land him another job. "He said many times that he wanted to contribute to the success of another baseball organization before his days on earth were complete," wrote his dutiful biographer Lee Lowenfish. That phone call never came. So Rickey was forced to fill his days finishing a long delayed manuscript on the history of the game and making various public appearances. The last words he uttered occurred during his induction speech to the Missouri Sports Hall of Fame on November 13. As the featured speaker for the evening, Rickey had intended to focus his remarks on the merits of spiritual courage. But he never got the chance to finish. "I don't think I can continue," he told stunned onlookers as he stepped away from the podium. Rickey collapsed from heart failure a moment later and was rushed to a nearby hospital where he lingered in a coma for a month before expiring. "He died the way he lived, with the audience in the palm of his hand," writer Bob Broeg said.

As the 1967 season approached, Cardinal fans received better tidings. Official word came down that Stan Musial had agreed to become the team's new general manager after Bob Howsam had departed to Cincinnati for a more plum job. "I had been retired as an active player for three years," Musial later told the *New York Times Magazine*. "I didn't have anything to do. . . . Golf a little. Take trips with the club. Talk trades with other teams. Come to think of it, I didn't even have to drive a hard bargain to get this job." As was the case with Schoendienst's appointment as field manager, Gussie Busch's chief motivation had been publicity. He needed someone to generate positive media coverage for the ball club in the wake of yet another uninspiring season. Fan favorite Musial would not disappoint him here, even though, as Curt Flood later pointed out, "his administrative gifts [had not been] exactly apparent when he was knocking the shit out of the ball."

Not that the team required another Branch Rickey. The talented core from the 1964 championship squad still remained minus declining veterans Bill White, Ken Boyer, and Dick Groat, whom Howsam had traded away. It didn't require any great leap of faith then to see the Cardinals contending for the pennant again. All they needed was a good start, a little luck, and some offense. Interestingly, they got all three in 1967.

## Chapter Three

# From Dynasty to Country Club

Like the Cardinals, the Boston Red Sox experienced their share of ups and downs through the decades. A charter member of the upstart American League, which was founded in 1901 by a former sportswriter named Byron "Ban" Johnson, the Sox, or the Americans as they were first called, were an immediate success. They decisively outdrew their more established National League crosstown rivals, the Boston Beaneaters, and secured their first AL pennant in 1903, largely on the Hall of Fame pitching arm of Denton True "Cy" Young, a 28-game winner. That fall the team played in the first World Series after they accepted a challenge from Pittsburgh Pirates owner Barney Dreyfess to meet his NL champions in a new best-of-nine postseason playoff series to determine the championship of the baseball world. With the help of the "Royal Rooters," a group of boisterous local fans who drove Pittsburgh's players to distraction with their spirited rendition of the Broadway show tune "Tessie," Boston prevailed, five games to three. "It was the greatest thing for baseball known in years," pronounced the *Boston Herald*.

The Americans repeated as AL pennant winners in 1904, but were not given the opportunity to defend their championship. That's because John T. Brush, the mercurial owner of the NL champion New York Giants, refused to allow his club to play the Americans in the World Series. Brush had been incensed at Ban Johnson for placing an AL team in New York, in direct competition with his Giants for fans and profits. His opting out of the Series was his way of getting even, despite charges in the media and among fans that he was a coward. Boston was declared

"World Champions by default" by the *Sporting News*, but this unofficial designation brought little consolation to Boston owner John I. Taylor, who had looked forward to reaping a financial windfall from the ticket sales a World Series would bring. Taylor, the pampered son of *Boston Globe* publisher and Civil War veteran General Charles H. Taylor, liked making money almost as much as he liked spending it. "He had a damn good time and gave other people a damn good time," a descendant said.

Taylor would leave a lasting imprint on the franchise. Aware that the crosstown Doves, formerly the Beaneaters, had moved away from the red hosiery that had been a distinctive part of their uniforms in 1907, Taylor prudently adopted the color for his own club, which heretofore had been outfitted in a blue design. "From now on we'll wear red stockings and I'm grabbing that name Red Sox," Taylor said. The rechristened Sox would go on to play in a glittering new steel and concrete ballpark that Taylor built in Boston's less than fashionable "Fens" area. Opened in 1912, that structure would become famous as Fenway Park—the "lyric, little bandbox of a ballpark" that novelist John Updike later mythologized in a famous *New Yorker* essay.

Taylor had sold his principal ownership stake in the team by then. The ball club passed on to former NL outfielder and Ban Johnson ally James McAleer, who in turn sold out to Canadian-born real estate magnate Joseph Lannin. Equal parts financial genius and hands-on manager, Lannin always wanted to know how his investments were faring, whether they be his extensive property holdings or his ball club. He had very little to worry about his team. After defeating the Giants in the 1912 World Series, the Sox went on to win back-to-back world championships in 1915 and 16. These teams featured such outstanding players as Tris Speaker, George "Duffy" Lewis, Harry Hooper, Bill "Rough" Carrigan, and a talented yet wildly undisciplined pitching sensation fresh out of reform school. George Herman "Babe" Ruth may have been a drinker and carouser without equal, but on a baseball diamond he was a dominant presence. Not only could he win 20 games from the mound, he could also hit a baseball, which eventually necessitated the Sox moving him permanently to the outfield after the team traded away Speaker, their best offensive player. "You know," Hooper told historian Lawrence S. Ritter, "I saw it happen, from beginning to end. But sometimes I still can't believe what I saw: this nineteen-year-old kid, crude, poorly educated, only slightly brushed by the social veneer we call civilization, gradually transformed into the idol of American youth and the symbol of baseball the world over—a man loved by more people and with an intensity of feeling that perhaps has never been equaled before or since. I saw a man transformed into something pretty close to a God. If somebody had predicted that back on the Boston Red Sox [during those years], he would have been thrown into a lunatic asylum."

The team managed to win one more championship in the war-shortened 1918 season, but the curtain was about to fall on Boston's once bright future. A New York theatrical producer named Harry Frazee had purchased the team from Lannin and in short order ran into money problems. To avoid financial disaster, Frazee entered into negotiations with New York Yankees owner Jacob Ruppert to sell Ruth, knowing full well the beer tycoon was the only person in the league that could meet his steep asking price. The details were quickly finalized. In exchange for Ruth, Frazee received $125,000 cash and a $300,000 personal loan, the existence of which both parties elected not to disclose publicly. The latter made perfect public relations sense, given that Frazee had put up Fenway Park as the security for the loan. Bostonians no doubt would have been aghast at the knowledge of a rival league operator like Ruppert holding the mortgage to their beloved ballpark. To Frazee, however, it represented a sound business move. "I can't turn that down," he reportedly said.

Frazee wasn't done wheeling and dealing, however. In need of more cash, he peddled away a steady stream of stars and soon-to-be stars—players like Waite Hoyt, Wally Schang, Everett Scott, Joe Bush, and Sam Jones—to Ruppert's Yankees. The result was the Red Sox collapsed to the bottom of the league while Ruth and his former Boston teammates carried the pinstripers to several pennants. As the estimable *Reach's Baseball Guide* reported in 1923, "Boston's last season reaped the fruits of four years' despoliation by the New York club, and for the second time in American League history this once great Boston team, now utterly discredited, fell into last place—with every prospect of remaining in that undesirable position indefinitely."

The final indignation came on April 18, 1923, when Frazee appeared as Ruppert's guest of honor during Opening Day ceremonies of the recently completed Yankee Stadium in the Bronx. The Red Sox obligingly went down in defeat, 4–1. To add further insult to injury, Ruth supplied the game-winning home run for the Yankees with two men aboard in the fourth inning. Wrote one bemused witness, "The fans were on their feet yelling and waving and throwing scorecards and half-consumed frankfurters, bellowing unto high heaven that the Babe was the greatest man on earth, that the Babe was some kid, and that the Babe could have their last and bottom dollar, together with the mortgage on their house, their wives and furniture."

The ballpark became known as "The House That Ruth Built," but a more apt nickname might have been "The House That Frazee Built," given the amount of high caliber talent the financially strapped Boston owner sent Ruppert over the years. "The Yankee dynasty of the twenties was three-quarter's the Red Sox of a few years before," Harry Hooper said. "All Frazee wanted was the money. He was short of cash and sold the whole team down the river to keep his dirty nose above the water. What a way to end a wonderful club."

Frazee sold the club to an ownership group headed by former St. Louis Browns executive Robert Quinn in the middle of the 1923 season. Woefully underfinanced, Quinn could do nothing to ameliorate the team's desperate situation. "I've been quoted as saying that the big mistake of my career was when I left the Browns in 1923 to go to the Red Sox as president and part owner," Quinn said later. "I don't remember ever having said that, but perhaps it is true, the way things turned out." Boston finished last eight times during his 10 1/2-year reign, which ended mercifully when multimillionaire sportsman Thomas Austin Yawkey purchased the club for $1.25 million in 1933.

Orphaned at an early age, Yawkey had been adopted by his mother's wealthy brother, William Hoover Yawkey, the owner of a vast lumber and mining empire that he oversaw from New York City. Summers were spent at a palatial family residence in Canada. Baseball great Ty Cobb was a frequent visitor because the elder Yawkey had been the principal owner of the Detroit Tigers from 1903 to 1908. "I was so young it didn't mean much to me but I got to know Ty as I got older," Tom later said. The two often hunted together. But that ended when the Georgia Peach let his famous competitive nature get the best of him one day. "Cobb and Mr. Yawkey and some of his friends enjoyed hunting in the Rockies for mountain goats," Carl Yastrzemski later recalled Yawkey telling him. "One of the men was sick with cancer. It probably was going to be his last hunt, and everyone agreed they'd let him get the first shot at a ram." Cobb had other ideas. When the party came upon a large ram during a climb, Cobb, always needing to be first, bagged the animal with one shot. "Mr. Yawkey got so mad that he jumped all over Cobb and they wrestled right there on the side of the mountain," Yaz said. They never reconciled.

Cobb would not be the only Hall of Famer with whom Yawkey became acquainted. Eddie Collins, the great second baseman for the Philadelphia Athletics and the Chicago White Sox, befriended the young man after Yawkey's uncle died in 1919, and encouraged him to enter the baseball business. "We used to have dinner together and one time he asked me if I'd be interested in buying a baseball club," recalled Yawkey, who had been a self-confessed "mediocre ball player" in prep school before moving on to Yale University in the early 1920s. "I said at the time I had never thought about it but it might be a possibility. I guess that's when the seed was planted."

When the Red Sox became available in 1933, Yawkey jumped at the opportunity to buy them with the sizable inheritance he had received from his uncle's estate. Enlisting Collins as his general manager and business partner, he had little difficulty convincing other American League owners to accept his bid for the debt-ridden franchise. "I know the Yawkey family," Tigers owner Walter Briggs said. "They've got money. I don't think the league should be a bank." A baseball mogul at the age of 30, Yawkey opened his checkbook and began an overhaul of the franchise. "I don't see how any man can get any real satisfaction out of taking a success and merely running it along," he said. "That's like landing a fish that somebody else hooked. The big kick comes from taking something that's down and seeing if you can put it up and across."

To demonstrate he meant business, Yawkey outfitted Fenway Park with modern amenities such as comfortable new grandstand seats and a hand-operated scoreboard, instituted a new farm system to sign and develop promising young Boston prospects, and purchased standout veteran ballplayers from other teams to beef up the club's lackluster major league roster. With regards to the latter, Yawkey acquired such premier stars as 31-game winning pitcher Robert Moses "Lefty" Grove from the Athletics and shortstop Joe Cronin from the Senators. Cronin's acquisition raised the most eyebrows. Known as a "Boy Wonder" for steering Washington to the 1933 AL pennant as a 27-year-old player-manager, Cronin's price tag came at a then record $250,000. "He's the man I want to run my ballclub and I'm going to get him," Yawkey had vowed before inking the deal with Senators owner Clark Griffith in 1934. "Boston's an Irish town. Cronin will be a tremendous favorite there."

While Cronin, a lifetime .302 hitter, did become a popular local fixture in the decade ahead, no championship banners were raised at Fenway. The closest the Sox came to first place was eight games out in 1940. The team had plenty of offense, especially when former Athletics slugger Jimmy Foxx (534 career home runs) was added to the mix in the 1935 offseason. But the club lacked the pitching to compete with the Joe DiMaggio-led Yankees of that era, winners of seven out of eight pennants from 1936 to 1943. Whereas the Yankees could send a passel of 20-game winners like Red Ruffing, Lefty Gomez, and Spud Chandler to the mound, the Sox could counter with only an aging Grove, who was reduced to being a .500 pitcher by 1940. "Yawkey couldn't buy a pennant," concluded one contemporary.

The free-spending Boston owner, however, paid off the mortgage note that Ruppert still held on Fenway Park. Only he paid it a lot sooner than expected. "I went to the Colonel [early in the 1933 baseball campaign] and told him I had already laid out a great deal of cash, and I wondered if he could carry the mortgage into the following year," Yawkey related years later. "He said yes, he was delighted to have me in the league." But Ruppert experienced an abrupt change of heart later in the season when Yawkey's Sox swept the Yankees at Fenway in five straight games. "The next morning my lawyer in New York called me to say it was a costly sweep," Yawkey said. "Ruppert's lawyer had just called, and they were demanding payment right now on the mortgage. Jake didn't like to lose five straight. So I sent the SOB (laughter) a check the next day."

Yawkey, who worshiped athletes, was also not averse to showing his players his appreciation by lavishing them with generous salaries, performance bonuses, and other perks. He even made available prostitutes from a bordello he silently owned near his off-season plantation home in South Carolina. "The girls were real happy when they went out to Mr. Yawkey's place," remembered one local. "They made good money. When the Red Sox would come down [from spring training], all the girls would go to his plantation and entertain. Not just for the night but for a couple of days." This officially sanctioned licentiousness, unthinkable for a Branch Rickey club, did not make for good team discipline, as Cronin came to learn. "Tom Yawkey was a bit of a rascal so it was tough on dad," remembered Maureen Cronin, the manager's daughter. "He'd be trying to get the players to come in at a certain time and the players would be out drinking with Tom Yawkey. A couple of times it was funny because dad would be waiting up in the hotel lobby and in would come Tom with a player and dad couldn't really say much about that." Nor could the Boston pilot say much about Yawkey's insistence on hanging around the clubhouse, dressed in team uniform, trying to be "one of the boys," and taking batting practice. "Yawkey loved the ballplayers," Cronin said.

The team's fortunes took a dramatic turn for the better when Collins made a memorable scouting trip to California in 1937, the only one of his tenure as GM from 1933 to 1947. Collins couldn't keep his eyes off a gangly, rawboned teenager who was playing outfield for his hometown San Diego Padres of the Pacific Coast League. "It wasn't hard to find Ted Williams," Collins said. "He stood out like a brown cow in a field of white cows." Though still relatively unproven as a baseball talent, Williams showed enormous promise at the plate. "When we first saw him," remembered San Diego teammate and longtime friend Bobby Doerr, "nobody on [the Padres] team knew who he was. He was just standing there by the batting cage, this tall skinny kid." Heads soon turned when he began taking swings. "Williams got in there and hit about 7–8 balls and [the veterans] started asking, 'Who's this kid?' One player said this kid will be signed [by a big league ballclub] before the week is out," said Doerr, a future All-Star second baseman with the Sox. Collins ended up picking up Williams's contract option for $25,000 to go along with Doerr's, making his West Coast jaunt the most eventful in club history. He acquired two Hall of Fame talents who would propel the team to pennant contention in the late 1940s.

Williams gave a tantalizing preview of things to come during his rookie season in Boston in 1939 when he hit .327 and drove in a league-leading 145 runs on 31 home runs. "I can't imagine anyone having a better, happier first year in the big leagues," he claimed. This positive attitude changed after Williams slumped to 13 homers and 113 RBIs the following season. Fans began to greet him with boos from the stands and Williams, an emotionally insecure person to begin with, responded in kind. "I blew up," he said. "Not acting, but *re*acting. I'd get so damned mad, throw bats, kick the columns in the dugout so that sparks flew, tear out the plumbing, knock out the lights, damn near kill myself. *Scream*. I'd scream out my own frustration." His relations with the notoriously negative Boston press were even worse. The six-time AL batting champion contemptuously viewed them as the "Knights of the Keyboard," more interested in finding imagined holes in his game and personal life than printing the truth. They "would come around pumping, pumping, always after something controversial, always listening at the keyhole, always out to put somebody on the spot," Williams complained. Dave "The Colonel" Egan of the Hearst-owned *Boston Record* was the worst offender. A Harvard Law School graduate with a contrarian bent, Egan relished getting under the Sox slugger's admittedly thin skin. "The man, of course, should be lying on a cot, talking things over with a psychiatrist and possibly unraveling his twisted mental processes," he once wrote of "baseball's terrible-tempered Mr. Bang." Williams could be equally dismissive of his nemesis. "There's one son of a bitch," he thundered, "that if someone came in that door and said, 'Dave Egan just dropped dead,' I'd say, 'Good.'"

To his credit, Williams never let his off-the-field battles affect his disciplined approach at the plate. This was, after all, where he made his living and he intended to live well as evidenced by his otherworldly performance in 1941, his breakout season. He batted .406 to become the last hitter in the 20th century to do so. Along the way, he also led the league in runs (135), homers (37), on-base percentage (.442), and slugging average (.735). "He must have hit a hundred line drives to right field that year that were sinking liners between the second baseman and right fielder," Doerr recalled. "On his bat, there would be a white spot on the fat part, where he was hitting every ball. Not just one bat, but a lot of bats. That's how sharp he was." Even for Williams, the magnitude of his accomplishment, which the late evolutionary biologist and baseball fan Stephen Jay Gould characterized as "a beacon in the history of excellence," did not personally sink in until the season was over. "Geez," he revealed to his road roommate Charlie Wagner, "I hit .406."

Williams was not the only young Sox player to blossom during these years. Doerr came into his own as a second baseman, leading the league with 118 turned double plays and a .975 fielding percentage in 1942. He also wasn't too shabby with the bat either, hitting 15 home runs and driving in 102. Bob Feller, the Hall of Fame right-hander from the Indians, could attest to Doerr's offensive skills. "I broke up two no-hitters on him, getting the only hit both times—both singles just over the infield," Doerr proudly recalled. Dom DiMaggio and Johnny Pesky provided further punch. Table setters for Williams at the top of the Boston lineup, these former minor league standouts were high average contact hitters who were always on base. The only problem, as far as Joe Cronin was concerned, was that Pesky sometimes felt the urge to steal a base. "Jesus Christ, Pesky, they told me you were raised in a ball park and now I find out you've got a hole in your head," the Sox manager scolded him. "You've got the best hitter in baseball coming up right behind you, and he hits the ball and you're going to score. You damn well won't run."

One highly touted player who might have made an even bigger impact than Pesky or DiMaggio was Harold "Pee Wee" Reese. The future All-Star double-play partner of Jackie Robinson on the Brooklyn Dodgers, Reese was considered the premier shortstop prospect within the Boston organization, if not all of baseball. But Cronin, looking to extend his own tenure at the team's lead defensive infield position by a couple of years, convinced Yawkey to ship Reese to the Dodgers for $35,000 in

1939. "Yawkey, who did not need the money, had virtually given away a diamond of a player without even giving him a shot," the author David Halberstam later concluded. Sox first baseman Tony Lupien was even more to the point. "Joe didn't want to move to third base," he said.

Despite the loss of Reese, the Red Sox appeared to have enough burgeoning talent to at last displace the Yankees from their traditional perch atop the AL in the early 1940s. Alas, the coming of the Second World War rudely altered that calculus. Outside of Doerr, who played through most of the 1944 season before being called up to the Army in early September, this promising young nucleus was forced to temporarily disband after 1942 due to the obligatory military service demands of the day. Williams, DiMaggio, and Pesky all exchanged their baseball togs for regulation US Navy uniforms. In their absence, the Sox filled out their depleted roster with 4-Fs, has-beens, and not-ready-for-prime-time youngsters, a sorry amalgam that plunged the team deep in the standings. The ball club "now wore more patches than Huckleberry Finn, and they started out like a Frazee or Quinn team at its worst," noted the historian Frederick G. Lieb. Things were so bad that a clearly over-the-hill Cronin was compelled to remain active as a player even longer than he wanted. Nevertheless, he found one final moment of glory when he connected for three pinch-hit homers in four at-bats in 1943. "I guess the old man showed them today," he crowed afterward.

With America's sweeping victory over the Axis powers in 1945, Red Sox fans eagerly looked forward to a revival of their team's fortunes the following season. They were not disappointed. Returning service veterans Williams, Pesky, DiMaggio, and Doerr quickly regained their prewar batting strokes and powered a red-hot Boston offense that led the AL in total runs (792), hits (1,441), batting average (.271), and on-base percentage (.356). The club's pitching was equally dominating thanks to the righty-lefty combination of Dave "Boo" Ferriss and Cecil Carlton "Tex" Hughson, two hard-throwing "good ole boys" from the Deep South who accounted for 25 and 20 wins, respectively. "We had a wonderful team," exclaimed Williams, who took home AL Most Valuable Player honors while hitting .342 with 38 homers and 123 RBIs.

Reeling off a pair of 17- and 10-game-winning streaks at the start of the season, the team left the rest of the competition, including an underperforming Yankees squad, in the proverbial dust. "It seems we were always in first place," said Pesky, a .335 hitter on the year. "Then in July, when we had a ten-game lead, we all knew we were in. It was an amazing year. There just didn't seem to ever be any real pressure." The question became not if the Sox could clinch the pennant but when. Fittingly, Williams provided the answer in Cleveland's cavernous Municipal Stadium on September 13, when the notoriously slow-footed slugger legged out an inside-the-park homer that gave Boston a 1–0 victory and the pennant. "That was the only inside-the-park home run I ever hit," Williams later admitted. "And it was the hardest. I had to run."

As satisfying and rewarding as the regular season was, the subsequent World Series loss to the Cardinals proved a major letdown. No one felt more disheartened by the team's disappointing performance than Williams. In what turned out to be the only Series appearance of his illustrious career, Williams hit a weak .200 with five hits, all singles. "I never got going, I never really felt swishy at the plate," Williams lamented. Overcome by the magnitude of the loss, the visibly depressed Sox star had a hard time mustering the energy to shower or leave the ballpark. "I couldn't believe we'd lost," he recounted. "I was shell-shocked. I was so disappointed in myself. Just sick inside. I gave my Series check to Johnny Orlando, the clubhouse boy who had always been there to give me consolation when I was down." Not long afterward, Williams was seen weeping openly before a crowd of curious onlookers.

Following the shattering Series loss, the Red Sox were still a formidable ball club despite losing 1946 pitching staff leaders Ferriss and Hughson to career-shortening arm injuries. Although the team slipped to 83 wins and third place in 1947, they came within an eyelash of winning consecutive AL pennants during the next two years. In 1948 they finished in a first place tie with Cleveland on the last day of the regular season, but lost a one-game playoff the following afternoon at Fenway Park. New Sox skipper Joe McCarthy, taking over for the departed Cronin, who had been moved to the front office to assume the duties of

The fiery Ted Williams led the Red Sox to the AL pennant in 1946, but fell short in the World Series. BASEBALL HALL OF FAME PHOTO ARCHIVE

a dying Collins, shocked the baseball world with his choice of playoff starter. He selected 37-year-old journeyman pitcher Denny Galehouse, the owner of a 109–118 lifetime record. He did this despite having Mel Parnell, his well-rested staff ace, available.

Why McCarthy, a Hall of Fame manager with seven championships to his credit, made this curious choice remains shrouded in controversy. Earlier in the summer Galehouse had pitched well in relief against Cleveland and McCarthy believed the former St. Louis Browns right-hander could replicate that success. "I was hoping he would do it again," the one-time Cubs and Yankees field general told the historian Donald Honig years later. "But he didn't." Indeed, Galehouse was pummeled by the Indians, giving up a pair of homers and four earned runs before departing for the showers after three innings of an eventual 8–3 loss. "Everybody thought I'd be pitching," said Parnell, a 15-game winner on the season. "I was in the bullpen, but I wasn't used. We were kind of stunned out there. In all fairness to Galehouse . . . his day had passed. It was the tail end of his career. We kind of felt it was a bad choice, simply because Denny was getting on in age. The old saying is that in a game like that you go with your best, and if you lose with your best, you have no complaints. I felt at that time I was the man for that game, because I was the leading pitcher on the staff and it was my turn."

The 1949 season brought more heartbreak and frustration. After a slow start, which saw the team mired in the second division in early July, the Sox caught fire in late summer and took first place behind the torrid hitting of Williams and infielder Vern Stephens. Stephens had been acquired in a blockbuster trade with the cash-strapped Browns for eight players and a hefty chunk of Tom Yawkey's wallet two years earlier. Together the two All-Star sluggers combined for 82 homers and 318 RBIs to pace a rugged Boston lineup that hit a league-leading .282 and scored 896 runs. "We had a great thing going," Williams enthused. Heading into the final two games of the season in New York, the Sox held a one-game lead over the Yankees and needed to win just one of the contests to clinch the pennant. It was not to be. In the first game, the visitors squandered a 4–0 lead and ended up losing, 5–4, when light hitting

Yankee outfielder Johnny Lindell broke up a 4–4 tie in the eighth inning with a solo home run blast into the left-field stands. "It's all McCarthy's fault," Lindell said afterward of his former manager. "When I came to the Yankees, he switched me to the outfield."

The second game was not as close but nevertheless provided its share of high drama. Down 5–0 in the ninth, the Sox staged a dramatic rally that fell two runs short when rookie Yankees manager Casey Stengel decided to stay with his ace starter Vic Raschi. Raschi, a no-nonsense right-hander from Springfield, Massachusetts, who would just as soon see his arm amputated than leave the mound in a tight game, recorded the final out after he induced Boston catcher Birdie Tebbets to pop out on an outside pitch. Just prior to this pitching sequence, Raschi had snarled to teammate Tommy Henrich to "get the hell out of here" when the first baseman tried to offer some encouraging words of support. A different and more debilitating kind of emotion seized the Red Sox on their way home. "The five-hour train ride to Boston was the longest I've ever been on," Williams confessed. "It was like a damn funeral train. Everybody was stunned. We had come so far, had made up so much ground. The whole year had just wound up terrible."

Drained by their near miss pennant drives, the Sox spent the 1950s mired in mediocrity, finishing no better than third place. Williams remained a potent offensive force, but other stalwarts such as Doerr, Pesky, and DiMaggio either retired or were traded, leaving huge gaps in the everyday lineup that the team's suddenly moribund farm system proved incapable of filling. "I think the Red Sox had a tendency to bring up the kids a little too soon," said DiMaggio who hung up his cleats early in the 1953 season. "They rushed them up, and they should have given them more time in the minors." A case in point was "can't miss" left-hander Maurice "Mickey" McDermott. Just 19-years-old when the Sox hastily promoted him to the majors, the tall, cocky New Jersey native dazzled most observers with his ability to deliver 98-per mile fastballs over the plate. But a combination of wildness, immaturity, and chronic alcohol abuse doomed him from rising above the level of a journeyman pitcher. "I got lost on the road to the Baseball Hall of Fame," McDermott later joked.

Ted Lepcio was a similar bust. A promising middle infielder with power who had been signed in 1951, the All-American from Seton Hall University got called up to the parent club the following year and batted .263 in 84 games. But the rigors of big-league pitching and the pressure to perform at a high level proved too much for Lepcio. His average went south and he was eventually relegated to a permanent spot on the bench. "Instead of sending him back for seasoning, [the Red Sox] kept him around, fighting for a job he wasn't ready for," complained one baseball executive. Traded later to the Phillies, Lepcio suffered the indignity of being described by his manager Eddie Sawyer as "the worst player I ever saw."

Contributing to the mediocrity on the field was an inept front office. While Joe Cronin had been a competent dugout manager, he proved to be completely out of his depth as the team's general manager. Having grown fat and indolent following his retirement as a player, Cronin spent his waking hours largely detached from the day-to-day running of the ball club. He apparently did not even make the time or effort to familiarize himself with the top minor league prospects the team had signed, including a talented young outfielder fresh off the campus of the University of Notre Dame. "He doesn't seem very big," was all Cronin could say upon meeting Carl Yastrzemski in 1958.

Cronin was equally languid in coming up with trades to improve the team. Although he did manage to pry away All-Star slugging outfielder Jackie Jensen from Washington in 1953, the majority of his deals were minor and underwhelming. "You can't do business with the Red Sox," complained one rival executive. "Cronin wants to sleep on everything. You think things are all settled and he starts backing out. Unless he's absolutely certain he will get the best of it, he won't deal. I gave up on him years ago." Where Cronin showed some vigor was loading the organization with a bunch of cronies and glorified coat-holders. "I don't think a single scout was fired when Cronin was GM," a journalist disdainfully noted. "Some of them were friends that went back to his days with the Pirates [the team he broke into the majors with in 1925]."

Regrettable as these shortcomings were, they were nothing compared to Cronin's glaring unwillingness to sign, develop, and promote talented ballplayers of color during his 11-year tenure as GM. It would not be until 1959 that the Red Sox finally integrated their roster, almost eight months after Cronin left the organization to become president of the American League. As a result, the team earned the dubious distinction of being the last ball club in the majors to have an African American playing for them. The sad irony is that the Sox could have been trailblazers when it came to breaking professional baseball's long-established color line.

In 1945 future Hall of Famer Jackie Robinson and two other Negro League stars, Sam Jethroe of the Cleveland Buckeyes and Marvin Williams of the Philadelphia Stars, were given a tryout at Fenway Park along with several white high school prospects. Despite performing impressively in a workout supervised by then Sox coach Hugh Duffy ["We hit that Green Monster real hard—all of us," Williams remembered], Robinson and his comrades were never given a second look. "We were fairly certain they wouldn't call us, and we had no intention of calling them," Robinson later revealed in his controversial autobiography, *I Never Had It Made*. The reason the ballplayers felt this way had to do with the "insincere" nature of the tryout. The Sox had agreed to stage one only after receiving pressure from a Boston city councilman about the team's lily-white employment practices. The councilman, Isadore Muchnick, threatened to initiate legislation that would ban Sunday baseball games if the Sox persisted in excluding blacks from job consideration. "I still remember how I hit the ball that day, good to all fields," Robinson said. "What happened? Nothing!"

Four years after letting Robinson slip through their fingers, the team passed on an opportunity to sign an even greater talent: Willie Mays. A Hall of Fame center fielder who would hit 660 home runs over a dazzling 22-year career, Mays was then a promising young star with the Black Barons, a Negro League team that had an agreement with a white Boston farm club operating in Birmingham, Alabama. In return for allowing the Negro Leaguers use of their home ballpark, the Sox farm club received "first refusal on any Black Baron players." Given Mays's exceptional abilities with the glove and the bat, it seemed a given the Sox would sign him to a contract. But the Boston front office determined that

Mays was "not the Red Sox type" and instead opted to sign his manager, aging Negro League second baseman Lorenzo "Piper" Davis, to a minor league contract. "There's no telling what I would have been able to do in Boston," Mays later said. "I really thought I was going to Boston." As for Davis, he would not last a full season in the organization, despite leading his Class A Scanton, Pennsylvania, team in hitting and stolen bases. He was unceremoniously informed by club officials that his release was due to "economic conditions." Not until infielder Elijah "Pumpsie" Green was brought on board in the late 1950s did the Sox even attempt to have another black compete for a roster spot.

While Cronin, who claimed the team had "no use" for Mays at the time, deserves a large share of the blame, there is no question he was taking the lead from his boss. For Tom Yawkey, a longtime resident of the Deep South, possessed views on race that were all too common of that era, namely that blacks were inferior and that they should be segregated from white society. To this end, he saw nothing wrong with employing field managers like Mike "Pinky" Higgins, who vowed there would be "no niggers on the ball club as long as I have anything to say about it." Incredibly, Higgins would be promoted to general manager in 1963 despite or perhaps because of this overt racism.

Yawkey himself is suspected of being the unidentified heckler who shouted, "Get those niggers off the field," when Robinson, Jethroe, and Williams were trying out at Fenway Park in 1945. "He is probably one of the most bigoted guys in organized baseball," Robinson once said. More significantly, Yawkey supported the findings of the highly classified Major League Steering Committee report of August 27, 1946, that condemned efforts to sign black ballplayers. "Certain groups in this country including political and social-minded drum-beaters, are conducting pressure campaigns in an attempt to force major league clubs to sign negro players," the report warned. "Members of these groups are not primarily interested in Professional Baseball. . . . They know little about baseball—and nothing about the business end of its operation. They single out Professional Baseball for attack because it offers a good publicity medium." That same year, fellow owner Larry MacPhail complained to Yawkey during a night of "talk and drink" at New York's famed

Toot Shor's restaurant that integration was going to "ruin" their business. Yawkey could only nod in agreement. "The buck stopped at the top," maintained the historian Glen Stout. "Yawkey was someone who almost had no life outside of being owner of the Red Sox. This was not a man who was going to take dramatic action. He was someone that allowed a temperament to proceed after it had disappeared elsewhere or was beginning to disappear elsewhere."

The bad racial vibes would continue in the Red Sox organization even after the team bowed to the inevitable and began signing African American ballplayers in large numbers after 1959. Pitcher Earl Wilson, the team's second black player, earned management's displeasure when he publicly complained of being discriminated against at a bar near the team's spring training facility in Winter Haven, Florida. "We don't serve niggers in here," he was informed. Wilson, whose initial Boston scouting report described him as "a well mannered colored boy, not too black, pleasant to talk to," soon found himself traded away to Detroit where he became a 20-game winner with the Tigers. "Tom Yawkey had his farmers on his farm," Wilson told the author and Red Sox historian Dan Shaughnessy. "They were black. What other people call great is bad for other people. Some probably thought Hitler was a great person. And they truly thought he was, but they wasn't Jewish and didn't have to deal with it. But once you're in that little guy's empire—everybody's got their cronies and junk, I don't know. I might have been a public pressure. You never know." For his part, Yawkey denied that race had anything to do with his organizational hiring decisions. "I have no feeling against colored people," he commented to a *Sports Illustrated* reporter in 1965. "I employ a lot of them in the South. But they are clannish, and when that story got around that we didn't want Negroes they all decided to sign with some other club. Actually, we scouted them right along, but we didn't want one because he was a Negro. We wanted a ballplayer."

Yawkey's anachronistic views on race were not out of synch with many Bostonians. Up until the 20th century, African Americans had represented a small but vibrant portion of city's population. Settled along the northwestern slope of Beacon Hill, this community had played an active role in the struggle for emancipation in the years leading up to the Civil War. During the war, many local blacks deepened their commitment to the cause by volunteering to join the 54th Massachusetts Volunteer Infantry, the first African American regiment raised by any northern state for the union army. When several hundred members of the regiment were killed during a heroic assault on Fort Wagner, at the gates of Charleston, South Carolina, in July 1863, their "common martyrdom," the late historian J. Anthony Lukas concluded, "helped cast a glow of brotherhood over the city's race relations."

Alas, this "golden era" of racial harmony did not last very long. Black Bostonians continued to be subjected to the same traditional forms of racial discrimination that had existed before the war in terms of housing, schools, jobs, and public accommodations. By the turn of the century, little had changed in a real socioeconomic sense, apart from the fact that blacks now lived predominantly in the lower South End and Roxbury sections of the city. As scholar Stephan Thernstrom observed in his seminal book *The Other Bostonians*, "There was virtually no improvement in the occupational position of Black men in Boston between the late nineteenth century and the beginning of [the 1940s]."

With the outbreak of the Second World War, however, came dramatic change. The city's black population doubled in size—the result of a larger national trend that saw millions of blacks migrate from the Deep South to urban centers in the North and Midwest due to the wartime economic boom conditions that existed there. Boston was no exception as many blacks found good paying jobs in war-related industries. But along with this influx came new problems. Blacks began to move out of their now overcrowded neighborhoods into formerly all-white ones. This development, in turn, caused panic among many whites, who felt their "turf" was in danger of being permanently overrun. Wrote Boston historian Thomas H. O'Connor: "Racial tensions quickly mounted as whites fears of blacks taking over their jobs, lowering the standards of their all-white schools, bringing down property values, and adding to the danger of crime in the streets."

Even with an integrated team roster, the Red Sox continued to struggle in the standings. Starting in 1961, when Carl Yastrzemski took over for a retired Ted Williams in left field, and extending to 1966, the club finished an average of 29 games out of first place. "We were the Mets before there was a Mets," Yaz said. Indeed, these "Red Flops," who were usually out of the pennant race by Memorial Day, featured one of the most colorful if dysfunctional cast of ballplayers to have ever donned a Boston uniform.

Taking top billing was Dick "Dr. Strangeglove" Stuart. Acquired in a trade with the Pirates, the brash right-handed hitting first baseman connected for an impressive 75 homers in his brief two-year stint with the team in the mid-1960s. But he struck out 274 times and committed a whopping 53 errors. "He wasn't called 'Dr. Strangeglove' for nothing," maintained Yastrzemski. So incompetent was Stuart with the glove that he once received a standing ovation from a bemused Fenway crowd for catching a hot dog wrapper that had blown onto the playing field. "I star gaze in the field," Stuart told the writer Arnold Hano in 1964. "I do not concentrate well. Basically I have a good pair of hands. The play I make worst is a groundball right at me. I tend to take my eye off the ball to check the pitcher and the runner. That's when I boot it. But if I have to go into the hole and come up firing, I will do it instinctively, and well. It is only when I think that I get into trouble."

Stuart presented almost as many problems in the clubhouse. His fun-loving, irreverent approach to the game grated on the nerves of his teammates and dugout bosses. He observed no set training rules, loudly overestimated his athletic skills, and frequently showed up drunk at team meetings. "Dick Stuart would try to take advantage of people," explained Dick "The Monster" Radatz, an All-Star reliever for the Sox in the early 1960s. Unsurprisingly, Stuart revealed to a *Sport* magazine writer that every minor league manager he had ever played for had challenged him to a fight. "I couldn't have licked half of them," he claimed. Given Stuart's physically imposing 6'4", 212-pound frame, this must rank as one of the few times during his lengthy pro career that the egocentric Californian was being modest. "He was the poorest excuse for a caring baseball player I've ever seen," commented Dick Williams, a teammate of Stuart who was about to retire and begin a long career in managing. "I don't care if he did hit 75 homers in two years with the Red Sox. He tried to hit nothing but home runs, and those players are no good for anybody. The Red Sox won a lot of games when he was there, didn't they?" Never shy about expressing his own opinions, Stuart was also not above second-guessing the competence of his superiors to their faces. "He was always telling me that I'd be lucky to bat two hundred against the pitching in the sixties," said Johnny Pesky, who managed the team to a pair of second division finishes in 1963 and 1964. "Then, he was always saying, 'John, did you ever hit a home run?' But, if you took the bat out of Stuart's hand, he wasn't even a good semipro player."

Starting pitcher Gene Conley was another eccentric who provided more laughs than victories during his years with the team. A rare two-sport athlete, Conley spent his winters backing up Bill Russell at center for the World Champion Boston Celtics of the National Basketball Association. But the physical and mental stress of playing professional sports for most of the calendar year had become too much of a burden for the tall right-hander. He escaped into alcohol which got him into considerable trouble one hot July afternoon in New York in 1962. "I'd had a terrible day at Yankee Stadium, and so had my teammates," he later recalled. "Even Yaz mishandled a ball or two. It was one big mess, a nightmare. So I'd gotten an early start and had a glow on when I got on the bus after the game."

Caught in a traffic jam, an agitated Conley felt that it would be a good idea to decamp from the bus and hit a local watering hole with teammate Pumpsie Green. "I didn't have anything specific in mind," Conley said. "I just figured we'd have a few drinks and felt it was worth $50 or $100 for a night in New York to rest and relax." Somewhere along the way, however, Conley believed it would make more sense to alter their travel itinerary. He decided they should go to Jerusalem, "to get everything straightened out between me and my Savior." Green wisely bowed out but Conley grew so determined to reach the Promised Land that he made it all the way to Idlewild Airport. His plan "to meet God" came undone when he was unable to produce a passport. "I was so disappointed, you just wouldn't believe it," Conley said. "I thought, 'What the heck.' Otherwise I would have gone." For his actions throughout this episode, Conley was levied a $1,500 fine by the team. He was out of baseball two years later. "Looking back, I guess I took that 100 percent stuff a little too far," said Conley who eventually sobered up and became a Seventh Day Adventist. "I always gave 100 percent on the field, and that's the way it should be. But I also gave 100 percent off the field, and sometimes that got me into trouble."

As the losses piled up, Tom Yawkey grew despondent. Though he had poured millions of his personal fortune into the ball club, he had precious little to show for his financial commitment apart from one pennant and a lot of headaches. Unwilling to recognize that his own managerial incompetence and racism were largely responsible for the team's poor performance, Yawkey instead lashed out against what he thought was the real culprit: the Boston media. They had taken to mockingly calling his highly paid, underachieving roster a "Country Club," which only served to enrage Yawkey further. "There is such a thing as human dignity and the American way of life in which I believe," he lectured a press room full of local scribes one day. "But when [reporters] go beyond that, I don't like it. They better not push too far or I'll take this team out of Boston. I am not bluffing."

Yawkey had been actively entertaining the idea of moving the team to another major urban market for years. In fact, when the Braves abandoned Milwaukee for Atlanta after the 1965 season (they had left Boston 13 years earlier), "Brew Town" became a prime target of interest for the Sox owner. But to suggest, as Yawkey did, that he was willing to pull up stakes in Boston solely from bad media coverage is stretching the truth. With Fenway Park in disrepair and the team's popularity plummeting (the Sox averaged only 8,000 fans per game by 1965), Yawkey was seeking the same kind of attendance boost and lucrative payday that the Dodgers and Giants had achieved when they uprooted their franchises for the greener financial pastures of California in 1957. "We've been losing money and sooner or later you come to the realization that it can't go on forever," Yawkey said. "There has to be a stop or you'll be bankrupt. And I don't intend to bankrupt myself."

Yawkey did not rule out the possibility of staying in Boston. Getting a modern publicly financed ballpark with expanded seating and parking to replace Fenway would go a long way in keeping his Red Sox around, he implied. "With a new stadium this club would be a financial success," he argued. "There's no doubt in my mind. Without one, it cannot be.

Tom Yawkey's astonishing incompetence and personal demons brought his team to the brink of disaster by the early 1960s. BASEBALL HALL OF FAME PHOTO ARCHIVE

And if I were disposed to sell or something happened to my health; the person who took over this club would find it almost impossible to exist financially in Fenway Park." The main obstacle was political. No one in Boston City Hall or the Massachusetts State House was willing to press voters to fork over their hard-earned tax dollars to build a sprawling stadium complex that would primarily benefit a multimillionaire like Yawkey. And this irked him. "In the past five years there have been a half dozen new stadiums constructed in the country," he said in reference to communities like Houston and Atlanta where the Astrodome and Fulton County Stadium were unveiled, respectively. "In all that time all we've done in Boston is talk. I wonder why? Why can those other cities build stadiums and not Boston?" In truth, Yawkey never felt particularly comfortable discussing such matters, especially with prying journalists.

"I can take any one of your stories and find 30 mistakes in it every day," he informed members of the Fourth Estate. "People who couldn't run trolley cars are telling me how to run a six million dollar business. I can fight. I'm 57-years-old and I've had every bone in my body broken at some time or other. I can fight. Maybe the guy I'm up against doesn't like broken bones."

Despite the defiant tone, Yawkey became an increasingly absent figure around Fenway Park as the 1960s wore on. Evidently there was only so much losing and off-field antics from his players that he could take. As one cynical writer put it, "Route 128 [a highway that encircles Boston] is like the Red Sox. Both are always being rebuilt and the jobs are never finished." More importantly, Yawkey was struggling to overcome health issues. Decades of heavy drinking and "good living" had taken their toll. Always heavyset, he now tipped the scales at 250 pounds with a blood sugar count that was astronomically high. Only a 1963 doctor's visit convinced him of the stark choice he now faced: "[c]hange his ways or forget about living." He opted for the former. "I was the kind of guy that always liked a few cocktails before and after dinner," he said in a 1965 interview. "But then I gave up liquor almost entirely. Once since at the owner meetings in Florida I had a couple of drinks when the fellas were sitting around talking baseball, but that's about all."

His newfound sobriety had a major effect on the management of his ball club. After years of front office mismanagement by Cronin and Pinky Higgins, who ended up serving jail time in Louisiana for killing a man in a car accident, Yawkey recognized that he needed to shake things up. Concluding the 1965 regular season, he summarily fired Higgins and handed over the keys of his struggling franchise to a respected longtime front office employee named Dick O'Connell.

A native of Boston's North Shore, the college educated O'Connell had joined the Red Sox organization in 1946, following a stint as a naval intelligence officer on the staff of Pacific Fleet Commander Chester Nimitz during the Second World War. "It was strictly by accident that I ended up in baseball," he later confessed. In need of a job out of the service, he thought he'd try his luck with the Olde Towne Team. The ball club had just purchased a minor league affiliate in nearby Lynn and was looking for someone to handle its business affairs. O'Connell had no problem convincing GM Eddie Collins that he would be a perfect choice. "He knew how to operate," remembered Johnny Pesky, who first met O'Connell while they were stationed together at Pearl Harbor during the war.

After quickly proving his worth in Lynn, O'Connell was promoted to the parent club where he was given increasing levels of executive responsibility. "He became a sort of an all-around troubleshooter," noted journalist and historian Al Hirshberg. Through it all, O'Connell did not let this hard-earned success go to his head. "Baseball, the whole game is trivial," he once said. "I knew it then and I know it now. Oh, it gives people pleasure, people in hospitals something to think about, something to listen to, but it is all so trivial." Later, when he was asked by an up and coming *Boston Globe* baseball writer named Peter Gammons to list his proudest accomplishment as Sox GM, he was equally modest. "You got me," he said.

This refreshing candor aside, O'Connell was not without faults. He could be frustratingly aloof and demanding of his fellow coworkers and underlings. "I don't know whether he means it or not," complained one disillusioned subordinate, "but he criticizes people behind their backs and has trouble dealing with people at times." Not that such criticism would particularly bother O'Connell. "All I ask in this organization," he said, "is that each employee do what he was hired for, and keep his nose out of other people's departments." What he cared most about was the bottom line, whether that meant the team turning an annual financial profit or contending for a pennant. "This can be a damned-if-you-do, damned-if-you-don't job," he reasoned. "It's a business where you try to put together the potential to win with a break here or a break there."

Unlike his predecessors, O'Connell had a more enlightened attitude when it came to matters of race. "I don't care what color a player is as long as he can play," he said. "If he is any good I want to sign him." He was as good as his word as he made a point of developing and promoting talented African American prospects including George Scott, Joe Foy, Reggie Smith, and future Hall of Famer Jim Rice, during his tenure. "To me," said Howard Bryant, author of *Shut Out: A Story of Race and Baseball in Boston*, "Dick O'Connell is the most underrated person in Red Sox history. He is the first Red Sox executive to look at the club and make baseball decisions and not crony decisions." For sure, he reinvigorated the entire baseball operation, bringing in bright young executives such as Haywood Sullivan to head player personnel, beefing up the scouting system, improving the ballpark, and exhibiting an overall professionalism that had been sorely lacking. "He wasn't part of the Yawkey Crony Club," Bryant maintained. "He was a Bostonian, he wasn't from the south. He was never the guy who was invited down to the plantation in South Carolina [like Cronin and Higgins]. He was a different guy. And because he was outside of the club, he was given free reign."

O'Connell also exercised considerable sway when it came to selecting a new manager. Following another ninth-place finish for the Sox in 1966, O'Connell decided it would be prudent to sack the dugout incumbent, former Brooklyn Dodgers star Billy Herman, an uninspiring Higgins hire who seemed to prefer the golf links to the baseball diamond. "He was always talking golf—how he did on this course, what club he used on a certain hole," groused Yastrzemski. "It just seemed to me that if you're trying to turn around a team, the team should be thinking about baseball. So should the manager."

To fill the vacant post, O'Connell turned to another Dodger product with an impressive minor league track record: Dick Williams. "From the start being around [O'Connell] was a blessing," said Williams who had just finished piloting Boston's Triple A Toronto farm team to its second straight International League championship in 1966. "He loved [kid ballplayers], and seeing as he showed up unannounced to watch a three-game series in Columbus that year and talked only to me, I assumed he was also interested in kid managers." O'Connell was, especially in stern disciplinarian types who were unafraid of asserting their authority over the clubhouse. Williams, an accomplished utility man throughout most of his 14-year big league career, fit the bill here. He played no favorites and demanded maximum effort at all time. He indicated as much during his first Boston press conference as Sox skipper. "If a player doesn't want to comply with the rules . . . well, see you later for him," he warned. "It's as simple as that." "Williams was tough," O'Connell acknowledged. "That's why I hired him. That's what we needed."

The Red Flops were history.

## Chapter Four

# Pursuing a Dream

Dick Williams was never one to wear rose-colored glasses. Proud, abrasive, opinionated, vindictive, arrogant, and demanding, the new Red Sox manager had no illusions about the difficult job that lay ahead. As his players arrived at the team spring training headquarters in Winter Haven, Florida, in late February, Williams realized he needed to radically transform the mindset of the perennially losing ball club. "I knew about the lackadaisical play, but I'd have to say that was management's fault," he later told the author Peter Golenbock. "Most of the players are going to do the least amount of work they can do unless you stay on them." He intended to be different, but the Boston media was understandably skeptical given the unbroken run of failure from previous regimes. "Another endless summer of Uncle Tom's Townies begins Saturday morning when recreation director Dick Williams asks them to try to touch their toes a few times and throw the baseball around just to get the feel of things," wrote Bud Collins of the *Boston Globe*. "He won't ask them to do anything the hard right away, like catching the baseball. They will have trouble doing that in August, and to ask them now would only break their spirits before the season has begun."

To demonstrate he meant business, Williams assembled the team on the first official day of camp and laid down the law—Williams' Law. "Well, I'm here on a one-year deal," he said of the $35,000 pact he signed with the club the previous October. "I can put you in the first division. I can put some pride back into you, and if you don't want to be proud of yourself as a ballplayer, I can find some distant places to send you." With

The intense and domineering Dick Williams shook things up in spring training.
PHOTO BY BOSTON RED SOX

those words, Williams did something that Johnny Pesky, Pinky Higgins, and Billy Herman had never been able to accomplish during their shortened managerial tenures—command respect. "The players understood they weren't going to get away with some of the things they had gotten away with, the lackadaisical play, not running out ground balls, giving excuses for not playing in certain ballgames," recalled pitcher Darrel Brandon. Williams further raised the bar by insisting everyone on the squad show up for workouts in peak physical shape. "During the winter we told each player what we expected him to weigh on opening day of the regular season," he briefed reporters. "At our last weight check, every man on the squad was already under the limit." To ensure they remained that way, Williams imposed a rigorous conditioning program of daily calisthenics and running. "Williams has a schedule mapped out for them that looks like something out of West Point," a writer half-jokingly said. For Williams, however, the issue was no laughing matter. "I feel this is important," he said. "Take last year's team. It got killed early in the season by losing 34 of 42 one run games. To me, that indicates that the club wasn't in top physical condition and didn't have it in the late innings."

Going hand in hand with a strict fitness regimen was the importance of fundamentals. "I took the whole club, position-by-position, around the diamond, explaining offensive and defensive possibilities," Williams said. "It took three days to do it, a good hour-and-a-half at each stop. I talked about things like when to pick up signs. It starts in the on-deck circle. The sooner you look, the coach will flash a sign—even before you leave the batting circle." The time and effort were well spent. The average age of the team was only 24.6 years, the second youngest in the league, and they needed the direction. "We didn't know how to study the game," said infielder George Scott, who was entering his second season with the Red Sox in 1967. "Dick Williams showed us how to do it that spring. He pressed the right buttons for everyone on that team." Williams was equally tough off the diamond, demanding that his players observe proper club etiquette when it came to showing up to meetings on time and making curfew. "He checks rooms with a vengeance," the *Sporting News* noted, "at times even going so far as to walk into the rooms late at night." Two players who challenged him early on these points, pitchers Bob Sadowski and Dennis Bennett, soon found themselves toiling for other ball clubs. "Bennett later threatened to sue me for saying he was a bad influence on the younger players," Williams claimed. "But the suit was never filed. Must have realized that truth is an unbeatable defense." The days of the old Country Club were clearly over and rival managers took notice. "He seems to know how to handle men," commented White Sox manager Eddie Stanky. "And I don't think he'll put up with any nonsense." Sam Mele of the Twins seconded that thought. "He's tough without making a project out of it," he said. "They'd better know that when he says something, he means it."

Carl Yastrzemski was the first to learn this painful truth. In his inaugural act as manager, Williams had stripped him of his team captaincy. "I'm the only chief," he said. "The rest of them are Indians." The bold move should not have come as a surprise. Williams made no secret he had found Yaz's leadership ability and overall baseball IQ wanting when the two had been teammates. "Carl, you run the bases just like [Jackie] Robinson," he told him. "The only difference is that you get caught." Williams later conceded he could have been more tactful about breaking the news of his star outfielder's demotion. "Yeah, and maybe I should have asked everyone on the team how many games they wanted to play," he said. "And maybe I would have lasted in Boston for six months. And had my goddamn living room repossessed. The hell with grace. I wanted wins. Isn't that what the fans wanted? My ass was on the line on a one-year contract, and during that time this team was going to do everything Dick Williams's way, not Millie Putz's way, nor Yaz's way. Eliminating the club captaincy was just my first way of passing that message along." To his credit, Yastrzemski did not complain, even though he suffered a slight dip in salary as a result. He preferred to lead through his actions on the field anyway and being team captain had distracted him from concentrating on his hitting and fielding. "I want to get one thing clear," he told Williams. "I'm here to play ball the best way I know how. Nothing else matters. I'll do anything you tell me to. All I want is for this club to have a good year."

While cutting down to size the team's best player was one thing, taking on the face of the franchise was something else altogether. And this is precisely the awkward position Williams found himself in when he told the last of the game's .400 hitters to hit the road. Ted Williams, the team's popular spring training instructor, had invited the ire when he openly criticized Williams's novel practice of having idle pitchers play volleyball to maintain muscle tone and strength. "Maybe some people don't like volleyball," the Boston skipper rejoined. "But I am the manager and the pitchers will continue to play volleyball." Humiliated, the Splendid Splinter packed his bags and walked out of camp muttering "Volleyball! What is this game coming to?" Williams didn't care. "He never said a word to me," he recalled. "That is, until the following October, at the World Series. He was full of congratulations then. Funny thing, not once did he mention volleyball." The biting commentary was emblematic of Williams's blunt communication skills as manager. "Our manager is a Dale Carnegie dropout," cracked one thoughtful observer. Players did their best to stay out his caustic line of fire, but as Boston's jocular reserve outfielder George Thomas quickly learned, sometimes escape was unavoidable. "George," Williams told him, "you are just as funny on the field as you are off the field."

Williams's penchant for getting under people's skins can be traced to a difficult upbringing in St. Louis during the height of the Great Depression. Living under the roof of an alcoholic and abusive father who had been out of work since the Stock Market Crash of 1929, Dick and his older brother, Ellery, lived in constant fear of when their next beating would come. "When he whistled, we came," Williams said. "If we didn't, that was disobedience, and that just killed him. And darn near killed us." Williams later admitted that by modern standards this kind of treatment constituted child abuse, but in his rough and tumble neighborhood it was the norm. "Back then it was just another case of a father dragging a son down to the basement steps, tying him to a pole, and whipping him," he asserted. Fortunately for Williams, escape from the constant physical violence at home came in the form of baseball. He and his brother became members of the "Knothole Gang" at nearby Sportsman's Park and passed many a happy hour there watching the Cardinals and Browns. Williams's schoolwork suffered but he didn't seem to mind. "I saw a lot of wonderful baseball," he said.

Inspired by such great St. Louis stars as Joe Medwick, Williams developed into a pretty good ballplayer himself. So good in fact that Brooklyn Dodgers scout Tom Downey signed him to a minor league contract upon collecting his high school diploma in 1947. His father, however, wasn't around to see the happy day. He had suffered a fatal heart attack two years earlier after witnessing his youngest son break his leg in a football game. "It was my fault," Williams said. "That's the first and only thing that ran through my head. My fault. My fault. If I hadn't been playing football so hard, if I hadn't gotten hurt, he would still be with me." To cope with these feelings of extreme guilt and remorse, Williams vowed to carry on his father's "tough traditions and spirit." "Unfortunately for some weak-kneed, prima donna baseball players, I think that's what happened," he said.

Reporting to his first spring training camp the following year in Vero Beach, Florida, Williams was struck by the level of organization and attention to detail that went into inculcating young prospects into the "Dodger way." This meant emphasizing such time-honored baseball fundamentals as executing a proper squeeze bunt, hitting the right cutoff man, and knowing when to take an extra base. "The Dodgers fundamentaled the devil out of you and that has a way of sticking," Williams said. "Total repetition. You can tell a player a thousand times and nothing will happen. Maybe on the 1,001st try, it will." The austere nature of the camp itself underscored these basic principles. Originally a naval air station, "Dodgertown USA" as it came to be known was a remote expanse of open fields and renovated military buildings north of Miami that provided "a baseball college atmosphere" to untutored players like Williams. "What an experience that was," he said. "We slept on old Navy barracks spring mattresses. We were called at 6:00 in the morning, you put on your uniform, you had to be finished eating by 7:30, you looked at a board to see what your schedule was that day and if you had the sliding pit at 8 in the morning you were [in] all kinds of trouble because you itched all day long [from the accumulated sand getting into your uniform]." Another downside was the sheer numbers involved. Apart from the big league club, every minor league team in the Dodgers system trained at the facility, making for some unexpected complications. "There was so many of us," remembered Williams, "that the instructors had no idea who was hurt, so players who were injured from the waist down just wore white sanitary socks instead of the blue stirrups. And those injured from the waist up wore a gray cap instead of a blue cap. Not that any of those distinctions mattered, because we were all treated the same—like we never played a day of baseball in our lives."

Williams was promoted to the team's Double A affiliate in Fort Worth, Texas, for the 1949 and 1950 seasons. Playing under Bobby Bragan, who went on to manage the Indians, Pirates, and Braves in the majors in the late 1950s and 1960s, Williams enjoyed his most productive years as a professional. He hit .300 both seasons and displayed some surprising pop in his bat, averaging 22 homers and 93 RBIs. More importantly, Williams was persuaded by Bragan, a one-time backup catcher with the Dodgers, that he needed to make a more serious commitment to the game. "In other words," Williams said, "he was the first to make me run with the pitchers because he thought I was fat, not to mention being the first to run me in 100-degree heat." Bragan's demanding style also impressed upon Williams the fine distinction between physical and mental errors, an approach he would pass on to his own players in the future. "A man has to know to know what he's got to do on the field at all times, and it's got to be automatic," Williams said. "Missing a cutoff man looks like physical action; to me it's a mental mistake. It shouldn't happen. I can't tolerate a guy missing signs. I won't tolerate it."

During the 1950 offseason, Williams experienced a minor brush with history. While playing for the Almendares Scorpions of the Havana Winter League, he encountered a young local pitching prospect with a wicked fastball who would eventually attract the attention of the Washington Senators. Scorpion management thought so highly of the headstrong and powerfully built left-hander that they gave him a uniform and permitted him to pitch team batting practice. Yet in his lone hitting encounter against him, Williams came away unimpressed. "He laid it in there, and I kicked his ass," he said. Alas, there would be no future in the majors for Fidel Castro. In 1959 he led a scruffy band of Marxist revolutionaries to victory over the ruling Fulgencio Batista regime to become the "Maximum Leader" of Cuba.

Williams finally made it to the big leagues in 1951 and cracked Brooklyn's starting outfield the following season. These were the famed "Boys of Summer" of Jackie Robinson, Duke Snider, Gil Hodges, Roy

Campanella, and Don Newcombe and Williams felt on top of the world. He became particularly close to Robinson, the fiery Hall of Fame infielder and racial trailblazer whom he described as "my big brother." "Jackie was the best ballplayer I ever saw," he said. "He did everything you could have a player do." And he performed at this elite level in the face of withering prejudice and discrimination, particularly in the Deep South. "At first, Jackie couldn't stay in the hotel with us in St. Louis," Williams recalled. "The next couple of years they allowed him to stay there. He and Don Newcombe and Campy (Roy Campanella), they had to go to another hotel in the black neighborhood. It got better but it still wasn't good." Any hopes for stardom of his own evaporated when Williams seriously injured himself on a diving catch against the Cardinals late in the 1952 season. "I had a three-way separation with my shoulder and collarbone," he said. "I had to get pins put in and since it was on my throwing arm, it was from that point I couldn't throw worth a lick." Through hard work, gritty persistence, and a willingness to play several different positions, Williams came back and performed as a utility player in the majors for the next 12 seasons. But thoughts of what might have been haunted him to his grave. "And to think I had finally become a starter Dodger outfielder," he lamented.

One unexpected benefit that did arise from the injury was that it allowed him to pay closer attention to events on the playing field and focus on in-game strategy. "I'd study the action on both teams—especially the men who I knew played well," he said. "It was this concentration, as much as anything else, that got me thinking about managing." He also honed to a finer degree his already exceptional skills as a bench jockey. "Westlake," he'd taunt weak hitting Pirates outfielder Wally Westlake, "is that a real bat or does it ALWAYS just hit the ball back to the pitcher." Teammates like All-Star shortstop Pee Wee Reese frowned upon such provocative behavior, believing it needlessly riled up rival ball clubs. But Williams thought the heckling contributed to victories because it got opponents distracted and out of their ordinary game rhythms. "My job was not to hurt anybody but to make Brooklyn a better team," he explained. When he wasn't antagonizing enemy players or fighting for a roster spot, the then single and uninhibited Williams devoted most of his time to satisfying the needs of his libido. "You see, I had developed a reputation on the Dodgers for being not just a loudmouth but a womanizer," he said. Indeed, when it came to philandering, according to the best-selling author Roger Kahn, who covered the Dodgers during this period, Williams was in a league of his own. "Last five girls I screwed, two was Filipinos, one was Spanish, one was colored and one was a Jew," he crudely boasted to Kahn in a Chicago dive bar one evening. Years later Williams disputed this account, claiming that Kahn gave the impression he had slept with the five women in only a week's time. "That's wrong," he corrected. "Took me at least two weeks."

In 1956 Williams went to the Baltimore Orioles in a waiver deal where he came in to contact with one of the most creative and innovative minds of the modern game—Paul Richards. The Orioles manager, known as "The Wizard" for his ability to turn around underperforming teams, predicated his entire game plan on run prevention—an emphasis that the impressionable Williams found logically appealing. "I heartily agree with that," Williams said. "Sure, I'd love to have a lot of power hitters, but I do think if you have a sound pitching staff and a strong defense, you're going to be able to scrounge two or three runs in the course of a ball game. And that should be enough to win, much of the time." Responding to Richards's tutelage, Williams hit .286 with 11 homers in 87 games but by 1958 offseason he was again on the move, going to the perennially awful Kansas City Athletics. Although he posted fine numbers with the Athletics—a career-best 16 homers and 75 RBIs in 1959—he was traded back to the Orioles for the 1961 campaign. Age and injuries had taken a toll by this time, especially on his worsening throwing arm. Baserunners could run virtually at will on him and he had little recourse apart from wryly observing he had become the first player in baseball history to be placed in a platoon with himself. "With a left-hitter batting, I'd be moved to left field, where there was little chance of the ball being hit to me. When a right-hander came to the plate, I'd be moved to right field for the same reason," he said. Williams could still hit, however, and this made him attractive to the Red Sox, who added him to their roster for the 1963 and 1964 seasons, his last as an active player. Boston was unlike any organization he had ever been associated. Whereas professionalism, hard work, discipline, and strict adherence to detail had been the hallmarks of the Dodgers and Orioles, the Red Sox seemed to operate on a different set of assumptions. "You had freewheeling," Williams said. "Nobody cared about advancing runners. They had that short left-field fence and everybody was trying to jerk it out of there."

If this wasn't disheartening enough, he witnessed Johnny Pesky's authority as manager undermined by uncaring veterans and a dysfunctional front office. "This was a country club," he said. "I saw guys lose every bit of pride they had playing on this team." For sure, some took greater interest in card games going on in the clubhouse than what was actually transpiring on the diamond. Williams, a good card player, was not above occasionally taking part in these games. During one rain delay, he fleeced a teammate out of a considerable amount of cash and then boldly announced to the locker room that if he ever became manager, he would ban such high-stakes contests. "They all laughed when I said this, but a couple of years later, while I was managing many of them, no money was allowed on the table of clubhouse card games," Williams said.

As the team floundered, Williams excelled as a pinch hitter, going 16 for 48 in 1963 and hitting 5 home runs in only 69 at-bats the following year. But the losing still hurt and he wasn't afraid to vent his frustration on his teammates whom he felt had adopted a complacent attitude. "I bitched about a lot of things," he admitted. "Players who didn't understand why had no idea how much it should hurt to lose, and how damning it should be not to care. Maybe those players never felt like they had to prove themselves to somebody. Well I did. . . . I wanted to prove that I wasn't a loser." His scrappy attitude and performance did not go unnoticed. "Every time I look down the bench and see Dick sitting there I get a wonderful feeling," Pesky said. "He's a nice guy to have around. Someday he's going to make fine managerial timber." Pesky didn't realize how right he was.

At the conclusion of the 1964 season, Williams was approached by Red Sox minor league director Neil Mahoney with a tantalizing offer. Knowing that Williams's playing days were over, Mahoney thought the 35-year-old, now married with two kids, would be the perfect choice to manage the team's Triple A franchise in Toronto, Canada. This was a bold, if not risky choice. Williams had no formal managerial experience but Mahoney had earlier identified him as leadership material when he heard him loudly sound off about the parent club's deficiencies. Impressed with his brashness and overall baseball savvy, Mahoney asked him if he would ever be interested in calling the shots. "Would I?" Williams responded. "Would I like to be able to do something about everything in baseball that bothers me? Would I like to be able to be able to teach people how to win, and maybe mold winners out of losers? What do you think?" Williams accepted Mahoney's offer without hesitation. "I guess it's time to back up my mouth," the future American League Manager of the Year told him.

Williams could not have fallen into a better situation. The Toronto roster was stocked with promising young prospects like Mike Andrews, Joe Foy, Russ Gibson, Gary Waslewski, Billy Rohr, and Reggie Smith, all on the cusp of making the big time. Williams had no trouble whipping this talented crew into championship form, leading them to consecutive International League titles. From the outset, Williams had an intuitive grasp of what would be required to make the transition from "bench jockey" to "dugout boss." As he observed, "When you're the player with the big mouth, the only thing you're accountable for is you. Your strikeouts, your hits, your errors. But as manager you are suddenly judged by an entire team, and your important statistics are whittled down to two. Wins and losses. Your wins. Your losses. And only yours." Then as later this relentless drive to succeed could be seen in the agitated way Williams conducted himself from the bench. "In a game, he is a bundle of restless energy," the sportswriter Jim Murray observed. "He chews gum so rapidly you'd think he would wear his teeth out. He never sits. He crouches—like a leopard waiting for the slow approach of fresh meat. The first sign of wavering on the part of his pitcher, he explodes from the dugout." Smiles or displayed lightheartedness of any kind were strictly verboten. "He is somber, serious," Murray continued. "He sees nothing funny about baseball. It is World War III, it is 'circle the wagons, they're out there. I can hear the drums!' You would think his ulcer had an ulcer."

A strict disciplinarian, Williams also set a no-nonsense tone in the locker room. When 6'2", 200-pound right-hander Mickey Sinks confronted him in his office before the start of the 1966 league playoffs and announced he would not pitch unless he received a guarantee of being on the Boston major league roster the following season, Williams demurred. "Mickey, if it was my decision, you wouldn't be put on the roster," he said. Enraged, the former Michigan State University star punched Williams in the face and threatened to do more bodily harm until Williams subdued him in a bear hug. "Take this son of a bitch away!" Williams thundered. As Sinks's obedient teammates hauled him off, Williams discovered that in all the excitement he had soiled his pants. "Smelled like an outhouse," he remembered. Sensing a teachable moment, Williams called a team meeting the next day and proudly displayed the ruined pants. "If this is what it takes to win," he informed the hushed gathering, "everybody in this room will be wearing diapers."

No diapers were required when the Red Sox prepared to wrap up spring training and head north for their season home opener against the White Sox at the beginning of April. For after several weeks of rigorous drilling, instruction, and mental preparation, Williams knew he had the makings of a strong ball club regardless of their ninth-place finish the year before. "We'll win more than we'll lose," he promised Boston fans. The basis for this optimism was understandable. The team was practically swimming in standout young talent. "Sometimes I'd just stand there looking at all these guys," Yastrzemski said. "It was the best collection of baseball talent we'd had since I'd joined the club." In the infield, Williams had proven power hitters George Scott and Joe Foy at first and third base, while Rico Petrocelli, 18 homers and 59 RBIs in 1966, was a lock at shortstop. All were 23 years old. Newcomer Mike Andrews, the IL leader in runs scored (97) the previous season, was penciled in at second. Catching duties were assigned to Mike Ryan, another Toronto product known for his accurate throwing arm.

The outfield looked even better with established All-Stars Yastrzemski and Tony Conigliaro at the corners and projected Rookie of the Year candidate Reggie Smith in center. All the Louisiana-born Smith had done was become the reigning IL batting champion with a .320 average at 22. "I've seen thousands of prospects . . . and Smith is by far the best," noted one rival scout. "He can do everything—run, throw, and hit with power, batting both right and left-handed." If there was an Achilles heel to the ball club, it was the pitching—a traditional Boston weakness. Outside of the 20-something duo of Jim Lonborg and Jose Santiago, who together accounted for 22 of the starting rotation's 25 victories the year before, there were slim pickings.

Despite the improved talent level, most baseball experts and prognosticators did not give the Red Sox much of a chance. They were seen as a lock for ninth place, well behind the defending World Series champion Baltimore Orioles, who were returning an All-Star lineup boasting the 1966 AL MVP and Triple Crown winner Frank Robinson. As one veteran scout put it, "Do rookies and second year men win in the majors? Possible. Not likely. Boston is too green in too many positions." Underlying the skepticism no doubt was the suspicion that the inexperienced team might bridle under the stern authoritarian ways of their new manager. Indeed, Williams was already on shaky ground with his 22-year-old star outfielder Tony Conigliaro.

"No two people were ever more unalike than Williams and I," Conigliaro said. They had a troubled history dating back to the latter's first spring training with the ball club in 1964. Stepping out of the dugout one day to warm up, Conigliaro received an unsettling jolt. "Suddenly, a ball came flying right for my head and I hit the dirt," he remembered. Confused and not a little incensed, Conigliaro quickly bounced back to his feet to stare in disbelief at his assailant. "Watch where you're going, bush," snarled Williams, who was then finishing up his big league career in a Boston uniform. Unwilling to let the incident go, Conigliaro got his revenge the following day, firing a well-timed strike at Williams's unsuspecting head. "Down he went, his cap flying off his head, and there was dust all over him," Conigliaro said. For added measure, Conigliaro told Williams to watch where *he* was going. Only the propitious intervention of a sympathetic veteran teammate prevented an enraged Williams from physically attacking Conigliaro. "This was a guy who'd been around a couple of years and he probably could have done a job on me," Conigliaro admitted. Ignoring the near fisticuffs, Boston manager Johnny Pesky ordered Williams to room with Conigliaro on the road during the regular season to expose the inexperienced youngster to some much needed veteran leadership. It was far from an ideal arrangement. "The setup lasted just two months, because during that time I never saw him," Williams later revealed. "Not late at night, not first in the morning, never. I was providing veteran influence to a suitcase. I told management they were wasting their time." For Tony Conigliaro always marched to the beat of his own drummer.

Born in 1945, Conigliaro grew up in a close knit, hard-working Italian American household on Boston's North Shore. His father made a living as a laborer at a zipper factory while his mother tended to raising Tony and his two younger brothers, future major league outfielders Billy and Richie. Young Tony's days revolved around playing baseball at a local park and getting into trouble. "I never got along too well in school," he said, "either with my teachers or classmates." In the second grade, his teacher became so angry at his "little wise guy" attitude that she locked him up in a classroom closet. "When she left the class later I was still in the closet," he said. "She had forgot about me." It took several hours before his concerned parents figured out what had happened and rescued him. "When they let me out of that closet I was the happiest little kid in the world," Conigliaro said.

His struggles in the classroom continued when his parents enrolled him at a private Catholic high school, St. Mary's of Lynn. "I just couldn't stand being cooped up," he said. "My mind was always off in the wild blue yonder." By this time it had become obvious to anyone paying attention that Conigliaro's future lay not with dusty books in a library, but with a bat and a ball. Mustering a zeal for the game that he never could for history, biology, or Latin, Conigliaro hit .680 and tossed four no-hitters in his senior year. He was hailed as one of the best prospects in Massachusetts and scouts from 14 teams lined up to get his name on a major league contract. But in the end, he decided to stay close to home, signing with Boston as an outfielder for $35,000. The Red Sox front office could not have been more delighted. "You can judge the physical abilities, but you can't always tell the intangibles," said team scout Milt Bolling, who had kept close tabs on Conigliaro throughout his high school playing career. "His intangibles, his drive, his confidence in himself, were just incredible."

All of these qualities were on display when he suited up for Wellsville of the New York-Penn League in 1963. Although Conigliaro missed the beginning of the season with a broken thumb, he still hit .363 and drove in 84 runs on 24 homers. "What had started as a near-disastrous year wound up surpassing even my own wildest expectations," he recalled. He won the league's Rookie of the Year and Most Valuable Player honors, but the conditions under which he played ball in this remote community along the Genesee River in southwestern New York left much to be desired. "It didn't take me long to find out why they're called the minors," Conigliaro said. "Whenever we had a road trip to make we used an old high school bus that should have been retired when Calvin Coolidge was president. There were no springs in it, just solid rubber tires and a lawn mower engine. There was no way I could sleep on this thing during those beautiful four-hour trips." Adding to the threadbare nature of the operation, the manager doubled as the bus driver.

With his season in Wellsville over, Conigliaro felt confident he could make the parent club the following spring. "Look at the outfield," he told his father. "Who do I have to beat out? There's Carl Yastrzemski. That's all." For sure, his chief competition of .247-lifetime hitting Lou Clinton and the oft-injured Gary Gieger were not exactly All-Star caliber, but Conigliaro was still only 19 with presumably much to learn. He didn't care. "I felt strangely confident and by the end of February I had my mind made up that I wasn't going to [Red Sox spring training camp in Scottsdale, Arizona] to be overlooked," he maintained. That self-assurance was not misplaced as he went on a batting tear throughout the exhibition game season, hitting well over .300 and leading the team in most offensive categories, including total bases with 39. "I sprayed the ball all over the place," Conigliaro recalled. "I was on base so much they almost had to keep me." In one game against the visiting Indians, he belted a Gary Bell fastball out of the ballpark in deepest center. "It didn't hit me right then, but I had hit this ball better than 430 feet; I later learned that I'd become the first hitter ever to clear that fence," he said. Making the moment all the more sweeter was the fact that his parents were in the stands. "As I came around third base I waved to them," Conigliaro said. "Yeah, just like in the movies, but I really did."

Comparisons were soon made to outfield greats like Joe DiMaggio and Mickey Mantle, but Conigliaro himself was more interested in the future Hall of Famer patrolling center field for the San Francisco Giants. "He's great," Conigliaro said of Willie Mays. "Some day I'd like to be like him. The people love him. The thing I like most about him is that he hustles just like any other ballplayer. Some ballplayers tend to get a little lazy. He's good to watch." So was Conigliaro according to Ted Williams. Working as the team's batting instructor that spring, the Red Sox legend marveled at the fluidity of Conigliaro's swing. "Don't change that solid stance of yours, no matter what you're told," he advised the young slugger. Frank Malzone became enamored with another aspect of Conigliaro's performance. "It was late in spring training . . . I was sitting on the end of the bench with Tony and a couple of other guys," the All-Star Sox third baseman later related to the author Peter Golenbock. "Something happened on the field, and some of the guys started laughing, and it really didn't call for laughing, but it was the [losing] atmosphere that was there." Conigliaro took exception and called out the veterans for their poor team attitude and lack of professionalism. "I sat there and smiled a little bit, because this kid was going to be a player. I could see it. He was so enthused about winning," Malzone said. Conigliaro took nothing for granted. As he had from the start of spring training, he went all out on the field. "Everytime I see my name in the batting order, I run to the outfield as fast as I can get out of the manager's sight," he claimed. "I don't want to give him a chance to change his mind if he sees me."

Conigliaro need not have worried. "He's the finest prospect I have ever seen in the Cactus League," Indians general manager Gabe Paul said. Installed as the starting center fielder for the team's Opening Day lineup at Yankee Stadium, Conigliaro confessed to having a few butterflies in his stomach. "Here I was, nineteen years old, less than two years out of high school, last year at this time I was supposed to be on my way to [the minors], and now, all of a sudden, here I was in Yankee Stadium," he said. Only a timely conversation with Carl Yastrzemski settled his nerves. He "told me his knees were knocking the first game he played for the Red Sox—and not to worry, everything would be all right," Conigliaro said. Bolstered by his team captain's soothing words of support, Conigliaro went out and had a memorable first game. He collected a single off of Yankee starter Whitey Ford in his second ever major league plate appearance and made a fine running catch in the second inning off a Tom Tresh liner to right center that was made all the more difficult by wet field conditions. "At the 407-sign I looked up and was blinded by the sun," Conigliaro recounted. "So I raised my glove to shade my eyes and the ball plopped in. For a split second I didn't even know I had caught it." Fans in the stands showed their appreciation with loud applause and no less an outfield authority than future Hall of Famer Mickey Mantle praised the effort. "Terrific," he enthused. "That was a tough ball to catch when the field is in good condition, and he made it with the field in poor shape."

Conigliaro garnered attention of a different sort when he boldly turned to the home plate umpire in his third at-bat and informed him that Ford, a well-known spit baller, was doctoring the ball with a foreign substance. "How can you let him go to his forehead, then to his mouth like that?" Conigliaro badgered. The umpire pretended to ignore the rookie's impertinent remark, preferring instead to silently wipe down the ball and relay it back to Ford. "He never said a word," Conigliaro said. As his sympathetic biographer David Cantaneo later observed, "It wasn't Tony's style to debut quietly." Indeed, prior to the contest Conigliaro learned that he was being fined $10 by the team for missing a mandatory team practice. "I figured I got off cheap," Conigliaro said. None of this immature behavior seemed to bother Johnny Pesky, who was looking for talented young players to improve upon the team's dismal 76–85 record of the year before. "He caught the ball and he took his rips at the plate," the Boston manager said of the Massachusetts native. "He didn't look bad at any time, which is unusual for a kid." What Pesky didn't say is that Conigliaro almost missed the game altogether. Looking out his hotel room that morning, Conigliaro saw it was raining and assumed the game was canceled. Only when an angry Pesky called him a few hours later did he learn differently. "Pesky told me I'd better haul all my tail to the stadium fast," he said. "I leaped into my clothes and raced for a cab." But his troubles weren't over. "The cabbie ran out of gas on the bridge leading to the stadium. I could have killed him," Conigliaro said. Pesky was beside himself when his flummoxed young charge finally reached the visitor's clubhouse. "For Chrissake, you've got a chance to play," he roared. "Don't screw it up." Conigliaro had better luck at the Boston home opener the following day.

Before an expectant crowd of 20,213 fans, he homered off White Sox starter Joe Horlen on the first pitch of his soon to be celebrated Fenway Park career, a fastball that he deposited over the Green Monster in left field. "No, I wasn't looking for anything special, just a good ball to hit and it was there, a fastball," Conigliaro told reporters afterward. "I thought it might be off the wall or even in the nets, but I never dreamed it'd clear everything though I hit it good." The blast paced the Red Sox to an easy 4–1 victory over Chicago while lifting Conigliaro's offensive exploits to the realm of myth according to the overheated prose of one local reporter. "It was the sort of thing that happens only in dreams . . . a dream of an unbelievable golden future . . . a man's dream of a past that never occurred," the *Boston Globe*'s Roger Birtwell wrote. Having a front row seat to this unfolding drama was US Attorney General Robert F. Kennedy and several members of his famed political clan, including Massachusetts Senator Edward M. Kennedy and future Ambassador to Ireland Jean Kennedy Smith. They had been specially invited by Sox management to attend the contest, which had been dedicated to the memory of their slain older brother, former 35th President of the United States John F. Kennedy. Other attendees included Stan Musial, Joe Cronin, Broadway performer Carol Channing, and former heavyweight boxing champion of the world Gene Tunney. As befitting his youthful cocky demeanor, Conigliaro betrayed no doubts about his ability to perform before such an august gathering. "Nervous?" he asked. "No, I wasn't nervous like I was yesterday in New York. I only saw two fastballs after that and they were bad. Yeah, my folks and brothers were here and I guess I could hear them yelling at me from the stands, especially in the bleachers."

Conigliaro finished his superlative rookie campaign with a .296 batting average and 24 homers. More than a few observers expressed astonishment at his rapid development as a hitter. "I wish he'd tell me how he doesn't get fooled," commented Dick Stuart on Conigliaro's disciplined approach in the batter's box. "I've been around a long time and get fooled lots of times. But this kid seems to wade into that curveball and sit back there for the fastball, too. He seems like a veteran up there." Standing close to the plate, too close according to many of his teammates, Conigliaro often dared opposing pitchers to challenge him inside with fastballs. More times than not, he came out the victor in these exchanges. "He was fearless of the ball," Pesky said. "He would just move his head, like [Ted] Williams did. A ball up and in; Tony would just move his head. He thought the ball would never hit him." Of course, it didn't hurt that he had superb hand-eye coordination. "Tony's got very good wrists and he follows the ball very well," Yaz explained. "I thought he'd strike out more often up here, but he seems to know what these guys are throwing already." Preparing to bat against hard throwing Angels reliever Bob Lee in one contest, he boasted to the Boston bench that he had gone 11 for 14 against Lee in the minors. After Lee subsequently retired him on a weak pop up, Conigliaro remained nonplussed. "That's 11 for 15," he said. He eventually had the last laugh in the ninth inning when he hit a two-out, game-winning grand slam off Lee. "That's 12 for 16," he beamed.

These heroics notwithstanding, Conigliaro could be a handful. He seemed to take great pleasure in testing the limits of his manager's patience, breaking team curfew, getting hung over and flouting club rules on a regular basis. "You're hurting the team," Pesky told him. Others were even more blunt in their criticism. "If Conigliaro had been 29 instead of 19 he couldn't have gotten through the 1964 season without a belt in the mouth from somebody," *Sport* magazine's Al Hirshberg wrote. Conigliaro did not disagree. "I think I did what every 19- or 20-year-old kid would have done in the same situation," he later reflected. "I threw temper tantrums and partied." And none of this seemed to bother coming of age Sox fans like future *Boston Globe* sports columnist Dan Shaughnessy, who saw Conigliaro as the baseball equivalent to Beatlemania. "Tony C was our guy," Shaughnessy confirmed. "He was young, handsome, built for Fenway, and best of all, he was local. He was no Southern Californian invading Fenway on a six-month work visa. He shared our accent and he knew how to drive the rotaries. The emergence of Conigliaro gave hope to Little Leaguers in Groton, Massachusetts, and Groton, Connecticut. Tony C made it. So could we."

Conigliaro soon discovered that he could capitalize on his celebrity status by branching out into other areas, most notably singing. Possessing a voice that drew favorable comparisons to Ricky Nelson, the former teen heart throb who became famous for such hits as "I'm Walkin'" and "Poor Little Fool," Conigliaro was no slouch behind the mike. He went on to record several songs that were released by the prestigious RCA-Victor label, including "Little Red Scooter" that became something of a local sensation. It "was a Jan & Dean-type rocker with a pulsing sax and a twangy guitar solo," notes Dan Epstein of Fox Sports. The early success only encouraged Conigliaro to believe he might have a viable pop music career in the offing. As he confided to a reporter after his rookie season, "I sing rock n' roll real good. Like the Beatles with a crew cut." Yet fading record sales and his own limited vocal range forced him to conclude that he was never going to be confused with any of the "Fab Four." Baseball would remain his chief avocation. "Singing and records are just for between seasons," he said. "But maybe I'll learn to read music. Anyway, I've got more hits than the Beatles—one hundred and seventeen last summer."

Conigliaro showed no signs of letting up after his standout freshman effort, averaging 30 homers and 88 RBIs over the next two seasons. By any metric, he had become one of the game's most fearsome young hitters. "If he takes care of himself and doesn't get hurt too often, he can be another Joe DiMaggio, good for 40 or more homers a season," Pesky predicted. Other contemporaries concurred. "Conigliaro is the most aggressive hitter I have ever seen in baseball in any league," said third baseman Ron Santo of the Chicago Cubs. "I have never seen a hitter glare at the pitcher the way Tony does and dare the pitcher to throw the ball. He defies them and they don't like it." Teammate Gerry Moses claimed that if he had to select one hitter to go to bat for him with his life on the line, he would have chosen Conigliaro without hesitation. "If he had been 0-for-20 and you needed a home run in the bottom of the ninth to win it, he'd get it," Moses said.

This "amazing aggressiveness" at the plate earned Conigliaro a coveted spot as the team's cleanup batter, but it was not without a downside. Now expected to go exclusively for the long ball, he swung at too many pitches outside the strike zone, thus bringing down his average. Conigliaro, a career .264 hitter, didn't seem to mind. "I don't care if I never hit .300," he told the *Christian Science Monitor*. "I stopped thinking about average the day I read somewhere that for a man with 300 at bats the difference between .333 and .290 is only 13 hits. I'll take the game-winning hit every time." What Conigliaro did care about was his alarming tendency to get hit by pitches. "Two years in a row, he got his arm broken from being hit with fastballs inside," Moses said. "Because they had to get him off the plate. They weren't trying to hit him. They were just trying to get him off the plate." Conigliaro saw things differently, often going after the pitchers who struck him. "You're taking my living away from me," he'd tell them. Making use of his knowledge of the martial arts, he once landed a karate kick on the left leg of Indians hurler Fred Lasher. "It's probable Conigliaro's aim was off a few inches," the author George Sullivan wrote.

Nor was his anger reserved exclusively for opponents. He had frequent clashes with teammates and a prickly relationship with new manager Billy Herman, who had been hired in 1965. Furious at Conigliaro's continued failure to make team curfews and showing up drunk one day before a game at Yankee Stadium, Herman decided he had seen enough. He called Conigliaro into his office and told him that he was being fined $1,000, a significant sum for a ballplayer in the 1960s. "I knew he was mad because his face was real red and his fists were clenched," Conigliaro recalled. The talk seemed to work, however. Conigliaro, who had been in a slump, proceeded to go on a batting tear and become the youngest player to ever lead the league in homers (32) at the age of 20.

While his bat heated up, his relationship with Herman remained cool. Conigliaro believed that Herman, who had been a Hall of Fame middle infielder with the Cubs in the 1930s, was more concerned with cultivating the goodwill of the writers covering the team than he was about seeing to the needs of his own players. "He was always sitting with the writers from town to town—all the players on the club noticed this," Coniglario said. "He wasn't a manager who protected his players." Regardless of the hard feelings, Conigliaro's career turned a significant corner under Herman. "Tony grew up a lot—the hard way," commented team closer Dick Radatz. "He made some mistakes. After all, he's only a kid who has gotten a lot of attention and had some trouble handling

The sweet swing of young slugger Tony Conigliaro. PHOTO BY BOSTON RED SOX

it. He embarrassed the ball club and maybe his parents, too, but it didn't deter him from playing. And make no mistake about it, the kid can play this game." Whether he could continue to play effectively for Dick Williams in 1967 remained an open question.

The Red Sox began their season at Fenway Park on April 12 against the Chicago White Sox. Managed by the irascible Eddie Stanky, who would later earn the ire of Boston fans for calling Carl Yastrzemski "an All-Star from the neck down," the White Sox were a pitching-rich team that boasted one of the finest starting rotations in baseball. But while Gary Peters, Joe Horlen, Tommy John, and Bruce Howard had all allowed under three runs per game in 1966, their team offense had been terrible, ranking second to last in the AL with a pathetic .231 batting average. Only Rookie of the Year center fielder Tommy Agee (22 home runs and 86 RBIs) posed any serious threat. Nevertheless, with the game-time temperature hovering around the mid-40s, Boston starter Jim Lonborg struggled early before finally settling down to pitch a 5–4 victory in front of 8,234 shivering fans. "It was very warm out there as far as I was concerned," Dick Williams quipped to reporters afterward. Rico Petrocelli made it seem so as the shortstop's scalding performance at the plate resulted in a perfect 3-for-3 day, including a homer and four RBIs. "I got some good pitches to hit, breaking balls down low," Petrocelli said. "If you don't get the pitches to hit then you can't hit. It's as simple as that." Petrocelli was particularly gratified that his hits came off Chicago spot starter John Buzhardt, a tough right-hander who had had an off-year in 1966 but won a career-high 13 games in 1965. "Buzhardt drove me nuts my first two years with the Red Sox," Petrocelli recalled. "He didn't throw hard, but I couldn't hit him. He'd throw me tailing fastballs in and sliders away in the dirt, and I'd chase them time and time again. He'd throw me 2-and-0 sliders for strikes, and I'd take them because I'd be looking for a fastball. But two years in the big leagues wised me up."

After dropping the next game to Chicago, the team journeyed down to New York City to play the Yankees for their home opener. Starting on the mound for the Red Sox was rookie Billy Rohr, a gangly 21-year-old left-hander from Garden Grove, California. In front a disappointing crowd of 14,375 that included such notables as widowed First Lady Jacqueline Kennedy and her six-year-old son John, Rohr got within a strike of becoming the first pitcher in history to record a no-hitter in his major league debut. But Yankees catcher Elston Howard spoiled the occasion by singling to right center on a 3–2 curveball with two outs in the bottom of the ninth inning. "It was the first time I ever got a base hit and got booed in New York," said Howard in the clubhouse afterward. Rohr, who had gone 14–10 with 10 complete games for Dick Williams in Toronto the previous season, induced next batter Charley Smith to fly out to end the game—a 3–0 Sox victory. "I would have liked to have [the no-hitter]," Rohr said. "But Howard gets paid to hit. He gets paid more than I do so I can't feel any animosity toward him for what he did."

Carl Drummond was another story. The home plate umpire called a questionable ball three on a curve in the dirt before Howard's hit. "I threw a 1–2 pitch to Ellie that everyone except [Drummond] thought was a strike," Rohr later told writer Steve Buckley. "Ellie knew it was a strike. The ump's hand kind of went halfway up, but not all the way up. And then Ellie singled to right." As impressive as the 122-pitch gem was, it was nearly upstaged by a spectacular diving catch Yastrzemski had made two batters earlier. Yankees outfielder Tom Tresh sent a screamer over his head to deep left field that Yastrzemski initially thought was going to leave the ballpark. Then he let his baseball instincts take over. "Running as hard as a man fleeing an aroused nest of bees," recounted longtime Sox broadcaster Ken Coleman, who called the game, "Yaz dove in full stride and reached out with the glove hand in full extension almost like Michelangelo's Adam stretching out for the hand of God." Yastrzemski caught the ball in mid-air before landing hard on the stadium turf and rolling over. He popped immediately back up to his feet amid roaring cheers and held the ball aloft "as if," Coleman wrote in his diary, "he were Liberty keeping the burning flame aloft." "I may have made better catches," Yastrzemski later claimed, "but I don't remember any."

Rohr became an overnight sensation, appearing on the popular *Ed Sullivan Show* and receiving a fawning telegram from Boston Mayor John Collins. But his time in the public spotlight would be brief. He would notch another victory against the Yankees nine days later and then suffer a baffling performance drop-off. By midsummer he was back in the minors. "He has the equipment," Dick Williams said. "He needs the desire." Alas, that competitive hunger failed to materialize. Rohr never won another game in a Red Sox uniform and found himself out of baseball by 1972. "Andy Warhol once said that everyone has their 15 minutes of fame—that was my 15 minutes," Rohr said. Rohr went on to become a successful medical malpractice defense attorney, yet he would be forever remembered by Sox fans for that one brief shining moment at Yankee Stadium. "That was a big turning point for the entire season," the late Boston sports writer Tim Horgan said. "You can look back and say it was just another game, but it wasn't. The Red Sox had been really awful. Nowhere. It gave everybody the confidence that they could beat the Yankees. It didn't matter that the Yankees were phasing out. There was always something special about beating the Yankees in Yankee Stadium."

By the beginning of June, the Sox, whom preseason oddsmakers had pegged as 100 to 1 longshots to win the pennant, found themselves one game above .500 at 22–21, only 4 1/2 games out of first. The term "Impossible Dream" soon entered the Boston vocabulary to describe the team's sudden rise to pennant contention. It was a nod to the popular song from the Tony Award–winning musical *Man of the La Mancha*, which was about an aging would-be Spanish knight seeking fame and glory. While no one confused him with the tragicomic Don Quixote, Carl Yastrzemski was withal the principal reason for Boston's unexpected baseball turnaround. Having worked out extensively in the off-season, a leaner and more muscular Yastrzemski became a beast at the plate, getting on base constantly, hitting for power and driving in key runs. By June he was batting .336 and among the league leaders in homers (18), runs (82), and RBIs (53). But his offense was only a part of the story. He was also emerging as a respected clubhouse leader. "I could sense as the season went along the guys were starting to rely on me," the normally aloof Yaz said. "It changed my approach. I found I could talk to some of them easily about their problems and I felt like they wanted me to. This was the big thing. It doesn't do someone any good if they don't want it."

Motivation wasn't an issue when the Sox stole one from the first place White Sox in a Fenway night game on June 15. Down 1–0 with two out in the bottom of the 11th inning, Tony Conigliaro slammed a two-run homer into the left-field screen for the walk-off victory. "After a split second of shocked silence, the homer triggered a wild celebration, one long, abdominal cry of relief—the fans reacted as if the pennant had been won," Ken Coleman recalled. "Tony's teammates poured onto the field and surrounded the plate to greet the hero. They overwhelmed him."

The Sox gained further momentum six days later when they took back-to-back games from the last-place Yankees in their return trip to the Bronx. Neither of the contests were particularly close but what transpired in the home half of the second inning in the second game convinced many long suffering Boston fans that this might be their year. For instead of supinely rolling over to the Yankees as they had done so often in the past, the Sox displayed a level of grit that reflected the team's feisty new competitive spirit. Nursing a 5–0 lead, Jim Lonborg hit Yankees pitcher Thad Tillotson squarely in the shoulder after the tall right-hander had plunked teammate Joe Foy in the helmet the previous frame. "Nobody had to tell me anything," said Lonborg, who had stepped into the team's stopper role with an 8–2 mark entering the contest. "I knew what I had to do. It was probably the only time in my career that I intentionally threw at anybody. Tillotson came up, knowing he was going to go down." Both benches emptied and a five minute free-for-all ensued. At the center of the brawl was Yankees center fielder Joe Pepitone and Rico Petrocelli, two hot-tempered Brooklyn natives. "Pepitone and Rico were [initially] exchanging words," George Scott said. "They were really going at it. Rico said they were kidding but that was a heckuva time to kid with both teams nose to nose. When Pepitone broke after Rico, I grabbed him and dropped him." Petrocelli ended up at the bottom of a large pile of players, but he never regretted his role in the fracas. "We [eventually] won 8–1," he later said, "and we sent a clear message to the rest of the league that we could not be intimidated."

Americo Peter "Rico" Petrocelli had never been the type to easily back down from anyone. The son of an Italian immigrant, Petrocelli had spent the majority of his childhood living in the rough and tumble Bedford-Stuyvesant section of Brooklyn, New York, where crime, violence, and urban decay were steadily on the rise in the postwar years. "You didn't hear much about drugs then, but it was around," Petrocelli said. Thanks in part to his six older brothers and sisters, who kept close tabs on him, Petrocelli stayed out of serious trouble. "We did a lot of family trips to Coney Island," he told the *Brooklyn Daily Eagle* in a 2014 interview. "That was always a big trip. Going to Coney Island always made for a special day. I loved the Parachute Jump. Yet, best of all, the biggest treat back then was Nathan's hot dog stand. And we also took family trips to Broadway in Manhattan. You know, the lights, the theatre district, that was always exciting when you were a kid." Playing baseball, especially in a city that then boasted three major league teams (the Yankees, Dodgers, and Giants), provided its own special thrill, too. For Petrocelli was a highly touted schoolboy ballplayer with quick hands and an explosive swing that professional scouts salivated over. Longtime

Red Sox scout Bots Nekola, who had earlier signed Carl Yaztremski, in particular liked what he saw. "We were interested in his bat," Nekola said. "I saw him hit some awfully long shots in [a] summer league, and I guess he was batting around .450."

An amicable negotiating period ensued, in which Petrocelli and his family were invited to Boston in late 1961 to check out Fenway Park and meet team owner Tom Yawkey. "We were so impressed by Mr. Yawkey and how well they treated us that I said 'This is it,'" Petrocelli remembered. He signed for a reported $40,000 bonus and after a brief apprenticeship in the minors, Petrocelli won Boston's regular shortstop job coming out of spring training in 1965. "I was surprised," he later said. "I was only 21, had played only three seasons in the minors, and hadn't exactly lit up Triple A pitching the previous summer." For sure, Petrocelli batted below .240, but the team had been impressed enough by his glovework to demote incumbent shortstop Eddie Bressoud, a 10-year veteran who had been Boston's lone representative at the 1964 All-Star Game. "They said I'd do all right if I only hit .220," Petrocelli recalled. "But I was so overmatched against those right-handed pitchers, I was afraid I wouldn't even hit .200." Petrocelli exceeded that mark, though just barely, hitting a forgettable .232 with 13 homers in 103 games. "Pitchers would set me up," he said. "I just didn't adjust. I couldn't figure them out." His lack of success gnawed at him to the point he became a moody and difficult person to be around. "Nobody could get on himself the way Rico could," his wife, the former Elsie Jensen, said. "He had a positive knack for it." After a bad performance, he would sullenly retreat to the basement of his suburban Boston home and play the drums, a lifelong avocation that occasionally led to some professional music gigs.

Petrocelli may have been his own worst enemy, but he did not receive much support from Red Sox manager Billy Herman. Herman was skeptical of rookies as a rule and thought even less of Petrocelli, whose attitude and fielding he believed did not measure up to major league standards. "He was from the old school," Petrocelli explained. "He didn't like the way young players went about things, even though we worked hard at improving our game." Despairing of Herman's icy treatment, Petrocelli seriously contemplated quitting the game until he was talked out of it by

Carl Yastrzemski. "Don't be ridiculous," Yaz told him. "You'll be the best shortstop in the business in a couple of years."

Petrocelli's problematic relationship with Herman reached a new low in 1966. Petrocelli removed himself midway through a night game at Fenway and went home. "My mistake was not telling Billy I was leaving," Petrocelli later told author George Sullivan. "I'm not proud of that and there's no excuse for it, merely the explanation that I was greatly upset when I did it." What prompted Petrocelli to take such drastic action was concern over his wife Elsie's personal health. "That morning she was stricken with tremendous pains in her right side," he disclosed. "I thought appendicitis. I also considered postnatal complications from the birth of our first child six months before." Petrocelli seriously entertained taking the night off, but his wife dissuaded him. He reluctantly went to the ballpark instead and was able to get through the early innings without incident. "Then," he said, "as we were heading off the field in the middle of the seventh inning, it hit me like a bolt."

He experienced a disturbing vision ("something approaching extrasensory perception") that told him his wife was in serious physical danger and needed his help. "My reaction was automatic," he related. "I had to get home immediately. I didn't think of the consequences. It was something I had to do. I never stopped running as I reached the dugout. I bounded down the steps and up the runway toward the clubhouse." There he flew by team trainer Buddy LeRoux and told him he was going home. LeRoux thought he was pulling a prank until Petrocelli tore off his uniform and took a quick shower. "As I was dressing," Petrocelli said, "Buddy tried his best to [talk me out of it] in his calm and persuasive way. But he could have saved his breath." Petrocelli floored his car home where he found his wife doubled over in severe pain on the staircase. "[He] rushed her to the hospital," Carl Yastrzemski said. "She had some sort of stomach ailment and, although not in danger, would have had to endure the pain for several more hours if Rico hadn't got there." Herman was not nearly as understanding. "Trade him," he told the front office. "Get rid of him. He doesn't want to play ball." Fortunately, cooler heads prevailed. Petrocelli was assessed a $1,000 team fine and the whole incident was largely forgotten—that is by everyone except Herman. He labeled Petrocelli a hypochondriac, an unfair characterization that took the emotionally intense shortstop by surprise. As Petrocelli complained to Sullivan, "I broke my hump for the guy; yet all I got from him was a bad name that took years to live down."

Petrocelli would fare much better under Dick Williams. "[Williams] figured Petrocelli right away," said team publicist Bill Crowley. "Rico is the kind of kid who needs the assurance that he's going to play every day whether he made two hits in his last game or two errors. It's when the doubts begin to creep in and Rico starts to wonder where he stands that he plays poorly. Herman used to give him the silent treatment. But Williams made him believe the job is his, no matter what happens." In fact, Williams went a step further. "He told the [club's] infielders that 'Petrocelli is the captain of the infield,'" Petrocelli recalled. "In other words, 'If he wants you to move, you move.'" This gesture of confidence was well received, but, truth be told, Williams did not need to be sold on Petrocelli or his importance to the team. "I just try to let the boy know I appreciate what he's doing," Williams confided to writer Al Hirshberg. "He's such a great shortstop that we're dead without him. I tell him so because he needs constant encouragement. But when he has real problems, he goes to Pop."

"Pop" was Eddie Popowski, a former Red Sox infielder whom Petrocelli had grown close to when the latter coached him in the minors. Williams named Popowski to his big league coaching staff at the beginning of the 1967 season. "I can remember when this kid didn't think he belonged in the big leagues," Popowski said. "He was confused and he had no confidence. What Rico needed was somebody to throw his arm around his shoulder occasionally and tell him he was doing okay." Popowski did that and much more, acting as a combination mentor, father confessor, and life coach. "He watched over me," Petrocelli confirmed. Suddenly, making a costly error or fanning with the bases loaded did not mean his life was over. With Popowski's steady guidance, Petrocelli learned to accept things as they came. "The other day I struck out twice and we won," he said. "Know what I told myself? 'Rico, what do you care as long as the team won, You picked a good day not to get any hits.'"

The more laid-back approach bore tangible results. Petrocelli became one of the finest all-around shortstops in baseball, finishing the season with a solid .259 average and 17 homers. "I don't have an explanation for my improvement at the plate, except I'm not worrying about my job, the way I did other years," Petrocelli told the *Christian Science Monitor*. "I've developed a philosophy that if I don't hit today I'll hit tomorrow." Petrocelli might have been able to add more round-trippers to his season's total, though, if he had played his home games in a different ballpark. Indeed, with its towering left-field wall, Fenway posed an unusual challenge for right-handed pull hitters like the 6'0", 175-pound infielder. Said Petrocelli: "There are several balls that just make the net and someone will say, 'Oh, what a cheap shot!' What they forget is most of them are so high up they'd be out of a lot of other ball parks. What you get is a lot of base hits against the wall that might be caught in other parks."

Outside the batter's box, Petrocelli had a much easier time, turning 73 double plays and making 223 putouts. No major surprise then he was named the starting AL shortstop to the 1967 All-Star Game, beating out more established mainstays such as Luis Aparicio of the White Sox or Zoilo Versalles of the Twins. "Rico plays the hitters properly now," Carl Yastrzemski remarked. "Up to this year, he might make a sensational stop but not have time to throw the man out because he had to run too far. Now, by positioning himself right, he doesn't have to move so much and he can complete plays he couldn't complete before." Yet Yastrzemski believed Petrocelli's biggest indicator of improvement lay in his overall attitude. "He's happy," Yaz said. "He knows he's needed. We all know he's needed . . . I could be out two weeks and we'd keep on winning. We'd keep on winning with anyone out two weeks-except him."

As good as the Red Sox were playing, nobody in baseball viewed them as serious contenders until after the All-Star break. Hosting the defending World Series champion Baltimore Orioles at Fenway July 13–15, the Sox took three out of four games from the injury-riddled club, who would finish the season in a sixth-place tie with the Washington Senators. They then moved on to Detroit where they won two more in an away series that saw Carl Yastrzemski record his 21st homer, the most he had ever hit in a season. Said Yaz: "For players and fans alike, the Sox were getting to be like Rohr's performance on [New York's] Opening Day; comes a certain point, you realize he's not just having a nice game—

he's pitching a no-hitter." The winning streak eventually maxed out to 10 when the team swept the Indians in a four-game set in Cleveland. They were now alone in second place, only a half game behind Chicago. As an astonished Arthur Daley of the *New York Times* wrote, "Perhaps the firm hand of Dick Williams, the new manager, has soothed the primas donnas and directed them toward more unified effort. Perhaps it's because Carl Yastrzemski and Rico Petrocelli are hitting like crazy along with increasing support from Tony Conigliaro and George Scott. Perhaps the supposed inadequate pitching suddenly discovered adequacy. Whatever the reasons, the BoSox have exceeded expectations." Arriving back to Boston's Logan Airport afterward, the ball club's plane was met by a mob of 15,000 wildly enthusiastic fans. "The crowd on the tarmac was a lot bigger than the attendance at a lot of our home games had been for years," Yastrzemski noted. "The fans rushed the bus, squeezing around it, pressing their faces to the windows. They started rocking the thing back and forth. We couldn't even get off. It was bizarre, it was new, it was scary, it was great. We looked at each other with wide eyes."

The Impossible Dream no longer seemed so impossible.

# Chapter Five

# El Birdos Soar

Red Schoendienst faced a far different managerial challenge than Dick Williams at the outset of the 1967 season. Unlike the Red Sox, who were among the youngest and most inexperienced teams in baseball, the Cardinals were a grizzled veteran crew that knew what playing in the heat of a pennant race was all about. To be sure, Bob Gibson, Lou Brock, Curt Flood, and Tim McCarver did not need an authoritarian type such as Williams constantly on their backs, goading them to make the correct throw or deliver the key hit. Rather, they required someone with a supple, more laid-back approach—a field manager who understood it sometimes took time for a ball club to properly jell. Schoendienst certainly met these criteria. Never a yeller or screamer, he accorded his players with the proper respect he felt they had earned in becoming professionals. As Bob Gibson later said, Schoendienst was "willing to treat us as the capable, self-motivated group of grown men we had proven ourselves to be in 1964."

Alfred Fred "Red" Schoendienst knew a thing or two about attaining results. The third youngest of eight children born to a Germantown, Illinois, miner and his devoted wife, Schoendienst came of age under difficult circumstances in the 1930s. The Great Depression was on and every day represented a struggle for survival for Schoendienst and his impoverished family. "Pop was always working whenever and wherever he could, and he would go hunting for rabbits and squirrels to bring us something home to eat," Schoendienst remembered. His home was without indoor plumbing or electricity and coal lanterns had to be hung at night to provide a source of light. Clothing was basic, consisting of old bib overalls that fit loosely on Schoendienst's tall, angular frame. When he or his siblings misbehaved, his muscular father would grab them by their overall straps and hang them like a picture frame on a nail protruding from the front porch wall. "After a while, he'd come by and pick you up and set you down," Schoendienst said. "No words, nothing. You learned not to get out of line, because he would just leave you there, hanging. Parents couldn't get away with that today. The kids would either sue them or somebody would file charges of child abuse."

School took a backseat to baseball and fishing during these formative years, as the fun-loving Schoendienst spent more time skipping classes than attending them. Realizing their son's chances of acquiring a college education were next to nil, his disappointed parents allowed him drop out of high school at 16 to join the Civilian Conservation Corps (CCC). A key component of President Franklin Roosevelt's New Deal program of economic and social reform, the CCC was a public works project that provided gainful employment to over a million restive young men like Schoendienst. Discipline was tight as corpsmen were required to wear dress uniforms and live in military-style camps across the country for $30 a month. "The only difference that I saw between the CCC and the Army was that you didn't have to fight," Schoendienst observed. Work assignments included building roads and bridges, fighting fires, providing flood control, and generally maintaining the nation's forests and parklands. "[The CCC] was probably one of the most worthwhile government programs ever created," Schoendienst said.

It was while working at the CCC camp in Greenville, Illinois, that Schoendienst experienced a freak accident that nearly robbed him of sight in his left eye and any chance he had of a future in professional baseball, a vocation he now seriously entertained. He was helping install a fence on a slope when a coworker's errant hammer blow caused a nail to deflect off a hedge post and go directly into his eyeball. "It was the most intense pain I've ever felt in my life," Schoendienst later revealed. "I knew exactly what happened, but I didn't know how bad it was. I just prayed I wasn't going to lose my eye." He was hospitalized for several weeks, but his doctors did not hold out much hope. Their prognosis was that the eye would have to be removed. Schoendienst strenuously protested and with the support of his mother he convinced one sympathetic specialist to try to save it. The resulting treatment was successful, though it left Schoendienst with 20/200 vision in the affected eye and episodes of diplopia, a condition where objects appear to double. This impairment notwithstanding, Schoendienst continued to play baseball. "There were some days I really had trouble seeing and picking up the ball from the pitcher, especially when it was cloudy," he later admitted. "Those days I was glad I wasn't facing a wild guy throwing 100 MPH, or it could have been really scary."

In 1942, Schoendienst hitchhiked to a Cardinals open tryout camp in St. Louis after the CCC had been officially dissolved with the onset of America's entry into the Second World War. Thin as a rail and unable to afford a decent meal, this "Huckleberry Finn of the diamond," as the writer Bob Broeg later described him, nevertheless impressed Cardinals general manager Branch Rickey with his steady glovework. He was offered a minor league contract with a signing bonus, he later joked, that consisted of a ham sandwich and a glass of milk. Assigned to the Union City, Tennessee team in the Class D Kitty League, Schoendienst demonstrated he was a legitimate prospect by recording consecutive hits in his first eight at-bats. But he surprised his manager Everett Johnson with an odd request after recording his eighth hit. A natural right-handed hitter, Schoendienst asked if he could bat left-handed against right-handed pitchers. As he explained, "Yeah, I've got a bum left eye and when a right-hander throws a curve ball, my nose gets in the way. Can't see the ball good with my right eye." He would remain a switch-hitter for the rest of his pro career.

After hitting .407 for Union City, Schoendienst made rapid progress through the Cardinals farm system over the next two seasons, helped in part by the large number of players who had either volunteered or been drafted ahead of him into the service. "I was glad to be playing baseball and I was determined to do the best job I could for as long as it lasted," he said. When Schoendienst reached the Cardinals' top minor league club in Rochester, New York, though, he was hardly welcomed with open arms. "Crying out loud," Rochester player-manager Pepper Martin said.

"I'm in last place, in a 10-game losing streak and now they're sending me batboys, babies." The former Cardinals outfielder was forced to eat his words when Schoendienst, whom Martin called "Shone . . . er . . . something," hit a very adult-like .337 in 137 games. "I became the youngest person to lead the [International League] in hitting since Wee Willie Keeler in 1892," Schoendienst said. Schoendienst's success on the field could not save him from his local draft board, however. In 1944, he was inducted into the army, but was medically discharged after serving only a few months in the infantry. Apparently, his damaged left eye raised too many red flags about his ability to serve effectively.

Returning to baseball, Schoendienst made the Cardinals starting lineup in 1945 and had a solid rookie season. Always a swift runner, he led the league in stolen bases (26) and drove in 47 runs on a .278 batting average. But perhaps his greatest coup was meeting his future wife, Mary O'Reilly, after a chance encounter on a streetcar following a home game. "[Mary] was a great fan, and that helped our relationship," Schoendienst said. They would marry two years later and have four children. By then, Schoendienst had already gained a measure of fame for recording the last putout of the 1946 World Series, a bad hop grounder struck by Red Sox pinch hitter Tom McBride that secured the Redbirds their sixth championship. Just as important, Schoendienst had established himself as one of the finest all-around second basemen in baseball, a distinction he would maintain well into the next decade. This was no small accomplishment. As he reminded one writer, his position was mentally and physically more demanding than it looked. "You've got two bases to protect—second base on most plays and first on some, mostly bunts," Schoendienst said. "You find yourself trying to read the mind of the batter and base runner all the time, and you're on the move more than any other man on the field."

In the middle of the 1956 season, Schoendienst was traded to the New York Giants as part of an eight-player deal that sent star shortstop and former NL Rookie of the Year Alvin Dark to the Cardinals. The move came as no shocker to Schoendienst. "The team hadn't won in a while, and some of us were getting older," the .289 lifetime hitter said. "I knew [the St. Louis front office] wanted to bring in some younger players, and that would require trading some of the older guys. I never heard any specific rumors, but I still kind of prepared myself for the news." Schoendienst played well for the rebuilding Giants, averaging .300 and raising eyebrows when he cut off the knob from a bat he borrowed from teammate Don Mueller. "I did it because the bat was too long and would catch me on the arm when I'd miss a pitch," he said. Soon enough, a "minor fad" developed among younger fans seeking to emulate the second baseman's style. They too started sawing off the ends of their bats, prompting one bemused reporter to later compare their behavior to that of a cult. Schoendienst typically took all the attention in stride and stopped using a saw in the clubhouse. "I simply ordered the same type of bat without the knob," he said.

Schoendienst played in only a handful of games for the Giants before he was back on the trading block the following summer. The contending Braves, who had moved from Boston to Milwaukee in 1953, were in the market for a veteran second baseman to plug a yawning defensive hole in the middle of their infield. And Schoendienst nicely synched with their needs. "I was pretty lucky," he later admitted. "I walked into a really good situation." For sure, he joined a Milwaukee ball club already loaded with established stars such as Henry Aaron, Eddie Matthews, Johnny Logan, Warren Spahn, and Joe Adcock. But the Braves had been unable to get by the Dodgers in the final standings the previous two seasons. With Schoendienst now on board, that was all about to change. "Schoendienst was getting a little old, but he was a master second baseman and he still had plenty of hits left in him from both sides of the plate," Aaron later said. "He made our team complete, and after the trade it looked as if nothing would stop us—except maybe injuries." Schoendienst, who hit .310 in 93 games, became the unofficial team captain as the Braves remained healthy and cruised their way to the 1957 NL pennant with 95 victories. "Some of the fellows on the club and some newspapermen thought I should have got the most valuable player award," Schoendienst pointed out. "But I didn't think I should have—and I didn't. Henry Aaron [44 homers and 132 RBIs] did. And he richly deserved it. But it was nice to know the boys felt that way." Schoendienst made a more modest contribution in the World Series, hitting .278 in a thrilling seven-game triumph over the Yankees. Still, he was a champion for the first time since

1946 and was especially appreciative of the respectful treatment he had received from Fred Haney in the Milwaukee dugout. "Fred was the kind of manager who was a friend of the players, but he also knew he was the manager and drew the line at becoming real buddy-buddy with them," Schoendienst observed. "That's one of the hardest things a manager has to do, be able to become the boss when the situation calls for it." Schoendienst would take this knowledge to heart when he later helmed the great Cardinals teams of the late 1960s.

The Braves repeated as NL champs the following season but Schoendienst did not play as big a role in bringing victory to the shores of Lake Michigan. He slumped to .268 and experienced long bouts of physical exhaustion. "Every game felt like three doubleheaders," he said. In spite of these obstacles, Schoendienst managed to have an outstanding World Series against the Yankees, whom the Braves lost to in yet another seven-game thriller. He hit .300 and tied Aaron for the team lead in hits with nine. He also scored the winning run in the fourth game after tripling to left center field at Milwaukee's County Stadium. But something was clearly off. "When [Schoendienst] reached third, he was exhausted, far more than a ballplayer should be," Yankees outfielder Mickey Mantle remembered. Schoendienst sought medical help and soon learned the terrible truth.

He had contracted tuberculosis, an infectious disease that most commonly attacks the lungs and results in severe weight loss, coughing attacks, and high fever. Before the discovery of the antibiotic drug Streptomycin in the 1940s, death claimed the majority of TB sufferers. "You've got a tough road ahead," his doctor cautioned him. "You'll have to lie flat on your back, hardly moving an inch, for perhaps as long as six months." Schoendienst did as he was told, though it was far from easy. He was confined to a sanitarium in St. Louis, forbidden to have physical contact with his children for fear they might contract the dreaded disease. His only source of amusement was a black-and-white television set, which he operated by maneuvering the control knobs with his toes. Baseball seemed a universe away. As his wife Mary recalled for a *Parade* magazine article she wrote in 1959, "There were no crowds to cheer him, no teammates to give him a hand, not even a scoreboard to tell him whether he was ahead or behind. But quietly and manfully and confidently, my husband began his year-long struggle."

The long recovery process did have setbacks. When his physician determined he needed to remove diseased tissue from his right lung, Schoendienst tried to hide his anxiety. "Well, it was the first time in my life I was ever cut, so I don't have anything to compare it with," Schoendienst said. "I guess it was quite an operation. But I had good doctors. I wasn't worried. They told me I would be cured. After the operation, I knew I was going to play ball again." Reinforcing this positive outlook was an unexpected morale boost he received from a high place. "Anyone with the competitive spirit that you have so often demonstrated can lick this thing," President Dwight D. Eisenhower warmly wrote him. "And you are not alone in this fight. Baseball fans across the country are pulling for you and wishing you a speedy and complete recovery. My own hopes and prayers will be with you."

Schoendienst made it back to the Braves at the close of 1959 season, appearing in five games and going hitless in three at-bats. "Part of the reason I was in such a hurry to get back was I was hoping I could contribute something down the stretch that would help the team win its third pennant in a row," he said. "Second base had been a problem spot for the team all year." The Braves ended the regular season in a first-place tie with the Dodgers, but were eliminated after dropping the first two games of a best of three playoff series. The Dodgers, now of Los Angeles, went on to defeat the Chicago White Sox in the World Series and Schoendienst was left to ponder an uncertain baseball future.

Even though he had not appeared in any of the Braves' postseason games, Schoendienst was confident he could return to the team's starting lineup. But his advanced age—he was now 37—and with Haney fired as manager, both worked against him. The new Braves dugout boss—former Dodgers skipper Charlie Dressen—was intent on starting a team youth movement and that meant there was no room for Schoendienst in his plans. "Had I been convinced that I couldn't play or perform anymore, I might have had a different attitude and gone ahead and retired," Schoendienst said. He ended up returning to St. Louis where he spent the remaining three years of his playing career pinch-hitting and acting as an assistant coach. This may not have been the storybook ending that he had hoped for, but his life-threatening battle with tuberculosis had taught him to keep things in perspective. For when Schoendienst first learned of his promotion to the Cards managerial post in 1965, he professed to feel no pressure. "I'm here on borrowed time," he said. And he intended to make the most of it.

The 1967 Cardinals had a certain swagger in their step when they gathered that March at Al Lang Field, their longtime spring training home in St. Petersburg, Florida. Although they had finished 12 games out in 1966, the team exuded a certain confidence, some have might even called it arrogance, about their chances in the upcoming season. "I went to St. Petersburg convinced we would win the 1967 National League pennant," Bob Gibson later revealed. "We had improved tremendously." Indeed, promising young Cardinal pitchers Steve Carlton and Nelson Briles had already seen significant action the previous year and were counted on to play even more prominent staff roles in 1967. Of the two, Carlton, 22, seemed to have the most upside. "Steve has a great curve now," said Howard Pollet, a former All-Star pitcher with the Cards in the 1940s who, like Carlton, threw from the left side. "It breaks sharply and it has a rotation that's hard for a batter to pick up. He looks a lot faster now and he certainly must be stronger, especially since he put on some weight." The club's infield defense also looked to get better with a healthy double-play combination of Julian Javier at second base and Dal Maxvill at shortstop. A starter on the 1964 championship squad, the acrobatic Javier went by the nickname "The Ghost" for his preternatural ability to avoid contact with opponents going hard into second. "Sticks and stones will break Javier's bones but never a sliding baserunner," wrote Joe Donnelly of *Sport* magazine. Hampered by a series of nagging injuries, Javier's ability to keep his steady glove in the Cards' lineup had been drastically put to the test the previous two seasons. "I had a talk with him when he came to camp last spring," Red Schoendienst said. "I figured if he could stay in there, we could move up real good. Then the first day of the spring schedule, he got hurt sliding into third." Maxvill, who would later serve as the team's general manager on two pennant winners in the 1980s, had been a regular at short since Dick Groat's departure in 1965. Like Javier, the 28-year-old electrical engineering major from Washington University wasn't much of a hitter (a .217 lifetime average), but his quickness and athleticism made him the glue that held the infield together. "He knew how to win, which was his biggest attribute," Red Schoendienst said. "He made the big plays at the critical moments in games." Maxvill would play in 14 major league seasons and earn a Gold Glove for his defensive excellence in 1968.

The Cardinals biggest upgrade by far, though, was on offense with the additions of Orlando Cepeda and Roger Maris. Cepeda had come over to St. Louis the previous May in a trade with San Francisco where he had starred for several years. A former NL Rookie of the Year, Cepeda entered the 1967 season with 243 career home runs. Only persistent knee problems had kept him from hitting more. When healthy, he was one of the most devastating power hitters in baseball. "Every club seems to have a big clutch hitter," Tim McCarver said. "The Giants have Willie Mays. The Phillies have Richie Allen. The Braves have Hank Aaron. Cepeda's *our* big man." Cepeda was expected to provide middle of the order protection to Maris, the all-time single season home run record holder with 61 in 1961. Maris had been acquired in an off-season trade with the Yankees. The fact he was available for only the price of journeyman third baseman Charley Smith spoke volumes to how far his baseball stock had fallen. Coming off consecutive injury-plagued seasons where the seven-time All-Star outfielder batted no higher than .239 and failed to top 13 homers, Maris was on the verge of hanging up his cleats. "I was sick and tired of the situation in New York," he said. Indeed, merciless booing from Yankee fans upset that he couldn't replicate his historic 1961 home run total and an unsympathetic front office made Maris open to the idea of retirement.

Only the fear of how such a move might be interpreted by the sensationalistic New York media—a group Maris had frequently clashed with—stayed his hand. "The writers would have made me look bad again," he said. "They'd say, 'Well. He's not going to play because he was traded away from the Yankees.' They would have jumped on me like it was a big news story. So I finally agreed to go ahead and play the year." Adding to his motivation was a guaranteed $72,000 salary and a rumored promise by Gussie Busch that he would sell Maris a lucrative Budweiser beer distributorship once his playing days were over. "He figured playing for Busch was a shrewd move toward a post-baseball career," Maris biographers Tom Clavin and Dan Peary wrote.

Irrespective of the reason he consented to the trade, Stan Musial was delighted to have him. "We know that Roger is an established major leaguer and a tremendous outfielder," the St. Louis general manager told the press. "We aren't looking at him and saying he is going to have a great year this year. Neither are we looking for any miracles from him. If he does what he can do—and we think he is now over his injuries, because we had him examined carefully—he can get runs for the Cardinals. That's what we need. We did not get enough runs last year."

Cardinal players were more cautious in their reaction. "We had all read and heard so much about him and now we would see for ourselves what he was like," Bob Gibson said. "Was he really the brooding, sullen, unapproachable ogre he was made out to be?" Mike Shannon privately harbored fears the aging slugger would become a cancer in the clubhouse and ruin the team's pennant chances. "The Cardinals were a close-knit team with a delicate chemistry," Shannon explained. "We had one star, Bob Gibson and a lot of good players who blended together. In New York, it was a star system—Mantle, Maris, Ford. And we had heard the stories about Roger fighting with the press, being moody and unhappy."

Maris felt equally in the dark about his new baseball home. He had spent his entire career in the American League and knew little of the Cardinals outside of competing against them in the 1964 World Series. That situation would change. "One day we were leaving the motel for the ball field when we saw Roger by himself waiting to catch the bus," Orlando Cepeda remembered. "We stopped the car and invited him to ride to the ballpark with us. This broke the ice." Cepeda and his teammates soon discovered that the angry and unapproachable Maris of the New York tabloids was "a decent guy." "After a couple of days everyone was impressed by Roger—especially his work ethic," Cepeda said. This work ethic could be seen in the diligent manner Maris labored to shed the extra weight he had put on in the offseason. "By the time spring training was over, he'd worked that weight down and was muscular and fit," Cepeda said. "He won the respect of the entire team and became one of us." Maris reciprocated the feeling. "I feel so much better here," he said. "I don't want to rap the Yankees for letting me go. Why should I? I had success there and was well paid for it. But this is great here—a real great organization and a nice guy as manager."

Roger Eugene Maris had always sought such stability in his baseball career. Originally signed by the Cleveland Indians out of high school, the shy but athletically gifted Maris had turned down a scholarship offer to play football for coaching great Bud Wilkerson at the University of Oklahoma. "I realized then that sitting in a classroom wasn't for me, and that I was just too impatient for any sort of college life, football or no," he said. Maris instead tried his luck at baseball, a sport he had difficulty wrapping his brawny arms around while growing up in Fargo, North Dakota, in the late 1940s. "It was my [older] brother [Rudy] who forced me to play baseball and I mean *forced* me," he said. "If he went to play, he grabbed me by the ear and pulled me out. If I had been bigger I might have put up an argument. But I didn't catch up to him until we were in high school, and by that time nobody had to force me to play."

Billed as one of the top prospects in the Indians farm system, Maris reached the majors in 1957 but had only a so-so year, hitting .235 in 116 games as an outfielder. He did jack 16 homers, though, and this was enough to convince many observers that he had a bright future. "He was a good all-around player," said longtime Cleveland sportswriter Hal Lebovitz. "He knew he was going to be much better than he showed as a rookie. Did I know he'd be the one to break Babe Ruth's record? Never. But I did like him as a player and a person? You better believe it." His Indian teammates were less enamored, seeing him as a quiet loner who kept his emotions tightly in check—that is until he hit two homers in a game one day. "He was so happy," remembered shortstop Chico Carrasquel. "He said, 'Chico, one of these years I'm going to hit 20 to 25 homers!" New Cleveland GM Frank Lane was thinking similar thoughts. He wanted Maris, now happily married with a child, to play winter ball in the Dominican Republic to work on his batting stroke. But Maris refused, citing a desire to be with his family. "That did it," Lane later recounted. "I made up my mind that this guy was going to be too difficult to handle to make it worth my while." Things didn't exactly go swimmingly with Cleveland manager Bobby Bragan either. Bragan, a tough and demanding baseball lifer, believed his budding young slugger had taken too long to return to the lineup after having pulled a muscle in his back at the start of the 1958 season. Maris took strong exception. "I couldn't play for Bragan," he said. "I didn't like him, and he had no use for me. He hauled me on the carpet one day and shouted, 'I am fed up with your loafing.'"

Having worn out his welcome in Cleveland, Maris was traded to the Kansas City Athletics in June where he went on to hit 19 home runs in 99 games. Though the Athletics were a distant also-ran, he took an immediate liking to the small-town atmosphere of Kansas City and appreciated the laid-back approach of the organization. "This club is different," Maris said. "They help you, but don't overcoach. They give you credit for using your brain and let you work out certain things for yourself." Maris had even begun to think he had found a permanent home in the big leagues but after suffering through a major batting slump in the second half of the 1959 season, he was put on the trading block again. This time the Yankees were the takers and Maris wasn't happy about it. "It doesn't thrill me, and it sure fouls things up," he said. "I just built a [house] and expected to spend a lot of time with my family. Now they traded me about as far away as they could."

Unbeknownst to Maris, he had been on Yankees general manager George Weiss's wish list for some time. Weiss had kept close tabs going back to his days with the Indians and couldn't resist pouncing when he became available. Rival league executives held a different opinion, seeing the move as yet another example of the wealthy Yankees fleecing a weaker, small market opponent of their brightest young talent. The A's certainly had made a practice of submitting to one-sided deals with the Yankees ever since industrialist-businessman Arnold Johnson—a close personal friend to Yankees co-owner Dan Topping—purchased the franchise in 1954. "It must be great to have your own farm system in the same league," former Indians GM and Tigers Hall of Fame outfielder Hank Greenberg sniped.

Looking resplendent in Yankee pinstripes, Maris emerged as one of the game's most feared power hitters over the next half-decade. It was easy to see why. "I'm getting better pitches to hit than I did at Kansas City last year," Maris told Walter Bingham of *Sports Illustrated*. "You hear people say it's easier to hit when you're on a bad ballclub. Don't believe it. Pitchers throwing against second division teams are generally loose. The ball is really moving. Once in a while in batting practice you'll see a pitcher with great stuff. That's because he knows he doesn't have to get anybody out, so he's relaxed. But a pitcher facing a team like the Yankees is likely to be in tight situations, which makes it tougher on him."

Teamed up with three-time AL home run champ Mickey Mantle in the middle of the Yankees lineup, the "M & M Boys" demoralized opposing pitching staffs, combining for 79 homers and 206 RBIs in 1960 alone. Yet their mutual success spawned talk of a heated personal rivalry that both players downplayed. "I'd be a liar to say I didn't want to hit more home runs than Mantle," Maris confessed. "A guy would be a liar to say he wouldn't want to lead the league, lead the club. But as far as him hitting a ball and me saying I wish it would hit the wall, that's a crock of baloney. I can make more money getting into the World Series than by being one home run ahead of him. We both do well, we both make money, that's all there is to it."

Mantle was of a similar mind, claiming that while both fed off the competition, they didn't let it interfere with their friendship or mutual admiration. "It is in the nature of people to look for the tension, the jealousy, maybe a feud between teammates," he said. "Those feelings may have been there with Ruth and Gehrig; according to the stories even their wives got into the act. It wasn't like that with Roger and me, but we kept it to ourselves. Our feeling was, let the press and the fans think what they wanted." The so-called animosity the two possessed for one another didn't prevent them from amicably sharing an apartment in Queens together or make fun of all the manufactured rumors swirling around them. Recalled Mantle, "I remember one morning Roger went out to get coffee and the papers and he came back to the apartment and said, 'Wake up, Mick, we're fightin' again.'"

Still, the New York sporting press, especially in the media capital of the world, could be relentless. And this where Maris ran into problems—he refused to play by their rules. "I came in during a transition period," he later said. "On one hand, you had a lot of older writers who wrote what happened on the field and nothing else. Then, you had Louella Parsons [gossip columnist] types who were just coming in and nicknamed 'Chipmunks.' They wanted to write about everything but the game itself." Including in their ranks such up and coming writers as Leonard Shecter and Stan Isaacs, the Chipmunks, so named for their chirpy disposition in the press box, were an irreverent bunch. "Not only were they younger than their predecessors, they were generally better educated, definitely more iconoclastic, certainly more egocentric, and probably less grateful to be covering the great New York Yankees," wrote David Halberstam. They looked for quirky and provocative angles to their stories, an approach that made Maris, a thoughtful and guarded man, uneasy. He wanted to keep interviews focused strictly on his performance while they wanted to know about his personal life and inner psyche. "I don't think it was the right way to do things, and it's something I will never understand," Maris said. Unsurprisingly, there were several explosive confrontations, including one where Maris took umbrage at a Shecter piece on his perceived poor handling of fame. "You fucking ripping cocksucker," Maris told him. In spite of these outbursts, Maris was not without defenders in the press box. "Roger made one mistake; he was honest," argued Jim Ogle, who wrote for *The Star-Ledger* of Newark, New Jersey. "He always told you what he thought, but he was dependable as the Federal Reserve. If he told you something, you could take it to the bank. The writers didn't understand that."

Maris gave them plenty to write about in 1961, arguably the greatest season any modern hitter has ever had. He drove in a league-leading 141 runs but set a new historic benchmark when he hit 61 homers to shatter Babe Ruth's single season home run record of 60 set in 1927. Fittingly, the historic blow came on the last day of the regular season at home against the Red Sox, the Babe's first team. Maris launched a waist high fastball thrown by Boston rookie right-hander Tracy Stallard into the deepest reaches of Yankee Stadium in his second at-bat. "As soon as I hit it, I knew it was No. 61," Maris said. "Then, I heard the tremendous roar from the crowd. I could see everyone standing, then my mind went blank. I couldn't think as I went around the bases. I was all fogged out." The loud applause descending from the stands lasted a full five minutes, but Maris was typically reluctant to acknowledge them when he got back to the dugout. His teammates forced his hand. "The other guys in the dugout practically pushed him out onto the field," remembered Whitey Ford. "Roger was so shy, he just popped his head out of the dugout, took off his cap, and waved it, and then ducked back in the dugout. Here the man had just broken the greatest and most glamorous record in baseball history and he acted like he was embarrassed."

It had been a long arduous journey to reach this career defining moment. Facing unprecedented scrutiny from the media and fans all year long, Maris nearly buckled from the intense pressure. "He just didn't seem to know how to cope with all the attention," Ford said. His hair began to fall out in clumps and he grew increasingly agitated by the hordes of reporters chronicling his every move on and off the diamond. "It put so much pressure on him that it's amazing what he accomplished," teammate Joe De Maestri said. "There would be fifty reporters standing around his locker. Roger's problem was that he tried to answer every question, not with a 'yes,' 'no,' or 'maybe,' but with a long dissertation. He would fall into the trap and just freeze up." The uncomfortable situation also carried over to other Yankees in the clubhouse, who resented being portrayed as mere bit players in this unfolding drama. "I remember a game where [Elston Howard] hit a home run in extra innings to win it after Roger hit one earlier," said second baseman Bobby Richardson, a close friend of Maris and future leader of the Fellowship of Christian Athletes. "After the game the writers went right by Ellie's locker to talk to Roger—that's the way it was." Not all Yankees minded the media freeze out. "Mickey [Mantle] used to laugh because they weren't bothering him anymore even though he was only a few homers behind Roger," De Maestri said.

Maris faced further unwanted attention when then Commissioner Ford Frick, an old friend and close business associate of Ruth's, announced that the Sultan of Swat's record would remain intact "unless bettered within a 154-game limit, since that was the schedule in 1927." Maris didn't hit his 61st until the 162nd game of the newly expanded major league schedule, thus requiring an asterisk in the official record book. "I thought it was a ridiculous ruling," Mantle later said. "It made no sense at all. Check further and you'll note that the same year, 1961, Sandy Koufax broke Christy Mathewson's National League strikeout record. Mathewson set it in 1903, when they played a 140-game schedule. But you won't find an asterisk attached to Koufax."

The asterisk would eventually be removed by one of Frick's fair-minded successors—the erudite Fay Vincent—but Maris never professed to give the issue much thought. "From the first time I was asked about it, I didn't give a damn about the asterisk," he protested to an interviewer from *USA Today* shortly before his death in 1985. "I could care less whether it was there and still don't . . . it really didn't make a hell of a lot of difference. No one was going to have the record unless he hit 61 home runs. It was such an immaterial thing, but yet everybody tried to make it such a big thing."

Maris never came close to matching his 1961 production again in a Yankees uniform. He had another solid year in 1962—33 homers and 100 RBIs—but his offense tailed off in the seasons to follow due to injury. Some Yankee fans, already resentful of the fact that Maris and not hometown favorite Mickey Mantle had broken Ruth's record, were less sympathetic. They lustily booed him at every opportunity. "He went through a kind of hell," said Whitey Ford. Maris did his best to ignore the abuse, but this proved impossible given the frequency and intensity of the catcalls. "Some kids feel they're big shots if they boo me," he complained. "I don't have to explain why I don't like certain fans. Would you like it if someone threw a beer can at you? How 'bout if someone threw a bottle at you?"

The boos only grew louder when Maris suffered a crippling hand injury during a contest against the Washington Senators at the start of the 1965 campaign. "There was a real sharp pop in my hand, loud enough that I could hear it," recalled Maris, who compared the sound to a pencil being snapped in half. "The hand swelled up right away, double its normal size. I ended up taking a pitch right down the middle to strike out."

At first, team doctor Sydney Gaynor could find nothing wrong with the hand, even though Maris was clearly in pain and unable to grip a bat. This led the Yankees front office as well as some skeptical teammates to conclude that Maris had lost his desire to play and was dogging it on the field. "I heard a few of them were thinking that and you can't blame them," Maris insisted. "I could show you my hand and nothing looked wrong on the surface."

A late season X-ray examination by a doctor outside the Yankees organization, however, revealed that Maris had broken a tiny wedge-shaped carpal bone in his right wrist. Maris had been right all along. "That was a terrible thing to do to a ballplayer like Roger," said Clete Boyer, a Gold Glove–winning third baseman with the Yankees. "All [team management] did was play games with him, hinting to reporters that the only pain was in Roger's head. How could anyone say Roger was dogging it? But that's what the front office basically said." "Everybody's going to draw their own conclusions," Maris commented years later. "There are just a lot of things that I don't understand, and I never will. A lot of things . . . I feel a lot of things could have been handled a lot differently than they were, and naturally I was quite disappointed in the way they were handled."

What was not disappointing was the offensive output Maris gave the Yankees during his seven seasons with the ball club. The 1960 and 1961 AL MVP hit 203 homers and drove in 547 runs, all the while finishing with a more than respectable .267 average in 850 games. "I don't claim to be a student of hitting," he once said. "I just concentrate on my timing and my swing. If some of my hits are homers, so much the better." Perhaps more telling, the team won five consecutive AL pennants and two World Series during this span. While he received significant help from Hall of Fame teammates Mickey Mantle, Whitey Ford, and Yogi Berra, Maris was the straw that stirred the proverbial drink when it came to extending the life of the great postwar Yankees dynasty. For before Maris had arrived in New York, the Yankees had slipped to third place and looked like a sure bet to remain there until his bat was added to the lineup. "In short," wrote historian Glen Stout in *Yankees Century*, "Maris made them the Yankees again or at least a reasonable facsimile of the team that had dominated the previous decade like no other. He was the piece that had been missing."

The Cardinals were counting on a similar outcome in 1967.

The team opened its 86th regular season campaign with a satisfying 6–0 victory over the San Francisco Giants at Busch Memorial Stadium on April 11. Pitching before a crowd of 38,117 fans, Bob Gibson struck out 13 Giants, including the first five batters he faced in the record-tying complete game performance. Only six other pitchers in baseball history had ever started a contest with as many strikeouts and among the illustrious names on this elite list were Hall of Famers Walter Johnson, Lefty Gomez, and Dazzy Vance. "He was busting the bats right out of their hands," Dal Maxvill said. Gibson, though, professed not to care. What mattered the most to him was the fact that he had beaten the Giants, a team he had come up short against all three times he had faced them the previous season. "I had pitched so many good games against this club, but I always seemed to get beaten," said Gibson, who had fanned a career-best 14 against San Francisco in one of the losses. "My slider was my best pitch tonight, but I had a good fastball, too."

Gibson's teammates did their part, too. They pummeled Giants starter Juan Marichal, who had been a 25-winner the year before, with 14 hits, the most the Dominican right-hander had allowed in a game his entire career up to this point. Lou Brock led the way with a towering three-run homer into the right-field bleachers in the bottom of the second inning. Brock also stole second after singling in the first. "I'm tied for the lead in home runs. I'm tied in runs batted in and I'm 1.000 in stealing bases," Brock joked afterward. "I think I'll go in [to the St. Louis front office] and ask for $100,000." The Redbirds outfielder wasn't alone in wreaking damage. Dal Maxvill had three hits and Roger Maris went 2 for 5 to the delight of the hometown fans. "It's nice to hear cheers like this for a change," he said. "It's been a long time." Maris would receive many more cheers that season as he hit a steady .261 and drove in 55 runs on 9 homers in 125 games. Unlike past campaigns, however, Maris held off on trying to pull every pitch. He used all fields, becoming, in essence, a spray hitter. "I took one look at Busch Memorial Stadium [and its distant outfield fences] and knew I'd have to change if I was going to help this ball club," he later told the *Christian Science Monitor*. "Yankee Stadium was built for a left-handed pull hitter. Busch Stadium is a pitchers' park. Lou Brock and Curt Flood proved the value of spraying the ball around, so that's the pattern I took."

To make room for Maris's bat in the lineup, Schoendienst moved Mike Shannon—the team's regular right fielder—to third base, a decision that initially was not greeted with a tremendous amount of enthusiasm in the Cardinals clubhouse. Bob Gibson, for one, thought it would weaken the club's infield defense. "It's a horrible idea," he said. "You don't really have to catch the ball," Shannon's skeptical teammates told him. "It's the hot corner. Just knock it down and throw him out." But Shannon, who drove in 89 runs in 1967, fooled everyone by making a smooth transition. He placed fifth in NL assists (239) by a third baseman and turned an impressive 18 double plays. "Talk about on-the-job-training," Dal Maxvill observed. "Shannon had his under the toughest possible conditions." Perhaps even more surprising, Shannon bore no animus toward Maris for bumping him out of his defensive comfort zone. Quite the opposite. He and Maris became fast friends and Shannon later served as one of 12 pallbearers at the slugger's funeral in 1985. "Moving to third was the greatest thing I ever did because it helped Roger come to the team and be happy," Shannon said.

The Cardinals had not received much love from the so-called baseball experts in the media prior to the start of the 1967 season. While they were considered a decent ball club with "[a]livelier offense, with both power and speed, plus strong pitching" according to *Sports Illustrated*, they were not expected to be in the final mix for the NL pennant. Even those covering the team daily —people like highly respected *St. Louis Post-Dispatch* sports editor Bob Broeg—did not give them much of a chance. "Fourth or better," he predicted in an April 11 column. "That's how the Cardinals look to these bifocals." With the unexpected retirement of 30-year-old pitching ace and 27-game winner Sandy Koufax from the defending champion Los Angeles Dodgers the previous fall, the league appeared ripe for the taking by the Pittsburgh Pirates. The Pirates had a powerful lineup featuring future Hall of Famers Roberto Clemente, Willie Stargel, and Bill Mazeroski and the reigning NL batting champ in Matty Alou. They were "everybody's favorites" to win it all. But the Cardinals proved they were the cream of the league, vaulting out to a 44–27 start in the first three months of the season and taking over first place to stay by mid-June. "Other teams might have had more talent, position by position, but I don't think there was a team at that period of time who got more out of their talent or players who worked better together," Nelson Briles said. The Pirates, by contrast, underperformed, eventually finishing with a mediocre 81–81 record in sixth place.

As the early Cardinal victories piled up, it became clear that Orlando Cepeda was having the best season of his career. Like Carl Yastrzemski with the Red Sox, the first baseman's every at-bat seemed to produce positive results for his team. "If there's one man on that St. Louis club that is going to beat you, it's Cepeda," said New York Mets manager Wes Westrum. "I always said he was going to lead the league and it looks like it's going to be this year." Cepeda was hitting a NL-best .356 by midseason and while he was unable to maintain that blistering pace, he did finish the season with a .325 average and a league-leading 111 RBIs. Those numbers, along with 25 homers and a career-topping .399 on-base percentage, were more than enough to make him the first ever unanimous selection for NL Most Valuable Player.

But statistics alone do not come close to describing the important contribution Cepeda made to the St. Louis locker room that season. More than anyone, he made the Cardinals "El Birdos," the affectionate nickname given to the team by coach Joe Schultz. An acknowledgment of the club's diverse mix of whites, blacks, and Latinos, El Birdos demonstrated in a time of great racial and cultural divisions in American society that individuals could put aside their differences and work together for the shared goal of winning. "All the guys seem to pull together," Bob Gibson said. "We go to dinner or out on the town in San Francisco or Chicago or Los Angles. We don't have three separate groups like some other clubs, where the Negro guys stay together, the Spanish guys stay together, and the white guys stay together." Looking back years later, Nelson Briles could only agree with his teammate. "We were very much aware how free from 'racist poison' we were," the pitcher said.

And Cepeda—or “Cha-Cha” as he was better known to his friends for his love of Cuban dance music—was a big reason why. In spite of or rather because of the fact he had felt the stinging lash of racial prejudice throughout his life, Cepeda had steadfastly refused to give in to such hate. He instead reached out to all his Cardinal teammates when he arrived in St. Louis and sought common ground. “Orlando is always trying to inspire the rest of us,” Dal Maxvill said. To be sure, Cepeda made a point after every Redbird victory to hop on a clubhouse table and lead the team in cheers. He would ask, “Who wins this game?” and the answer would inevitably be a loudly affirming “El Birdos.” Such gestures of inclusion forced even the normally skeptical Curt Flood to buy into this progressive-minded team approach. “Victorious on the field and victorious off it, by God,” he later enthused. “A beautiful little foretaste of what life will be like when Americans finally unshackle themselves [from racism].”

Growing up in Puerto Rico in the 1940s, Orlando Manuel Cepeda had to contend with the pressures and expectations associated with being the son of a famous ballplayer. His father—slugging shortstop Pedro Anibal “Perucho” Cepeda—once hit .464 and was celebrated as the “Babe Ruth of Puerto Rico.” Young Orlando lived in awe of him, even when his behavior on the diamond was less than exemplary. Perucho would frequently get into fights with other players and fans and fly into a rage over a 0-for-5 day at the plate. Once, he was arrested for going after a heckler in the stands while the game was still in progress. When he was brought down to the police station for booking, the desk sergeant on duty remarked, “Ah, Perucho, not again.” “My father had a bad temper,” Cepeda later told writer Lennie Megliola. “Worst I ever saw. I don’t know. Maybe that’s why he was such a good ballplayer. He demanded a lot from himself.” Perucho also demanded a lot from his son who was following in his baseball footsteps. Once, after Orlando had failed to register a hit in his first two at-bats of a sandlot tournament game, Perucho, popularly known as “The Bull,” stormed onto the playing field to give him a tongue-lashing. “If you don’t get a hit next time, don’t even come home after the game,” he roared. Confronted with this ultimatum, Orlando banged out a double.

Perucho was not all sturm and drang. He possessed an enormously appealing personality that drew in people from all walks of life. Recalled Cepeda, "He used to take me downtown. Every few seconds, someone would stop us and talk to him. They all idolized him; they wanted to buy him something. We never had to spend any money. They still talk about him." Perucho, whose dark skin color barred him from playing in the all-white majors during these years, relished the attention. He remained active as a player well into his mid-40s and would often entertain fans by performing acrobatic somersaults on the field. "He wanted to show them he was not too old to play," Cepeda said. Adding to Perucho's celebrity was the respect he received from great Negro League stars such as Satchell Paige, who made an annual trek to Puerto Rico to play winter ball. "It was a special treat whenever [Paige] paid [my family] a visit, which he did quite often," Orlando remembered. The social calls were not entirely baseball-related, however. "It's no secret . . . that Satchel Paige was a genuine ladies' man," the future Cardinal related. "One of his favorite ladies was our neighbor, a woman named Tommie. After visiting Tommie he'd stop by our house to talk with my father and enjoy a good cup of coffee, which my mother always had waiting for him."

By the time Orlando had signed with the Giants in 1955 as a wiry 17-year-old, Perucho had been retired from the game for several years. He was also in declining health, suffering from the ravaging effects of malaria. "He argued all the way to the hospital that he wasn't sick," his son said. "Then he fell into a coma and was dead in a week." His loss shattered Orlando, who was about to make his professional debut with the Salem, Virginia, Rebels of the Class D Appalachian League. "I was really too upset to play," he said. "It took me two months to get over his death. He had always wanted to see me play as a pro. His death was the saddest moment of my life." If this wasn't bad enough, Cepeda was now burdened with the responsibility of being his family's principal breadwinner, as his profligate father had never saved much money from his years of playing ball. "My brother Pedro was in the service, so my mother was left alone," Cepeda revealed. "She had no money. I was lucky to be playing baseball. I could support her. I paid for the funeral with money from the Giants."

First baseman Orlando Cepeda's 1966 trade from San Francisco rejuvenated his career. BASEBALL HALL OF FAME PHOTO ARCHIVE

Cepeda's transition to stateside life did not go smoothly. He had little command of the English language and being a black Puerto Rican in the heart of the segregated South made him the target of venomous attacks from racist white fans. They would yell to him from the stands that if he was back at his island home, he would be cutting sugar cane in the fields.

"They don't even know Puerto Ricans are American citizens," he said. "They think of us as some kind of animals." Nor were things much better outside Dixie. "On our first road trip to a town in Iowa, I couldn't get into a restaurant," he recalled. "They wouldn't serve me, I didn't know what was going on. I was lost. I was looking for help. No one gave it to me." The combination of these personal attacks and the grief he still felt over his father's passing made him withdraw into a deep personal shell. "In the evenings and on Sundays I'd sit alone in a room in the black section of town, listening to the sounds of gospel music from the church across the street," he recounted. "Looking back, I don't know how I did it. I couldn't hit anything. My father was on my mind. Every time we made a road trip, I'd be by myself. I never knew such loneliness."

Cepeda hit rock bottom when his unsympathetic manager John Crosswhite called him a "Sonovabitch" after striking out six times in a doubleheader. An angry Cepeda informed Giant higher-ups he could no longer play for the man. "He has insulted my mother," he explained. Salem released him but luckily for Cepeda, he was reassigned to the Giants' Kokomo, Indiana, affiliate in the Northern League. Here he found a more supportive manager in Walt Dixon, who doubled as the team's first baseman. "The club really wanted me," Cepeda said. "Walt and his wife took good care of me the entire year, and my teammates were a good bunch of guys." He had averaged only .247 with a single homer in 26 games for Salem, but now he busted out at the plate, hitting a league-leading .393 along with 21 home runs, 21 doubles, and 91 RBIs.

Two more outstanding seasons in the minors followed, but there remained doubts among some in the Giants front office about Cepeda's ability to play at a higher level. "In their minds, he wasn't a prospect," wrote Cepeda biographer Bruce Markusen. But after having a standout spring training in 1958, in which he hit 8 homers and drove in 22 runs, Cepeda silenced the critics. He became the Giants starting first baseman when the former New York–based ball club opened their inaugural season in San Francisco at home against the Dodgers on April 15. As Cepeda recalled, "It was a warm, breezy day, the sun was shining, and we were making history." Indeed, the Giants' traditional archrivals from Brooklyn were now taking up residence in nearby Los Angeles, making this the first West Coast major league contest ever played. And Cepeda rose to the occasion in the bottom of the third inning by hammering a 3–1 changeup from Dodger reliever Don Bessent into the right field stands of Seals Stadium, a Depression-era ballpark built for the Pacific Coast League's San Francisco Seals. The Giants won the game 8–0 and Cepeda was on cloud nine. "Right from the beginning, I fell in love with the city," he later said. "There was everything that I liked. We played more day games then, so I usually had at least two nights a week free. On Thursdays, I would always go to the Copacabana to hear the Latin music. On Sundays, after games, I'd go to the Jazz Workshop for the jam sessions." Cepeda had even greater fun crushing fastballs from opposing pitchers. "I have the ability to hit, and I always have confidence that I can hit," he once told an interviewer. "I am not a scientific hitter. It doesn't matter how you stand. You remember Bob Speake. He used to be with the Giants. He had the best swing I've ever seen, but he always hit .200 or something. I don't know how to hit. It's just what you do when the ball is right here—right over the plate. I follow the pitcher's arm and wait for the ball and keep my head down—like all those golfers."

On the year, Cepeda submitted a batting line that read .309, 25 homers, and 96 RBIs. He was unsurprisingly named a unanimous selection as the NL's Rookie of the Year, only the second time it happened since the award's inception in 1947. "The public loves a slugger and this boy is the Rocky Marciano of the batters' ring," lauded one local newspaperman. Some intrepid observers even began comparing Cepeda to his All-Star teammate Willie Mays, who was entering his seventh season in the majors and already considered the greatest center fielder to ever play. "Cepeda's supporters feel he is basically a sounder hitter than Mays," wrote Tim Cohane of *Look* magazine. "They concede that he will never equal Mays defensively, but they argue that his bat may ultimately resolve the comparison in his favor." Where Cepeda had a clear edge over Mays was in the fan preference department. "While the Giants wanted to make [Mays] the showpiece of the franchise," notes Mays biographer James S. Hersch, "San Francisco didn't need a packaged icon from the East Coast. It wanted to find its own heroes. And it did in [Cepeda]." Yet as the accolades poured in, the money did not. His top annual salary never exceeded $53,000 during his nine years with the Giants, seasons in which he averaged .308 and was among the league leaders in several batting categories, including home runs and RBIs. "I would argue with the Giants in the early years," Cepeda said. "I felt I deserved more money. They said that I was lucky to be playing in the United States. They said it was better than picking sugar cane back home. They tried to put you in a position where you couldn't argue."

Cepeda did put up a fuss when the team tried to move him to third base his sophomore season. Much heralded first base prospect Willie McCovey had been called up from the minors in the middle of the year and Giants manager Bill Rigney wanted to find a spot for him in the club's everyday lineup. Cepeda felt completely disrespected. He had, after all, been chosen the team's MVP the previous season and had developed a reputation for being a smooth fielder around the bag with an accurate arm. "I didn't want to vacate first," Cepeda said. "It was my position, and I felt that I had earned it." Rigney, though, insisted and Cepeda, who was now being called the "Baby Bull" in honor of his late father, reluctantly went to third. The experiment lasted exactly four games. Cepeda made three errors on eight chances for an embarrassing .625 fielding percentage. "In one game I threw the ball so far over McCovey's head that it sailed into the stands where it hit a lady in the face and emptied the seats," Cepeda said. Rigney switched him to the outfield for the remainder of the season, where he played alongside Mays in left. But in the years to follow, he would spend most of his playing time at first. He later conceded to *Sports Illustrated*'s Ron Firmte that he could have handled the situation better, but that his own stubborn pride stood in the way. "I just wasn't ready mentally," he concluded.

The same words could have been used to describe his Giant teammates from this era. Despite the presence of five future Hall of Famers (Cepeda, Mays, McCovey, and pitchers Juan Marichal and Gaylord Perry) on the roster, the club had the unfortunate tendency of coming up short in big games and in the final standings. The one year the Giants did qualify for postseason play—1962—the team dropped a heartbreaking World Series to the New York Yankees in seven games. The Series came down to the last at-bat at San Francisco's recently opened Candlestick

Park, a forbidding concrete and steel edifice located in the rundown Bayview-Hunters Point section of the city. With his team trailing 1–0 and the tying and winning runs in scoring position, Willie McCovey lined a two-out scorcher to right that Yankees second baseman Bobby Richardson barely gloved to end the game. "I watched helplessly," commented Cepeda, who was in the Giants on-deck circle as the play unfolded.

Cepeda had every reason to feel frustrated. After having one of his best statistical years in a Giants uniform—.306 average, 35 homers, 26 doubles, 191 hits and 105 runs scored—he was a complete bust in the Fall Classic. He hit an embarrassing .158 with only three hits and four strikeouts. Still, Cepeda was not prepared for the shabby treatment he was about to receive. He was abruptly told by Giants management his salary would be slashed by $7,000 the next season. The reason given had to do with a bizarre plus-minus player ratings system devised by Giants manager Alvin Dark, an ill-mannered taskmaster who had replaced the fired Bill Rigney the previous year. "Our players get a plus anytime they do a little extra to help win a game," Dark explained. "Anytime a player misses a sign or fails to drive in a runner from third with less than two outs in a key spot, he's charged with a minus." According to Dark, Cepeda's banner 1962 season had been "terribly minus."

Cepeda could not believe what he was hearing. He had been playing all year on a badly injured right knee requiring eventual surgery and had still managed to put up good numbers. Now this insult. Cepeda, who was eventually able to wrest a small salary increase from the ball club, believed the unfair criticism was motivated by anachronistic racial views. As he later said, "Some people think that because we are Latins—because we did not have everything growing up—we are not supposed to get hurt. But my knee was hurt. Dark thought I was trying to not to play. He treated me like a child. I am a human being. Whether I am blue or black or black or white or green, we Latins are different, but we are still human beings. Dark did not respect our differences." Indeed, so tone deaf was Dark to the cultural sensitivities of the Latino players on his roster—standout performers like Cepeda, Marichal, and Felipe Alou—that he felt there was nothing wrong with arbitrarily banning the speaking of Spanish on team premises. "SPEAK ENGLISH, YOU'RE

IN AMERICA," instructed a sign Dark had erected in the clubhouse. Cepeda was beyond mortified. "I said this is ridiculous. I said I'm proud of my language. I'm Spanish. This is going to be the worst thing if we talk English. Because we can communicate better in Spanish. How come when you people go to Puerto Rico you speak English? We don't care. So why do you care what we speak."

Dark was dismissed as manager at the end of the 1964 season, but Cepeda's troubles with the team continued. New manager Herman Franks, a longtime Giants coach specializing in stealing opponents' signs, accused Cepeda of not putting out his best effort. This was news to Cepeda. His right knee still bothered him as he had progressively worn the cartilage down to the bone. "If I said it hurt, they thought I was faking," Cepeda said. "I could hardly get my uniform on and off, it hurt so much. It was so swollen. They would see how swollen it was. They put on a blank face." Cepeda was limited to only 33 games in 1965, logging a forgettable .176 average. The Giants had seen enough, however. Looking to unload what they saw as a malingering clubhouse presence, they made Cepeda available to other ball clubs at the start of the 1966 season. Cardinals GM Dick Howsam was immediately interested, yet aware of the risks involved. "We knew we wanted a right-handed power hitting first baseman," Howsam said. The only question was if Cepeda's knee could hold up to the rigors of everyday competition. After close consultation with Cardinals manager Red Schoendienst and team physician Dr. I. C. Middleman, who pronounced Cepeda's knee "75 percent sound," Howsam rolled the dice. He traded Cards left-hander Ray Sadecki—the 1960 NL Rookie of the Year—for the six-time Giants All-Star. "I knew if we didn't get a fourth place hitter, maybe neither Schoendienst or I would have a job much longer," Howsam said. As it turned out, Howsam left St. Louis anyway when the Cincinnati GM's post suddenly became available at the end of the year. Not that any of this front office deck shuffling concerned Cepeda. He was just sad to be leaving San Francisco, a city he had come to regard as a second home. "When I got the news . . . that I was traded, I had a lump in my throat," he said. "Willie Mays came over to my locker and said goodbye. I couldn't even answer him."

Cepeda did not remain sad for long. His new Cardinal teammates embraced him and the added dimension he now gave to the club with his long ball power. "He came here and he took the pressure off all the hitters," Lou Brock told *Sport* magazine's Leonard Schecter. "Curt Flood and I are basically singles hitters. Having Cepeda means we score runs and don't have to strain." Cepeda, whom Bob Gibson called "a big, good-natured guy," also provided infectious energy and enthusiasm to a floundering team that was frankly in need of some after a disappointing title defense in 1965. "He's always optimistic," Brock claimed. "You can get bugged in this game, you know. But Cepeda is always there, very energetic, full of fire, and it's catching." For his part, Cepeda was just glad to be free of controversy. "[The Cardinals] allowed me the latitude to be myself and to be appreciated for that," he said. "That was very important to me. The last few years in San Francisco, no one seemed to realize that all I wanted to do was play baseball. It got so that I was afraid to make an error at first base. I never felt up against a wall in St. Louis." For sure, when he did boot a ball in a contest one day, a supportive Red Schoendienst told him not to worry about it.

Such soothing words would never have left the lips of Dark or Franks and that was the point. "I am more happy here," Cepeda said. "They let me know they are very happy. Everything I do is good for them. They make me feel good." The positive karma initially brought only modest results on the field. Although he won the NL Comeback Player of the Year Award in 1966, he drove in 58 runs on 17 homers, numbers well below his normal production levels. "I thought I did a good job considering that my knee still wasn't perfect," Cepeda said. But he wanted more than a good year to justify the substantial risk the Cardinals had taken in trading for him. "I want to pay them back," he declared. He got the opportunity in 1967.

Among the Cardinal players who made Cepeda feel the most at home was Tim McCarver. "Orlando, you're here now," the All-Star catcher told him. "Screw the Giants. Screw Herman Franks. We really want you here." The sincere welcome caught Cepeda off guard. "Tim is from [below the Mason-Dixon Line], and my past experience taught me to tread carefully with people from the Deep South," he later explained.

James Timothy McCarver had long made a habit of surprising people. The son of a beat cop turned private investigator, McCarver's postwar upbringing in Memphis, Tennessee, resembled less "Leave It to Beaver" and more "Rebel Without a Cause." He ran with a tough crowd and was no angel when it came to respecting authority. "On a delinquency scale of one to ten, maybe I would have come in at around five or six," he later reflected. A subpar student in school, McCarver was quick to anger and preferred using his fists to learning his multiplication tables. One concerned family neighbor even predicted that he was destined for the electric chair. "To be blunt, I was probably lucky to emerge as a halfway decent citizen, considering that I was constantly sprawling and brawling all over the place," McCarver said. Fortunately, athletics saved him from getting into more serious trouble and for this he had his "tomboy" sister Marilyn to thank. "Marilyn played both tackle football and baseball with me," he said. "She was the one who turned this right-handed kid into a left-handed hitter." Her efforts, though, were not without cost. "The legend around the McCarver family is that I broke so many windows playing for Marilyn's team that they stopped using baseballs and began substituting tennis balls in their games," McCarver said.

Young Timothy's hitting prowess eventually attracted the attention of major league scouts, who began showing up at his games at Christian Brothers High School, a private all-boys Catholic preparatory school in Memphis. "They never talked about my signing but they'd talk to my parents and friends and parents of friends," McCarver recalled. Yet baseball was not the only sport he competed in. He was also a standout football and basketball player, though his mother once disputed the latter. "I wouldn't say he was a good basketball player," she claimed. "He was too darn rough to be real good." College athletic scholarship offers from top programs around the country poured in nevertheless, including one from legendary Notre Dame Athletic Director Edward "Moose" Krause. "Moose wanted me to come to Notre Dame and to play baseball and football once I got there," McCarver said. "The scholarship offer made it imperative that I play both sports, but football was clearly my first love." Ultimately, though, McCarver decided to go the professional baseball route. "Money was the deciding factor, plain and simple," he said. The

Cardinals outbid the Yankees and the Giants to sign him for $75,000, a then sizable amount that exceeded all the money McCarver's father had earned in his lifetime. As he later joked, "The Cards offered me a little bit more [than Notre Dame]."

McCarver was less flippant about his first pro experience catching for the Keokuk, Iowa, Cardinals of the Class D Midwest League in 1959. "This was a jolting experience in my life," he said. "I had always been better than those I played with but suddenly the caliber of play went up dramatically. Now I was playing with guys in their early 20s. Unlike me, their bodies had already formed. The pitching was a lot better, the runners were a lot faster." While his confidence may have been shaken, the 17-year-old quickly learned to adapt to the new level of competition. He hit .360 and was called up by the parent club for eight games at the end of the season. He did not leave much of an impression apart from the unfashionable dime store quality clothes on his back, which he later claimed made him look like a fugitive "out of a nineteenth century poorhouse." "That's the worst-looking fucking outfit I've ever seen, bar none," one unsympathetic Cards teammate told him. "I was really scared," McCarver later admitted. "The newness of [the majors] did it, I guess. And it was something so special in my eyes. I grew up with the idea that the major leagues were something super, with superhuman players." McCarver's biggest influence during these formative years was George "Big Daddy" Crowe, a former power-hitting first baseman with the Braves and Reds who had become a roving minor league hitting instructor for the Cardinals. Crowe took an immediate liking to McCarver. "He changed me from an open [batting] stance to a close one," McCarver later told Rick Hummel of the *St. Louis Post-Dispatch*. "Had he not done that, realistically, I don't think I would have made it. I don't think I would have been able to hit big league pitching. . . . [He] made more sense talking about hitting than anybody I'd ever talked to."

McCarver shuttled between the majors and minors over the next three seasons before finally landing a permanent roster spot with the Cardinals in 1963. "He got as much out of the minors as he was going to get," his new manager Johnny Keane said. "There wasn't any use in sending him back." In fact, Keane became so impressed with McCarver's work behind the plate, that he felt comfortable trading starting catcher Gene Oliver to the Milwaukee Braves for washed up former 20-game winner Lew Burdette. McCarver's subsequent play gave Keane no reason to doubt his decision. Aside from providing superlative defense, the muscular 6'0", 180-pound receiver punched out 117 hits in 127 games for a .289 average. McCarver became a pivotal factor in the Cardinals late season pennant drive that saw the team fall just six games shy of the Dodgers. "Give the credit to McCarver," teammate Bill White said. "He's been great." On this point, there was universal agreement. "The kid reminds me of Mickey Cochrane," posited retired backstop Wally Schang, a .284 lifetime hitter and contemporary of the Hall of Fame Yankees and Tigers catching great in the 1920s. "I don't know if McCarver can hit with Cochrane, but he's got Mickey's same aggressiveness and speed. And, as a kid, McCarver's a pretty good hitter right now." Veteran shortstop Dick Groat agreed. "You just can't find kids like this," he said. "He was born mature. He hits the good pitchers and he doesn't strike out much. You got a man on second, you can look for Timmy to move him up because he's going to get a piece of the ball. I keep referring to him as a kid. Well, he's not. He is a mature youngster. He is 22 chronologically, but he's a heck of lot older baseballwise."

McCarver demonstrated this maturity by the firm manner in which he took charge of the Cardinals' pitching staff down the stretch. "The pitchers," said Groat, "had as much confidence in him as he had in himself: 'Do I want to throw that pitch? I've been in this league a little while, why should I listen to a kid catcher?' But with Timmy, that didn't happen. From August on, he was the boss." Nelson Briles, who became McCarver's batterymate for five seasons, believed the receiver's secret was his fiery competitiveness and his ability to maintain focus. "I have never pitched to a catcher who could call a better game, strategize behind the plate, know what's going on," Briles claimed. "He was really into the game. He paid attention to game situations, paid attention to the way hitters were hitting, paid attention to their stance and if they had changed. And watched what was going on."

McCarver also exhibited a brand of personal grit that was rare even for catchers of his All-Star ability. When batters foul-tipped balls off the top of his head, for instance, the former All-West Tennessee linebacker refused to show any outward signs of pain. "It never seems to hurt him, though I don't know why the hell not," an amazed Ken Boyer said. "We ride him a little bit about it—we tell him, that's why he let his hair grow this year. We call him Goathead." Yet as deadly serious McCarver was on the diamond, he could be a cut up away from it. He was a notorious clubhouse prankster and would often entertain his teammates with a

Tim McCarver was in peak form behind the plate in 1967. BASEBALL HALL OF FAME

spot-on impression of "Crazy Guggenheim," a popular ne'er-do-well character played by television comedian Frank Fontaine on *The Jackie Gleason Show*. Wrote *Sport* magazine's Myron Cope: "One must bear in mind that Tim McCarver has a true gift for buffoonery—a born stage presence, if you will—that compensates for material that is sometimes less than socko. Though without formal schooling in the drama, he is one of those guys who walk headlong into slapstick situations with no intention of doing so."

There was nothing clownish about McCarver's performance in the 1964 World Series against the New York Yankees. He recorded a hit in all seven games, which tied a postseason record, and hit the game-winning homer in the pivotal fifth game off reliever Pete Mikkelsen. "Mikkelsen's best pitches were his palm ball and sinkerball, but on a 3–2 count he threw me a fat fastball up in the strike zone," McCarver remembered. "I didn't think I hit it that good, but in Yankee Stadium you didn't have to hit it that hard to get it out in right. I remember touching first, but after that I could no longer feel my legs as I circled around the diamond. I had to look down to make sure my feet were touching the bases." McCarver's euphoria did not abate when he reached home plate. He was greeted by Bill White, the respected team veteran and future NL president whose approval the 22-year-old had craved. "Well, son, you really did it for us today, you're all right," White told him. McCarver, who hit .478 in the Series, could not have asked for higher praise.

McCarver showed no signs of drop off in the seasons to follow. He continued to hit well [a .275 average] and earned the nickname "Bulldog" for his ability to defend home plate. As longtime Cardinals coach Joe Schultz once said, "He doesn't scare from anybody." But entering the 1967 season, no one, not even McCarver, was prepared for the kind of hot start he was about to have. After switching to a heavier 34-ounce bat model, McCarver found himself among the league leaders in hitting, compiling a .348 average by the beginning of July. His motivation for abandoning the 32-ounce bat he had been using stemmed from an earlier encounter he had with San Francisco's Willie McCovey and Willie Mays. "[They] kidded me about the [lighter bat]," McCarver said. "They called my bat a 'baby bat' and McCovey would pick it up and act like he was using a toothpick. And you know what? Now McCovey's using the baby bat."

While McCarver's offensive numbers eventually came back down to earth due to injury—he ended the season with a .295 average—he was selected to play in the All-Star Game held at California's Anaheim Stadium on July 11. Joined by fellow Cardinals Orlando Cepeda, Lou Brock, and Bob Gibson, McCarver made a strong showing for the National League squad. He collected a double and a single in a 2–1 NL victory that went a record 15 innings, a mark since equaled in 2008. But it was McCarver's Cardinal batterymate who garnered the most plaudits. Gibson pitched two innings of clutch shutout relief late in the contest to keep the NLers in the running. "Most of the American League's guys considered me a fastball pitcher," Gibson explained afterward. "So I knew they were going to crank up. But most of the pitches I threw were breaking balls. They didn't expect that."

Gibson got his own taste of the unexpected four days later when he was seriously injured in a scheduled start against the Pittsburgh Pirates. He was transported by ambulance to St. Louis Jewish Hospital where X-rays confirmed his worst fears—his ankle was broken and he would be out for the next six weeks in a walking cast. "I was really depressed," Gibson said. He had every reason to be. He was well on his way to his third consecutive 20-win season with a 10–4 mark at the time of the injury. "I was in the prime of my career and another big year would put me in a pretty good income bracket," he said. What's more, Gibson's team was enjoying a comfortable four-game lead over the surprising Chicago Cubs in the NL. The Leo Durocher–led club had finally surrounded veteran slugger Ernie Banks with a talented young nucleus (Billy Williams, Ron Santo, and Don Kessinger) and was on the verge of its first winning season since 1947. Now the Cardinals would have to fend for the pennant without their best pitcher in the dog days of late July and August. Gibson's teammates were understandably left wondering about their chances. "We've lost him for six weeks," Mike Shannon mused. "What's that—eight or 10 starts? You know he wins six of those starts. Even if he's going bad, he wins five of them." Publications like *The Sporting News* saw no reason to sugarcoat things either. "Did Card Dream Go Down with Gibson?" the magazine speculated. Befitting his emerging role as a team leader, Tim McCarver tried to head off such negative talk. "Sure the injury to Gibby's a bad break," he said. "But all it means is that we have to bear down all the more. We can't look for excuses. When you start looking for excuses, you start finding places to use them."

To fill Gibson's spot in the rotation, Cards manager Red Schoendienst turned to Nelson Briles. The 23-year-old right-hander had been used exclusively in the bullpen all season, though Schoendienst had planned to make him a spot starter after the All-Star break when the team was scheduled to play several double headers. "When Gibson broke his leg," he later said, "that just gave Nellie more opportunity sooner." Indeed, after dropping two of his first three decisions, Briles became an unstoppable force. He went 9–0 down the stretch while holding opponents to under two runs a game. Perhaps his most impressive performance came against the Giants at San Francisco's Candlestick Park on August 22. Facing a lineup top heavy with power hitters like Mays, McCovey, and Jim Ray Hart, Briles blanked them 9–0 on four hits and three strikeouts. Mays, McCovey, and Hart went a combined 0-for-10. "I can explain it all to you if you have a couple of hours," Briles joked with reporters afterward. Overall, Briles compiled a 14–5 record on the season with a league-leading .737 winning percentage and a club-best 2.43 ERA. "People thought I had come out of nowhere when I replaced Gibson in the starting rotation," Briles later said. "Actually up to the All-Star break I had pitched in 36 games. I had six saves, and I'd won four ballgames." Be that as it may, there can be no minimizing the impact Briles's performance in the second half of the season had on the team's fortunes.

After the Cubs had drawn even with the Cards in the league standings on July 24 with a 3–1 victory at Busch Memorial Stadium, the Cardinals went on a blistering 40–16 tear. Briles accounted for nearly a quarter of the wins as the Cardinals coasted to a 101–60 pennant-winning finish, 10 1/2 games over the second place Giants. The Cubs meanwhile faded to third, 14 games out. Inexperience and a lack of quality starting pitching beyond 23-year-old fireballer Ferguson Jenkins (20–13) doomed their chances. "Nellie was the guy who won the pennant for us," Dal

Maxvill maintained. "Everyone played a part—Orlando Cepeda, Gibson, everyone. But Nellie's performance stands out because his performance filled a void. If Orlando, say, had been hurt and someone filled his void, then I'd say that someone won the pennant for us. But it was Nellie who picked us up on his shoulders and carried us the rest of the way."

Nelson Kelley Briles was an unlikely candidate for team savior. The son of itinerant mill workers, Briles spent the bulk of his childhood in Chico, California, a small town nestled in the agriculturally rich Sacramento Valley east of the Sierra Mountains. The second youngest of five children, including twin brothers, Briles had an early brush with death when he stumbled into a bog. "It's a lot like quicksand," he remembered. "I sank so far that you could barely see the top of my head." His father was fortunately in the vicinity and pulled him out of harm's way by grabbing a fistful of his thick dark hair. "My mother had been closer by," he said. "But she couldn't bend over. She was pregnant."

Despite the near tragedy, Briles had happy memories of these years. His hard-working blue collar parents did everything they could to provide a better life for young Nellie and his siblings. "I'll never be able to repay them," Briles said. "Words just can't express my feelings." Words also couldn't describe his growing attachment to baseball. "I was committed to [the game] from Little League days on," he said. "I wanted to go to college where they had a good baseball program, because I knew you could develop and get more money for signing that way." Away from the diamond, Briles tried his hand at acting, something that would become a lifelong passion. "I do love the theater," he once said. "I think actors are just as great performers as athletes are." Briles played the lead character—frustrated Washington Senators fan Joe Hardy—in a school production of *Damn Yankees*. While donning grease paint for the role, he met the love of his life—fellow classmate and stage performer Ginger Moore. "I was a little bookworm and he was the big hero in high school," remembered Moore, who married Briles in 1965. "He had the lead in the play and I had just seven lines as a member of the Joe Hardy Fan Club. I had just moved to Nelson's city and I was very unimportant."

After graduation Briles enrolled at Santa Clara University, where he went 11–2 as a freshman starter. The team was stacked with talent, including future major leaguers Tim Cullen and Johnny Bocabella. But Briles still managed to stand out with an explosive fastball and a fierce competitive attitude. He put both to good use in a Canadian semiprofessional league he played in that summer. He won 16 games for a subpar Medicine Hat, Alberta ball club that finished near the bottom of the standings. "The fans there were avid," Briles recalled. "The Medicine Hat ballpark was on a river and we saw the biggest and most bugs anywhere. That's the only place I know where the game had to be interrupted because of bugs. So many bugs swarmed over the lights that the bulbs would pop. The lights had to be turned off for a while in hopes the bugs would go away."

Briles continued to impress the following season at Santa Clara when he was given the opportunity to pitch against the San Francisco Giants in an exhibition game. Briles struck out future Hall of Famers Willie Mays and Willie McCovey, while allowing just one hit and three walks in five scoreless innings. The moment was extra poignant for Briles as his father had passed away a short time before. "That was my biggest game ever," he later said. "That game was for my father." Giants manager Alvin Dark wanted to sign the precocious undergraduate on the spot but Briles held off when the two could not see eye to eye on a signing bonus. "The Giants had just given [Santa Clara teammate] Bob Garibaldi a $100,000 signing bonus and were reluctant to spend more than $10,000," John Devaney of *Sport* magazine later reported.

Briles, a physical education major who liked to dabble in foreign languages like French and Spanish, had been enjoying his time in college. He was engrossed in his studies and had continued to act on stage, including a memorable stint as a court musician and a priest. "Actually, I was just helping out a drama teacher in college," he later told the *New York Times*. "She was directing [William Shakespeare's] *Twelfth Night*, and I took two or three of the small parts because she needed someone." His future wife Ginger especially liked the elaborate costumes he wore for the parts. "We got a kick out of those tights, bouffant skirts, long-sleeved blouses and funny hats," she said. Nevertheless, when the Cardinals approached him with a $60,000 contract offer, Briles knew he couldn't turn the money down. Mounting family financial obligations in the wake of his father's death left him little other choice. "I was satisfied," he said.

Briles was assigned to the Double AA Tulsa Oilers of the Texas League in 1964 where he came under the tutelage of Grover Resinger. A former minor league third baseman, Resinger taught Briles the importance of mental preparation and concentration. "It didn't mean throwing strikes," Briles said, "but rather to set up the hitter and pitch with a purpose." The lessons sunk in. Briles had solid numbers with the Oilers (11 wins in 28 games with 132 strikeouts) and was promoted to the parent club the following season. The only catch was the Cardinals slotted him as a reliever rather than as a starter. Briles voiced no opposition to the new role. He appeared in 37 games for the Cards in 1965 with a 3–3 record and 4 saves. "I was young and I didn't mind relieving as a rookie," Briles said. "I liked the challenge of working out of pressure situations. You learn what you have to do and what you have to make the hitter do. Relieving helped me to be a success."

But not in 1966. Splitting his time between the bullpen and the starting rotation, Briles lost 15 games, including seven consecutive decisions from late July onward. It wasn't entirely his fault. The Cardinals were a low-scoring outfit that season and could manage only a handful of runs when the rugged 5'11", 195-pound Californian took the hill. "I tried not to fight myself but everything I did went wrong," said Briles, who experienced victory only four times that long season. "I started to fight the bad breaks we were having, our not getting any hits when I pitched and finally wound up beating myself," he said. Determined to turn over a new leaf the following spring, Briles took the advice of Cardinals pitching coach Billy Muffet and adopted a no-windup delivery. While the benefit of this approach was that it allowed the pitcher to disrupt a hitter's timing and therefore throw more strikes, Briles had difficulty getting the hang of it. "The whole secret is the rotation of the hips," he explained. "The rotation of the hips is what gives you the momentum to be able to drive off the mound."

Though he eventually got the motion down, Cardinals manager Red Schoendienst determined Briles's chief value to the team was coming on in relief. "I didn't like it," Briles said. "I knew I had the ability to be a starter. . . . But my job was to do the job in the bullpen. It was no time to balk, to use a baseball term. We knew we had a chance to win the pennant." And Briles, whom teammates praised for his warm, accommodating manner, did not want to provide any kind of clubhouse distraction. "I just had to stay ready and if the situation arose, I would get a chance to start," he said. "That was my slogan: Be ready if the situation arises." For sure, Briles answered the bell when Gibson went down in July. "Rather than looking at it as, 'Boy, there's a lot of pressure on me, I'm trying to fill his shoes,' I had a positive approach to things. You always have to be [prepared] to walk through the door of opportunity, because it might only open one time for you, and if you're not ready to take advantage of that, that might be the only opportunity you ever get." Briles did not squander his opportunity.

The same was true for fellow pitchers Steve Carlton and Dick Hughes. The son of a Miami, Florida, airlines worker, Carlton had a breakout season in 1967. He won 14 games and led the staff with 168 strikeouts. But the moody left-hander, who would go on to earn 329 victories en route to Cooperstown, did not win any team awards for congeniality. "Lefty always had a tough time being human," Tim McCarver once told Jayson Stark of the *Philadelphia Inquirer*. "If you talked to him, he would really prefer not to be a member of the human race." This personality tick was mainly due to insecurity. He "was always certain that each inning would be his last," Curt Flood observed. "'I haven't got it,' he would moan to me on the bench while our side was at bat. 'I'm shot. I'll never make it. They better take me out.'" After patiently listening to such defeatist talk go on for a while, Flood would usually cut him off. "I used to give him the old Knute Rockne," he said. "'Goddammit, Carlton, you gotta hang in there. You're all we've got. Now get your ass in gear and earn your money.' And he would drag his miserable self to the mound and throw the best left-handed stuff since Koufax, dying with every pitch."

Hughes, who wore thick black-framed glasses to compensate for near-sightedness in both his eyes, did not possess the same kind of lights-out natural ability that Carlton had. A 29-year-old rookie who had bumped around the minor leagues for several years, the Arkansas-born

Hughes put it all together in 1967, winning 16 games with a team-best 2.67 ERA in 27 starts. "I've watched him pitch in three minor leagues with 11 different teams and always he tried to be cute," noted one rival scout. "But somebody must have gotten to him in spring training, He doesn't pitch to spots any more. He just goes out and overpowers people." For sure, the once wild right-hander's ability to place his fastball and throw strikes was instrumental in his securing the club's fifth starter's spot over veteran hurler Al Jackson that spring. "He proves that if you don't walk anybody, and keep the ball inside the park, it takes a lot of singles to beat you," Red Schoendienst said. Although a torn rotator cuff to his right throwing shoulder the following spring derailed his baseball career, there were few better right-handers than Hughes in 1967.

Another Cardinal who fueled the team's second half surge was Curt Flood. Absent from the club's starting lineup since July 13 due to an injury to his right throwing arm, the center fielder returned to action two weeks later. Although clearly still in pain, Flood hit over .400 in his first 17 games back and finished the season with a team-leading .335 batting average, fourth best in the league. He also collected his fifth straight Gold Glove for defensive excellence. "Flood's value is on view game after game," *Sport* magazine's George Vescey wrote. "He gets on base, he drives in runs, he sacrifices himself to move a runner, he hits-and-runs, he steals. In the field, he seems to nuzzle against the center-field fence, but he catches line drives in shallow center field. He throws to the right base, he cuts off potential doubles before they scream into the alleys."

Curtis Charles Flood always played to win. The youngest of six children to a hospital custodian and a house cleaner, Flood spent his early years in the run-down, segregated neighborhood of West Oakland, California, getting in and out of trouble. Parental supervision was at a minimum as his mother and father worked long hours trying to keep the family afloat financially. "We didn't starve, but we were poor," Flood said. In his parents' absence, Flood roamed the streets stealing food or anything else he and his delinquent friends could get their hands on. "We would sneak around the unloading area at a nearby cannery to grab what we could find," Flood later said in his biography *The Way It Is* with Richard Carter. "Or we would ambush a fruit truck at a stop light, leap aboard the back, break open a crate, stuff our mouths and pockets and drop to the street before the light turned green."

One day at the age of 10 Flood went too far. He came upon a truck parked at a local factory and discovered the keys were still in the ignition. "I had played driver a thousand times, but this was for real," he said. "Without deliberation or doubt and, as best I can recall, without thought or consequences, I turned the key and the motor started, exactly as I knew it should." The joy ride that followed lasted exactly two blocks before he got into a major car accident. The local police held him in a detention center for a day before his parents were notified to pick him up. The family reunion was not a pleasant one. "When we got home, my trembling father told me that I had done $300 worth of damage," Flood recalled. "He then visited $300 worth of hardship on my behind. It was painful and unnecessary: I had already decided to avoid further traffic with the police."

With the active aid and encouragement of a local coach named George Powles, a former Pacific Coast League player who had a hand in developing such future major leaguers as Billy Martin, Vida Pinson, and Frank Robinson, Flood began to turn his attention to baseball. "Powles gave us coaching and direction," Flood said. "We always seemed to be at his house, nine or ten of us at a time. He wanted to know where we were, what we were doing. He'd pick us up in his car, drive up to a game, make sure we ate and then drive us home." More importantly, Powles, who was white, was color blind when it came it came to interacting with his players. "The beauty of George was that you did not have to adulterate your blackness to win his confidence and approval," Flood said. "He neither preached nor patronized. He emitted none of the smog of the do-gooder embarked on a salvage operation."

In fact, Powles's agenda was quite simple and straightforward. "[He] had no motives more exalted than good baseball and the benefits it offers," Flood maintained. "To inspire unfortunates with glimpses of a larger life was furthest from his mind." Flood's contemporaries agreed. "[Powles] taught us what it takes to win," Frank Robinson said. "He taught us fundamentals. He brought it all into focus." In Flood, though, Powles saw a fragile talent, one who needed some special coddling to fully develop. To that end, Powles encouraged the future Gold Glover to put on fan-friendly fielding exhibitions before games to boost his confidence. "I raced all over the diamond like a terrier, gobbling up every ball I could reach," Flood remembered. "The applause warmed me. If I had ever been short of self-esteem, the problem disappeared in the recognition I got for doing something socially acceptable and doing it well."

Flood's only problem was his size. When he graduated from high school in 1956, he stood a mere 5'8", 145 pounds. Nearly every major league scout dismissed him as a prospect, except for Bobby Mattick of the Cincinnati Reds. He signed Flood to a $4,000 minor league contract along with an invitation to the Reds spring training camp in Tampa, Florida. "[Mattick] did not consider me too small." Flood said. "Perhaps he thought I would grow." Flood looked every inch the raw, untested rookie when he reported to Tampa spring training, however. He overswung on pitches and demonstrated a marked inability to hit a curve ball. "The hitch [in my swing] was there," Flood acknowledged. "It started when I took a big, wide sweep at the ball at the top and it showed up again when I moved into the ball. My hands were actually backing up, though I didn't believe it [at the time]." These batting deficiencies were nothing compared to the indignities he suffered in his first encounter with the Jim Crow South. "Until it happens you literally cannot believe it," Flood later reflected. "After it happens, you need time to absorb it." Flood was specifically referring to the region's "separate but equal" system of racial injustice, which held all blacks were inferior and had to be cordoned off from the ruling white society at large. Case in point: when he was not working out with the Reds, Flood was forced to stay at Ma Felder's, a second-rate boarding house far across town that was reserved for blacks only. "When I saw who was there—Frank Robinson [who had signed with the Reds three years earlier] and four or five other black ball players—my knees began to knock," Flood said. "I was at Ma Felder's because white law, white custom and white sensibility required me to remain offstage until wanted," he said. "I was a good athlete and might have an opportunity to show it, but this incidental skill did not redeem me socially. Officially and for the duration, I was a nigger."

The feeling of being personally marginalized did not go away when Flood suited up for the High Point-Thomasville Hi-Toms of the Class B Carolina League. "It's hell down here," he wrote his parents back in California. Indeed, despite winning league MVP honors with a .340 average and club record 29 homers, Flood was loudly dismissed as a "black bastard" and "jigaboo" by most of the hometown fans. Conditions weren't much better on the road. "When the bus stopped at a gas station, Flood was not permitted to use the rest room," Flood's thoughtful biographer Alex Belth has written. "If he had to relieve himself, he would have to do so along the highway, where he would try to hide himself from the traffic along the side of the bus."

Flood endured even greater humiliation, if that is possible, when he was promoted to the Class A Savannah Redlegs of the South Atlantic League the next season. Recalled Flood to historian Geoffrey C. Ward: "I thought I was beyond crying, but one day we were playing a doubleheader. . . . After the end of the first game you take your uniform off and you throw it into a big pile and the clubhouse manager, he comes and he gets your uniform and he dries them and he cleans them and then you play the second game in the same uniform." Only this time the routine was slightly altered. "The clubhouse guy came by with one of these long sticks with a nail on it and he very carefully picked my uniform out from the white guys' uniforms and my little sweatshirt and my jock strap and everything," Flood revealed. "Sent my uniform to the colored cleaners which was probably 20 minutes away and there I sat while all the other guys were on the field. These people [in the stands] have really been giving me hell all day long, and now I'm sitting there stark naked." When the uniform finally arrived back from the cleaners, Flood hastily put it on and rejoined his teammates on the field. But the reception he received from the crowd was anything but cordial or understanding. "Boy you'd think that I had just burned the American flag," he said. "They called me every name but a child of God."

Flood received a far warmer welcome when the Reds called him up at the end of the 1957 season. He appeared in three games and hit a homer for his first major league hit. But when he asked Cincinnati general manager Gabe Paul for a raise, he got the proverbial cold shoulder.

"I thought the man's heart would break when he replied that a raise was out of the question," Flood recalled. "He agreed that I had done a pretty fair job, for a beginner." Paul then launched into a long soliloquy about the burdensome financial pressures the Reds were allegedly under as a franchise and how he was certain Flood would understand. "The constructive thing [for me] to do was sign a 1957 contract for $4,000, accept promotion to a higher minor league and do my very, very best," Flood said. Unwilling to rock the boat at this early stage of his career, Flood reluctantly complied.

Little did he know, however, that this would be the last contract he would sign with the Reds. For newly installed St. Louis GM Bing Devine had become aware of Flood's steady climb through the minors and was of the mind he would look good in Cardinal red. A deal was struck. In exchange for Flood and another outfielder, Cincinnati received a pair of top right-handed pitching prospects named Marty Kutyna and Ted Wieand. "I certainly had some fear and trepidation," Devine later admitted. "This was my first big-league deal." But Cardinals manager Fred Hutchinson, the former Detroit pitcher who had earned *Sporting News* Manager of the Year honors for the season just concluded, put his mind at ease. "Awww, come on," he said. "I've heard about Curt Flood and his ability."

Despite Hutchinson's vote of confidence, Flood struggled in his first three seasons with the Cards. He had difficulty hitting above .250 and saw more time on the bench than he did as a starter. He was in his early 20s and still developing as an outfielder, but his progress had been stalled by playing for Solly Hemus, Hutchinson's plodding and unimaginative dugout successor. Put simply, Hemus had a low opinion of Flood as a ballplayer. "You'll never make it," Hemus bluntly told him. "Talk about disasters," Flood said. "In a rational environment, I might have gone to Hemus and asked for a better opportunity . . . But this was major-league baseball and I was a second-year man without an iota of bargaining strength. Stars might sometimes be able to challenge a managerial decision and win the debate, but second-year men who tried were not often around for a third year." Only when Johnny Keane replaced Hemus as manager in 1961 did Flood perform up to his enormous potential.

"[Keane's] first words to me, ever, were, 'Hey, you're going to play center field for me—good, bad or indifferent—now get your butt out there,'" remembered Flood, who likened his new manager to "a wonderful uncle." "He gave me the break that made me a major-league ballplayer."

Flood batted .300 or better in four of the next five seasons and became a three-time All-Star (1964, 1966, and 1968). Better patience at the plate and a superior knowledge of the strike zone accounted for the improvement. "[Flood] waits and waits on you until he gets the pitch he knows he can lick as well as anyone I've seen," noted Dodgers ace right-hander Don Drysdale. "There are days when it's next to impossible to get him out." Flood helped himself further by learning to hit balls pitched on the inside corner of the plate to the opposite field. "Before that, he had pulled too many pitches down into the ground to third base and shortstop," apprised former Cardinal great Joe Medwick. "He's better off hitting the inside pitch on the hit and run because he gets more wood on the ball."

Flood tied Roberto Clemente for the league lead in hits (211) in 1964 and was a major reason why the Cardinals snuck by in the pennant race and defeat the New York Yankees in the World Series. "Curt was one of only three men who played consistently fine ball all season," Keane later told writer Al Stump. "On a late day in September, for example, he was four-for-five and two-for-four when we beat Pittsburgh twice and took the league lead." Keane also credited Flood in the same interview with pulling off a game-ending double play against the Phillies in July that "saved our shirts, vests and pants." The circumstances were these: Philadelphia's Johnny Herrnstein had sent a one-out screamer toward distant center that Flood made a sensational over-the-shoulder running catch on with the tying run on first in the bottom of the ninth. He then in one fluid motion spun and threw a strike to second that cut down the runner. The Cardinals had been leading by a run. "The ballgame is over," Keane said. "We win one that could have broken our heart."

Flood's spectacular play was not atypical. By the mid-1960s he was considered by many to be the finest defensive outfielder in baseball, going 226 consecutive games from September 3, 1965, to June 4, 1967, without making an error. "Curt Flood tracked down everything," Tim

McCarver said. "Flood, like Mays, could catch up to fly balls all over the outfield because he had extraordinary anticipation." His own teammates were often taken unawares by his defensive wizardry. "[Cardinal pitchers] would think they gave up gappers based on the straightaway [defensive] alignment, but when they turned around expecting the worst they saw Flood standing in the gap waiting for the ball," McCarver continued. "How did he know? His anticipation was based on the count and his understanding of who was pitching, what he was throwing, and how hard he was throwing." That was Flood. He left little to chance.

The Cardinals officially clinched their eleventh National League pennant on September 18 with a rousing 5–1 road victory over the Philadelphia Phillies. Appropriately, Bob Gibson, who had returned to starting duty only two weeks before, got full credit for the win. He threw a complete game and held the Phillies to only three hits. "It made me feel good to pitch the pennant-clincher, but I was happier I had gone nine innings," Gibson said. "I was still far from satisfied. I had a lot to make up for." His teammates chose to bask in the moment, though, spraying each other with beer and champagne and carrying a fully uniformed Red Schoendienst into the visitors' showers for a traditional soaking. Stan Musial would follow his old friend in short order. Meanwhile, Orlando Cepeda was bursting at the seams with joy, jumping up and down and exhorting everyone in the alcohol soaked room to celebrate. "How many more do we gotta win?" he shouted to his fellow El Birdos. "None, none," came the resounding reply. When Lou Brock spotted Cardinals owner Gussie Busch—making one of his rare locker room appearances—the outfielder thanked his boss for trading for him four years earlier. Busch, who had been spending most of his time setting up two new breweries for his vast beer empire, was moved by the gesture. He warmly grasped Brock's hands and said, "Let's win the World Series now, 1-2-3-4."

If only it would be that easy.

# Chapter Six

# Coming Through

While the Cardinals breezed to the NL crown, the Red Sox found themselves in what *Sports Illustrated* called "the longest, daffiest and most desperate American League pennant race in history"—a four-way scrum with Chicago, Minnesota, and Detroit that would not be decided until the final day of the regular season. And for an ultra-competitive player like Carl Yastrzemski, who had never been on a team that finished closer than 19 games out of first place, the situation was the baseball equivalent to heaven. "When I first joined the Red Sox in 1961, it was a bad ballclub getting worse," he told *Sport* magazine. "We didn't finish down among the league's patsies because we wanted to. Even in our worst years, we wanted to win. But if you don't keep your nose to the grindstone, you won't. We not only didn't have the talent-we kept our noses so far away from the grindstone, we couldn't even see it . . . We were the country club of big league baseball. The only place you found discipline around our ballclub was in the front office dictionary. Curfews meant nothing to us. And neither did fines." That is, until Dick Williams took over. "Williams has given us something else that no manager in my time ever did-respect for ourselves and each other," Yaz said. "In the old days, everybody laughed at mistakes, even when they cost ballgames."

With those days now long gone and the Sox in a position to seriously contend for the first time since Harry Truman resided in the White House, Sox GM Dick O'Connell diligently went to work improving the team. He had already picked up veterans Jerry Adair and Gary Bell in early June to fill major holes in the roster. Adair, a durable good-field, no-hit second baseman with the Orioles and White Sox, had responded well to his new change in scenery. He provided infield depth while hitting .291 in 89 games. Williams, in particular, was enthused by the move as he had played alongside Adair with the White Sox a few years earlier and knew his worth. "I don't know how O'Connell . . . got the White Sox to part with Jerry and I don't care," Williams said. "The point is we needed a spare glove man, preferably a veteran who could play anywhere in the infield and not hurt us defensively." Bell, who later gained everlasting fame as Jim Bouton's irascible roommate in the best-selling, tell-all baseball memoir *Ball Four*, proved equally valuable. After starting the season a dismal 1–5 with the Indians, he rebounded with a respectable 12–8 record and 3.16 ERA in Boston. "Heck, we've won four games with Cleveland we wouldn't have, because of Bell," joked a fellow Red Sox. "We beat him twice when he was an Indian, and he beat 'em twice since he came to us. His timing has been marvelous."

As significant as these moves were, they nevertheless fell short of addressing the ball club's most glaring weakness: the lack of quality veteran catching. Up to this point, the team had tried to get by rotating a trio of former Sox farmhands (Russ Gibson, Mike Ryan, and Bob Tillman) behind the plate, but they had collectively failed to measure up either offensively or offensively. The latter was especially troubling given the overall inexperience of Boston's young pitching corps. Ironically, O'Connell found a ready solution to this dilemma in Elston Howard, the same individual who had ended Billy Rohr's dramatic no-hit bid back in April. Howard was nearing the end of a remarkable 13-year run with the Yankees in which he had succeeded Hall of Fame great Yogi Berra as catcher. All the former Negro League standout had done was win the 1963 AL MVP award, earn two Gold Gloves and appear in 12 All Star games and 9 World Series. But the Yankees were in a rebuilding mode in 1967 and eager to shed an expensive veteran salary.

With money never being much of an object to a Tom Yawkey outfit, especially one fighting for a pennant, a deal was quickly struck on August 3. Howard went to the Red Sox for a $20,000 waiver fee and two minor league pitching prospects. Although Howard was reluctant to leave New York due to his longstanding ties to the Yankees organization and the city, he soon came around to the idea after realizing he would be back on a contending team, his first since 1964. "That would be the greatest thing that ever happened to me if I got into a World Series with this club after getting traded—greater than all the other honors," he said. It also didn't hurt that Yawkey, never known for his inclusionary hiring practices, had personally reached out to him. "We need you," the Sox owner pleaded. "We're fighting for a pennant, we've got a young pitching staff, and we need your experience." While the 38-year-old receiver struggled at the plate (he hit only .147 in a Boston uniform), he more than made up for his offensive deficiencies by providing a steadying influence on emerging pitchers like Jose Santiago and Jim Lonborg. "Ellie had that one quality about him—experience," Lonborg said. "[He] wasn't assertive but, boy, the way he framed pitches [for the benefit of umpires], the way he'd sit back there as a receiver, it looked like a huge funnel that went right down the middle of his glove. He had very soft hands and he moved very smoothly behind the plate. When you're throwing like I was throwing, you don't have to be assertive [as a catcher]. You just have to think about making the right calls." Invariably, Howard did just that. "I always thought Howard was the best catcher I had ever seen for calling a ball game," Yaz said. "He could handle pitchers and no one was better at setting up a batter. He knew us all."

The son of college educated parents, Howard's initial career path involved books, not balls or strikes. "My folks gave me every educational opportunity available," he said of his comfortable middle-class upbringing in St. Louis in the 1940s. "This placed me in a position to go on to college." But Howard, a standout four-sport athlete in high school, had his head turned when fellow African American Jackie Robinson joined the Brooklyn Dodgers in 1947. Suddenly the notion of talented athletes of color like himself playing in the majors was no longer a far-fetched notion in a rapidly changing postwar American society. "I wanted to try baseball," he explained. Passing up on several college scholarship offers, he signed with the Kansas City Monarchs of the Negro Leagues, the same team that Robinson had made a name for himself during his climb to the big leagues. "We had some pretty good ballplayers," he remembered. "Ernie Banks, Gene Baker, Bob Thurman, Curt Roberts, Hank

Thompson and Willard Brown were all on that club, and they all made the majors."

Used primarily as an outfielder, Howard impressed everyone with his keen batting eye, hitting a robust .375 and capturing the attention of the Yankees, who signed him to a minor league deal in 1950. At the time the Yankees were on the receiving end of much public criticism for being the only major league team in the Big Apple not to have an integrated roster. "The Yankees are not averse to having a Negro player, but we are averse to settling for a Negro player merely to meet the wishes of people who insist we must have one," Yankees GM George Weiss said. "The first Negro player in Yankee uniform must be worth having been waited for." Weiss, who fretted that white suburban Yankee fans might "be offended to sit with niggers," initially believed that Vic Power was that player. A highly touted first base prospect from Puerto Rico, Power had signed with the Yankees in 1951, but soon ran afoul of team management for his reputation in the minors of being a "hot dog" and stepping out with white women. He ended up being dispatched to the Philadelphia Athletics for several lesser talents while establishing himself as a six-time AL All-Star over the next decade. "He was not a Yankee type," author David Halberstam wrote.

With Power's trade, Howard emerged as the most likely candidate to integrate the Yankees. But he would have to bide his time. The front office continued to drag its feet under Weiss and the team's famously misanthropic field manager was not exactly bowled over by Howard's outfield skills. "They finally get me a nigger and he can't run," Casey Stengel complained. Still, Howard, an unusually proud and patient man, bit his lip and soldiered on. He was converted to a catcher under the tutelage of former Yankee great Bill Dickey and made the parent club coming out of Florida spring training camp in 1955. "He's a good boy," Stengel said. As the "Ole Perfesser's" racially derogatory remark indicates, although ticketed for the big leagues, the 26-year-old Howard still had to put up with the petty humiliations other African American ballplayers of this era had to endure, especially when playing exhibition games in the Jim Crow South. "The camp would break at the end of the day, and you had to go back across the tracks to the black section to dress while the white boys would go back to the hotel to dress," he said. "They would all get on the bus, but I had to jump in a cab in my uniform and go back there to dress." Needless to say, such frustrating experiences took a significant toll on his mental health. "Elston—I don't know if he internalized it—he was very angry and very moody and of course he couldn't let it out at the ballpark," said the former Arlene Henley, a fellow St. Louis native who married Howard in 1954. "He would come home and he wouldn't talk and it was a stress. You always felt like you were on view, on stage. You had to be this perfect person."

While some teammates like shortstop and future Yankees broadcaster Phil Rizzuto went out of their way to be supportive, others were downright hurtful and insensitive. Hall of Fame Yankee outfielder Mickey Mantle later confessed that he and teammate Billy Martin "used to tease Ellie a lot." "When we got into a hotel on the road, we'd tell Ellie to deliver our bags to our room," Mantle related. "People who didn't know us might think it was cruel of Billy and me, or that it was racial. But we were just having fun and Ellie understood." Howard did understand, but not in the way Mantle supposed. Putting up with such callous behavior was simply the unfortunate price he had to pay for wearing pinstripes. "Elston wasn't a flaming crusader," his wife later told the writer Bill Madden. "He just really wanted to play for the Yankees because, let's face it, no matter what you say about them, they were the best. He didn't care what other people had said about them or their racial attitude. To him, they were the best team in baseball and he wanted to be part of that."

Splitting his playing time between the outfield and catching, Howard posted impressive rookie numbers, belting 10 homers and hitting .290 in 97 games. "The switching around hurt me a little," he later conceded. "You have a tendency to worry about a position you're not used to. . . . But if it helps the club out I'll do it. I don't mind." His qualified acceptance of the situation was also tempered by the fact that the Yankees starting catching position was then held by 10-year veteran Yogi Berra, a lifetime .293 hitter and three-time AL MVP. "I was second string," Howard admitted, "so thank God I could play other positions. That kept me going." Interestingly, the highlight of his rookie season occurred in his very first game as a major leaguer at Fenway Park. Before collecting his first hit and RBI, Howard was deeply touched by the enthusiastic reception he received from the Beantown faithful. "When I came to bat for the first time the fans gave me a standing ovation," he recalled. "Not just an ovation, a standing ovation. I couldn't believe it."

Howard earned more accolades for his clutch outfield play during the Game 5 of the 1958 World Series against the Milwaukee Braves. He made a spectacular diving catch on a Red Schoendienst liner in short left field that helped team starter Bob Turley out of a late innings jam and preserve a victory for the Yankees. "I knew I had to get the ball," Howard said afterward. "I skinned my knee and my stomach doing it." In spite of his postseason heroics and a .314 batting average for the year, Stengel continued to platoon Howard in the seasons ahead. "I never felt like I had it made," Howard confessed. His situation improved when Stengel was unceremoniously squeezed out as manager following the Yankees' close loss to Pittsburgh in the 1960 World Series. New skipper and former team backup catcher Ralph Houk let it be known that he intended to move Berra to the outfield and make Howard his starter behind the plate. It was a decision he never regretted. "He couldn't move around back there as quick as Yogi—he was a lot bigger, he was like six inches taller than Berra—but he had a good active arm and he knew what he was doing," Houk said. Indeed, Howard became a master at keeping opposing hitters off-stride. "Ellie was smart," Houk confirmed. "Just because a batter couldn't hit a curveball, say, Ellie wouldn't sit back there and call for the curve all the time. He knew how to mix the pitches." Howard was also adept at helping his pitchers "bend the rules." When Hall of Fame lefthander Edward Charles "Whitey" Ford needed an "accomplice" to help him doctor balls after umpires and opponents had grown wise to his cheating, Howard was more than happy to oblige. "He had one of the clasps of his shin guards sharpened so it could cut a nick in the baseball," Mickey Mantle said. "He would 'accidentally' drop a ball, and as he picked it up, he would rub it across the clasp and there would be a nice little nick in the ball for Whitey. Nobody ever figured out what was going on."

Howard rewarded Houk's faith in him by having the best years of his career. In 1961 he hit a career-best .348 with 21 homers and won league MVP honors two years later. "This is the high spot of my career, no doubt about it," Howard gushed. "I've always been happy just to be a Yankee . . . but this just tops everything." Contributing to his success was a new approach to hitting that Yankees batting coach Wally Moses convinced him to adopt. "We decided in the spring [of 1961] that I ought to close my stance and ease up on my swing," Howard revealed. "I was swinging my head off the ball. Moses told me to swing with my arms—use my wrists—not my body. I also began using a heavier bat, a 36-inch, 35-ounce one. I used to use a 33-ounce one." Yet even in his moment of greatest triumph, the ugly specter of racism once again intruded. A photograph of his family had been published in newspapers around the country and not everyone was pleased to see he was married to a light skinned African American woman. "I got a letter from a man in Maryland," Howard recalled. "He said, 'mister, you're married to a white woman.' I wrote him back. 'Mister, you're a crazy man.'"

Like the rest of the elite Yankees players of this period, his performance in the field began to dramatically tail off after 1964, the last time the team would win a pennant until 1976. Advancing years and the daily wear and tear of catching had finally caught up with him. But Howard was not quite ready to retire from active playing. He still felt he could contribute, albeit not at the high level he had grown accustomed to during his salad days. The Yankees held a different view, however. So when Boston came calling late in the 1967 season with a proposal to acquire the veteran receiver, there was little resistance on their end. The Red Sox "feel they can win it with you handling their pitchers," Houk assured Howard before officially showing him the door. "We're not going anywhere and this will be a great opportunity for you to get yourself another ring." Howard, who had always wanted to retire a Yankee, could not argue with this logic. Besides, his wife thought it was a good idea. "I wanted him to go because I had no love affair for the Yankees," Arlene Howard said. "I liked Boston anyway and under the circumstances, I said 'why not.' It turned out to be a good experience." That it did.

As the weather grew warmer at the beginning of August, the Sox cooled down, dropping six of their first eight games to Kansas City and Minnesota. "This stuff doesn't taste any good after losing one like that," said Yastrzemski of his ritual postgame beer following a disheartening 8–6 defeat to the cellar dwelling Athletics on August 2. With the losses mounting, Dick Williams's patience grew shorter, especially with George "Boomer" Scott. He and Scott had developed a strained relationship since spring training when Williams began splitting his playing time at first base with the veteran Tony Horton. "He didn't realize that I'd play him at first throughout the year, that Horton couldn't carry his jock and would later be traded," Williams said. "He didn't understand that I was just trying to give Horton a chance before turning him loose. That's what spring training is for, isn't it? Giving somebody a chance?" Things went further downhill when Williams insisted that Scott maintain a playing weight of 211 pounds during the regular season. The tall, broad-shouldered 22-year-old had displayed an alarming tendency to pack on the pounds and Williams thought this lack of personal discipline made him sluggish in the batter's box and more prone to striking out. Scott disagreed and clashed repeatedly with Williams on the issue. "He called me names that I don't think were justified," Scott later said. "I honestly think it wasn't his thought to try to harm me or hurt me but I wondered if he respected me as a player." Although Scott was flirting with a .300 batting average since the All-Star break, Williams decided he needed to make a bold statement. Just prior to opening a three-game series with the Angels in Anaheim on August 11, he benched Scott after the latter had shown up in the clubhouse several pounds over his prescribed weight. "I don't know how he did it in one day," Williams later reflected. "Anyway, I didn't play him the whole series—oh, I guess he pinch hit once—but I had to be firm."

More than a few of Scott's teammates were perplexed and angered by the move. "It didn't matter that [he] . . . was hitting better than .300 against Angels pitching," Yastrzemski later complained. "We were to learn that you could have a pennant on the line and Dick would still try to make his points." Indeed, without Scott's bat in the lineup, the Sox lost all three games to the Angels, prompting California shortstop and former Sox farmhand Jim Fregosi to joke that there were nine managers in the league and "one dietitian." But Williams remained unapologetic, despite his team dropping all the way to fifth place, two and a half games out. "This is the way I've operated all season," he stubbornly insisted, "and I'm not going to change now just because we're in a race." For his part, Scott good naturedly tried to shrug off the controversy, attributing it to a banana split he had consumed before his weigh-in. "I'm a country boy and I like to eat," he explained.

Nothing had ever come easy for Scott. Growing up in a struggling single mother household in Greenville, Mississippi, in the 1950s, he labored long summer hours in the sweltering local cotton fields. "The reason you did that, all that money was turned over to your parents to make ends meet," Scott said. "Nothing can be worse than getting up at four in the morning waiting for a truck to pick you up to go pick and chop cotton from six or seven in the morning until five or six in the afternoon." If that wasn't taxing enough, he often worked without the benefit of gloves, which he feared would only "slow down my pickin'." As a result, his hands became a gnarled and bloodied mess. For all his pain, however, he earned very little in terms of compensation. "I got $2.50 for every 100 pounds of cotton I'd pick," he said. "I'd picked about 200 pounds a day—but that's really pickin'. Ask anyone that's ever done it."

Money was an ongoing problem. A star athlete in football, basketball, and baseball in high school, Scott was temporarily forced to drop out during his freshman year when his mother experienced difficulty paying the family's bills. "Yes that's right," Scott later said. "We needed money at home. My mother was having a hard time making ends meet and I wanted to go to work." Luckily, his financial plight did not go unnoticed by his coaches who worked diligently with the school's administration to keep him athletically eligible. "We got George a job in a dry cleaning plant, and [the principal] rearranged his classes so he could work," remembered Andrew Jackson, his basketball coach. "He put in a couple of hours every afternoon after school, and the money he earned help relieve things for him." His high school didn't come away empty-handed. Scott led the football and basketball squads to state championships and starred on the baseball diamond. Along the way, Scott became one of the most celebrated student-athletes in Mississippi, in addition to being transformed into a local folk hero. "There were 50 younger boys following him when he left the gymnasium," Jackson said. "He looked like the pied piper."

College athletic scholarship offers soon came pouring in, including an opportunity to play hoops with John Wooden's legendary UCLA basketball program. But Scott decided to go the professional baseball route when he picked up his high school diploma in 1962. Once again, his family's precarious financial situation played a role in his decision-making process. "I got tired of watching my mother struggle," he explained. "I didn't have the mind that I could go to college and see my mother struggle for another four to five years."

Signing with the Red Sox for an $8,000 bonus, Scott toiled in their minor league system over the next three years. They were not especially easy or happy ones for the intensely private and insecure young man. He experienced difficulties adjusting to professional pitching, hitting only .238 his first season. "I didn't think I could possibly make it," he confessed. "I had no confidence." He might have ended up returning to Greenville and seeking another line of work if not for the timely intervention of Bobby Doerr the following season. Now employed as a roving instructor in Boston's low minors, the former All-Star second baseman took an immediate shine to the free-swinging Scott, whose determined mental approach to the game reminded Doerr of Ted Williams. "We got him to move his hands up a little higher and he got hitting the ball pretty good," Doerr said. "I think he ended hitting .290 or something. But he really made a big improvement when he started to be a little more cautious of not hitting home runs, but (just) hitting the ball."

Given this new lease on life at the plate, Scott went on to terrorize Double A pitching in 1965, hitting .319 to go with 25 homers and 94 RBIs. "It's a true thing I have going for me that other boys don't," he later said. "Number one is that I have great strength. I don't have to try and do anything with the ball. All I have to do is try and hit the ball and let the ball go where it wants to go. I can hit the ball out of any part of the ballpark, see. But see, I have to learn that. When I try to pull the ball I'm dead. Everybody [gets] me out. When you try to pull the ball you chase bad pitches. You can only learn by experience."

One experience Scott did have while steadily advancing through the Sox farm system was far less salutary. Playing for Winston-Salem of the Carolina League, he had the misfortune of running up against some insensitive teammates who thought it would be an amusing idea to scare him by donning Ku Klux Klan–style garments in the locker room. "They said George jumped about ten feet in the air and when he landed he was in the bathroom," recalled his manager Bill Slack, a Canadian who was unfamiliar with the historic racial mores of the American South. Only the soothing reassurance of Slack convinced Scott that there was no real threat on his life. But this didn't mean an end to the racial abuse he faced while playing for Winston-Salem. "I mean [the fans on the road] were calling him everything," Slack said. "They were calling him 'jungle bunny' and 'nigger' and 'black boy' and 'Sambo.' I couldn't understand it coming from Canada." As a native son of the Mississippi Delta and the Jim Crow South, Scott had more than a passing acquaintance with this kind of racial intolerance and bigotry. But unlike Bob Gibson and Curt Flood, baseball peers who regularly fought back against such injustice, Scott stoically chose to do nothing. In fact, the whole burgeoning civil rights movement of this period held little interest to him. "I go my way," he explained. "I let other people go their way. I don't bother nobody. I let everybody tend to their own business."

In 1966 Scott earned a promotion to the parent club straight from spring training and proceeded to open eyes. He hit a scorching .330 out of the gate while displaying the kind of raw power (18 homers by early July) that had led the Boston scout who had signed him, Ed Scott, to compare him to future Hall of Famer and home run champion Henry Aaron, a previous signee. "This boy is going to be a hitter," he said. His success didn't come without a price. "I [have] been hit more up here than I [have] been hit the while time in the minor leagues," he told the writer and author Leonard Schecter. "They got me in the side, in the elbow twice, in the foot. Six, seven times. But I don't worry. Nobody can hit you in the head. That's the [first] thing that moves. You got to be up there in a trance to get hit in the head."

Scott, who used the colorful handle of "taters" to describe his prodigious home run blasts, became the talk of baseball and was voted the overwhelming favorite to start at first base for the AL during that year's midseason All-Star game in St. Louis. "When he learns the strike zone, he can't miss being truly great," predicted former Cleveland GM Frank

Lane. "I see no reason why he shouldn't hit .340 to .350 every year and get 30 to 40 homers without any trouble." Scott also made true believers of his teammates. "It's not only his strength that amazes me, it's his agility," Carl Yastrzemski told a reporter. "He's the most agile big man I have ever seen. He weighs 220 pounds, but he moves around the infield like he's 170 pounds. I guess like everyone else I figured he'd be clumsy. I hadn't seen him until spring training and I just took it for granted he would be on of those slow guys who couldn't handle the glove too good. But, he fooled me. He's fast and he's quick in the field." His defensive prowess around the first base bag, which eventually earned Scott eight Gold Gloves over his 14-year big league career, was especially appreciated by the team's pitching staff. "He probably had the softest hands of any big guy I've ever played with, with regards to ground balls," Jim Lonborg remembered. "If it hit his hands, he could scoop it up. It was great to look back into the infield and see George Scott there playing behind you."

As well as he played in the first half of the 1966 season, he was just as terrible in the second half, slumping all the way down to a .245 batting average with just nine home runs. "Everybody knows how badly I flopped . . . going for bad pitches and making plenty of mistakes," he said afterward. "What you don't know is that I replayed every one of those games at my home. . . . I went over every pitch I could remember. I took stock in what I had to do." It furthermore didn't aid his mental preparation that the Red Sox under the taciturn leadership of the Billy Herman were an absolute disaster of a ball club, finishing one step removed from the AL basement. Scott found it extremely difficult to accept all the losses. Long after most players had showered and gone home, Scott would sit and brood in the locker room over what had transpired. "Carl Yastrzemski used to come over and ask me, 'What are you still doing here?'" he recalled. "I explained to him, that this was something new to me. I had always been on winning teams from Little League all the way up through high school ball. Wherever I played I won. So this was the first taste of losing that I really experienced, and it was something new to me."

The winning returned in 1967 and Scott's performance between the baselines was a major reason why the Red Sox were in the thick of the pennant fight. But some observers felt his early August run-in with

Williams over his body weight threatened to derail what was shaping up to be his finest season. "He'll probably go on road trips in the future with heads of lettuce sticking out of his coat pockets and carrots out of his trousers," wrote Clif Keane of the *Boston Globe*. "There'll be rabbits following him everywhere he goes, but that's the way it's going to be with Dick Williams—quit or sit." Such concern, however jocular it may have been, was overstated. For when Williams reinstated Scott in the starting lineup in a home game against the Tigers on August 15, a trimmer-looking Boomer lived up to his nickname by blasting a homer into the left field screen in his first at-bat during a 4–0 Sox victory. He followed up this impressive power display with another one the next day, launching a pair of moon shots in an 8–3 dismantling of Detroit. To say Williams was pleased was a gross understatement. "The manager was in such high glee he was at the top step of the dugout to greet George for the second time, and the guessing was that George's two homers had gone 420-feet and 390-feet respectively," noted Keane. The Boston first baseman would finish the season in fine form, batting .303 with 21 homers, 82 RBIs, and a .373 on-base percentage. Regarding his earlier contretemps with Williams, Scott had this to say: "I guarantee that if [he] had to do it all over again, he would do it different."

As Scott's "Battle of the Bulge" receded in importance, real misfortune befell the Red Sox. In the fourth inning of a Friday night home game against the Angels on the 18th, Tony Conigliaro was struck in the face by a fastball thrown by California's Jack Hamilton, a tall fireballing right-hander enjoying the finest season of his eight-year big league career. "The sound was terrible," remembered Petrocelli, who was standing in the on-deck circle when the beaning took place. "It was the kind of sound you'd hear if you smashed a piece of fruit. I can still hear that sound." Conigliaro collapsed to the ground in crippling pain, his once envious matinee idol looks now marred by a broken left cheekbone and hideous facial bruising. "Funny," he later wrote, "you never go up there thinking you're going to be hit, and then in a fraction of a second you know it's going to happen. When the ball was about four feet from my head I knew it was going to get me. And I knew it was going to hurt because Hamilton was such a hard thrower."

Not even the defensive act of throwing his hands up to his face at the final moment of impact provided much protection. "The roof fell in on me," Conigliaro revealed. "My skull absorbed the full shock. Grabbing my head, I squeezed it hard, trying to stop the shriek that filled it, and at the same time I was gasping for breath. 'Oh God,' I prayed, 'Let me breathe.'" His concerned teammates and coaches rushed to his side but were horrified by what they found: a writhing Conigliaro coughing up blood and struggling to remain conscious. "I looked at his face and saw it blow up like a balloon as the blood flowed into that area," Petrocelli said. Some wondered if he was close to death. Others could only avert their eyes, including Conigliaro's usually hard-bitten manager. "My heart nearly stopped," Dick Williams confessed. "In a few minutes he started flipping his legs around in agony." The fans in the stands felt equally uneasy. "I remember the hush," wrote future *Boston Globe* sports columnist Bob Ryan, then a wide-eyed Boston College undergraduate attending the game. "The sound of silence from 31,027 people is an eerie sensation. There was no hubbub, no low buzzing, as Tony lay at the plate. He wasn't popping up and running to first base. That was obvious. It was also obvious something very bad had just taken place."

For his part, Hamilton denied any malevolent intent. "I haven't hit a batter all year," Hamilton informed the assembled media afterward. "I certainly wasn't throwing at him. I was just trying to get the ball over the plate." What Hamilton failed to mention and what many Sox players came to strongly suspect, including Yastrzemski, was that he was adding something a little extra to his fastball that evening. "Was it a spitter? I don't know, but I thought so because of the way it acted," Yaz maintained. "Guys who throw spitters know how to keep them low or else they sail and then *no one* knows where it's going. This one went right toward Tony's face. . . . The ball was coming in with such velocity and lift that he just couldn't judge it." Adding an element of foreboding to the occasion was the fact that just prior to Conigliaro's fateful at-bat, a smoke bomb had been tossed onto the field as a prank by some overzealous fan. "It was kind of eerie," recalled younger brother Billy Conigliaro, who was watching the horrific incident unfold from the stands with his parents. "You almost felt something was going to happen."

Conigliaro had in some respects invited the beaning by the overly aggressive approach he took in the batter's box. "Tony stood right on the plate," Mike Andrews related. "He would not give in to a pitcher, any pitcher. And he'd freeze. It was inevitable he'd get hit in the head." No less than Ted Williams thought the same thing. On the 17th, the old slugger had bumped into Ed Penney, a Conigliaro friend and business associate, at his summer baseball camp in southeastern Massachusetts and took the opportunity to share his concerns. "Tony is crowding the plate," Williams told Penney. "He's much too close. Tell him to back off. It's serious time now. The pitchers [in a tight pennant race] are going to get serious." When Penney dutifully conveyed this message to Conigliaro prior to the Angels game the following evening, the confident young Boston star could only express bemusement. Although he was batting .287 with 20 homers and 67 RBIs at the time, he had found himself mired in a dispiriting 1-for-21 offensive slump. He thought it would be a bad idea to concede any additional portion of the plate to rival pitchers by backing off as Williams suggested. Instead, he stubbornly insisted on moving in closer. It was a critical lapse in judgment that ended up costing him dearly.

"Death was constantly on my mind," Conigliaro said. "I thought I was going to die." He was not exaggerating. Team physician Dr. Thomas Tierney told him afterward that had the pitch been a couple of inches higher, he "would have been dead." The vision in his left eye was another matter. His retina had been damaged and along with it his ability to discern objects at a distance. While this might not have constituted such a big deal if he were an accountant or lawyer, the fact he earned his living hitting 90-mile-per-hour fastballs out of the ballpark did.

His season, which had started out with so much promise, had come to a disappointing end. Whether he could effectively return to the majors the following year was anyone's guess. In the interim, all Conigliaro could do was root for his teammates and hope for the best. It wasn't easy. "For the first time I realized how much I loved it all, how I missed the guys and the excitement of being with them and all the laughs we had," he sadly reflected. "I missed the games, the competition, especially now with the ballclub fighting for the pennant. There wasn't anything in the world

I would rather have been doing than playing baseball. I didn't want to go out with the best-looking girl in the world or with this actress or that model. I didn't want to own my own nightclub. I didn't want anything but to play baseball. You don't know how much you miss something until it's taken away from you."

With Conigliaro out of commission, Dick O'Connell was left in a difficult bind. Not only did the Sox GM need a starting right fielder but he needed one with power to make up for all the homers Conigliaro regularly supplied in the middle of the lineup. The only problem was there was no one even remotely ready on the team's major league roster or in the minors to fill that void. That the rest of the ball clubs in the AL and NL were aware of this put O'Connell at a tremendous disadvantage. For the asking price in any trade for a player of comparable ability would be unavoidably high, if not prohibitively so. What to do? As O'Connell was pondering his options, a serendipitous event occurred that would provide him with the very solution he was seeking.

In Kansas City, temperamental Athletics team owner Charles O. Finley had gotten into a major spat with his prize young first baseman—outfielder Ken Harrelson. "The Hawk," as he was known to fans and teammates on account of his prominent nose and quirky personal behavior, had publicly criticized Finley for the latter's sacking of Athletics manager Alvin Dark, a respected mentor and close friend. His exact words were that Finley's actions were "detrimental to the game." Finley, however, had learned from an inaccurate media account that Harrelson had called him "a menace to baseball" and demanded an immediate written retraction. "Charley," Harrelson countered, "I'll be glad to retract the word 'menace,' but I won't retract anything else." Furious at this response and Harrelson's overall lack of contrition, Finley opted to take extreme action. "As of this moment," he seethed, "you have your unconditional release from the Kansas City Athletics. As of this moment, you are no longer a member of the Kansas City Athletics."

The 25-year-old Harrelson, who was averaging .305 in 61 games with the A's, was taken aback by what he had just heard. "I knew [Finley] was going to do something when he read what I said, but I had no idea what it would be," he claimed. Now he knew and he was frankly filled with dread. "I was afraid that Finley might have blackballed me with the other owners," he later told William Leggett of *Sports Illustrated*. His fears were misplaced. Several teams proceeded to line up and eagerly bid on his services, making him baseball's first bona fide free agent of the modern era. "Nine clubs made me offers, seven in the American League and two National League clubs," Harrelson said. Initially, Harrelson leaned toward the Braves owing to his local roots. "I'm a Georgia boy, and I like the park there," he said. It also didn't hurt that he was a close golfing buddy with Atlanta GM Paul Richards, who was chomping at the bit to team Harrelson up with Hank Aaron, Joe Torre, Clete Boyer, and Rico Carty in an already power-laden Braves batting order. "The more I thought about it the better the idea seemed," Harrelson later confessed. "I'd be home in a town where I have a lot of friends. I could run down to Savannah whenever I felt like it. Atlanta sounded great."

Harrelson wasn't prepared for Dick O'Connell's refusal to take no for an answer, however. In the bidding war from the beginning, the dogged Sox front office chief was determined to land his target. "Kenny, we've got to have you here in Boston," he told the veteran slugger. When Harrelson informed him he had already made a verbal commitment to sign with another team, O'Connell remained unmoved. "How much will it take for us to get you up here?" he asked. Having nothing to lose, Harrelson replied a $150,000. "You've got it," O'Connell answered. Harrelson was ecstatic. Deep in personal debt entering the negotiations, he now had more money than he could have ever dreamed possible. His financial future seemed secure. "It's really unbelievable," he exclaimed. "This is something a ballplayer works for all his life. When I said what I did [to Finley], I never realized it would come to this. Would you believe it? Some people ask me whether I planned all this. Can you beat that?" Apart from the huge paycheck he would be receiving, Harrelson also liked Boston's chances in the AL pennant race. "They fight you tooth and toe-nail," he commented to the *Christian Science Monitor*. "They never quit. . . . But it's more than that. I have a feeling that history is repeating itself and we're going to have another Red Sox–Cardinals series as we did back in 1946."

The product of a divorced household, Harrelson was raised by his single mother in Savannah, Georgia, in the years following the Second

World War. Though money was often tight, Harrelson never did without. "We lived in a poor section of town, but our house was well kept, and we had nice things in it," he recalled. School was another matter. He frequently skipped classes, preferring to hang out at local pool halls where he hustled adult patrons of their cash. When he did bother to show up at school, he often got into fights with his classmates. "I got promoted from grade to grade because any teacher who had me once had had it," he admitted. If Harrelson fell short in the classroom, he positively excelled on the playing field, becoming a standout athlete in baseball, football, basketball, and golf. He also tried amateur boxing but wisely gave it up after one of his opponents fractured his jaw. "All I saw was the ceiling," he said.

When he wasn't engaging in fisticuffs or playing sports, Harrelson claimed his "favorite occupation" was purchasing clothes. "I've always been a clothes rebel," he boasted. "I remember black and pink were very big in Savannah one year. Everybody I knew—girls as well as boys wore black-and-pink combinations. The kids would have pink sweaters and black pants or black sweaters and pink pants, that sort of thing. When I got tired of it, I added a color or two. Maybe I'd wear pink and gray one day and pink and white the next." Invariably, classmates took his lead and acted accordingly. "I wasn't exactly the St. Laurent of the sixth grade, but I noticed after a while many of the kids changed colors when I did," he said. "I'm sure they were just as sick as I was of whatever happened to be hot at the time, but nobody would make the first move. I did because even in those days I wanted to be different."

His later elevation to the big leagues only enhanced this predilection. In the middle of the 1960s it was not uncommon to see Harrelson strolling around clubhouses in brightly colored Mao jackets with large gold medallions dangling from his neck. "I hate to see a guy who wears nothing but basic black, brown and gray," he said. "Men's fashion has come along terrifically in the last few years, especially sportswear, but a lot of men are still afraid of it." His adherence to style also extended to his on-field baseball uniform. He insisted, for instance, that his pants snugly conform to the contours of his muscular legs. "I suppose I'm the fussiest-dressing ballplayer in the business, but I can't help it," claimed Harrelson, who was reported to have owned 300 sports jackets, dozens of sweaters and over 40 pairs of shoes in his prime. "As long as we win, I don't care if I go 0 for 4—but, dammit, I insist on looking good going 0 for 4. Let 'em say the Hawk isn't swinging the bat, but don't ever give 'em a chance to ask who's the guy in the baggy pants striking out all the time."

Upon his high school graduation in 1959, Harrelson decided to accept a $30,000 signing bonus offer from the A's and begin his professional ballplaying career. It was not a hard decision to make. He had recently married his high school sweetheart and the money was simply too good to pass up. Although basketball was his favorite sport ("I had no qualms, none at all, about putting that spheroid in the air," he said), baseball was not far behind. To him there was no beating the close-knit team camaraderie associated with the game. "There are eight other guys on the same side with you," he pointed out. "You're trying to help them and they're trying to help you."

After posting impressive power numbers in the minors (he once led the Eastern League with 38 homers), Harrelson earned a promotion to the parent club in 1963. There he began his tumultuous relationship with Charlie Finley who had riled the baseball establishment by dressing his A's in gaudy green and gold uniforms with matching white shoes. "It's my ballclub and they'll wear what I want them to," he declared. Finley further caused a stir by adopting a mule as the team's official mascot. Named after its eccentric owner and benefactor, "Charlie O." traveled with the team on the road and would come to occupy a memorable place in Harrelson's career, courtesy of a team promotion gone bad. Always seeking publicity for his then also-ran ball club, Finley thought it would be a great idea for one of his players to ride the mule around Yankee Stadium before a ballgame. Thinking there would be "some money or a gift" involved, Harrelson eagerly volunteered his services. Big mistake. When the appointed time came, the prickly beast showed Harrelson exactly what it thought of his novice riding skills. "Charley O. began cantering, and I lost control of him," Harrelson recalled. "I got scared, the mule sensed it, and the next thing I knew, he was madly dashing along while I frantically hung on to whatever part of his anatomy I could get a grip on." Attending fans erupted in laughter but Harrelson was in no laughing mood. "All I wanted . . . was to get off the damn animal," he said.

Harrelson continued to turn heads when he became the first major leaguer to use a "batting glove" during a 1964 night game against the Yankees. "I was taking BP and had a blister on my left hand [due to his having played 27 holes of golf earlier in the day]," he explained. "I remembered I had my golf glove in my pants, so I ran upstairs and got it just before the game started. I put it on." He was glad he did. The glove afforded him a better grip on the bat and the results spoke for themselves. "The first time I go to the plate," he said, "[Yankees starter Whitey Ford] hung me a curve ball, and I hit it over the left-center-field wall about 450 (feet). I hit another one later in the game." Little did Harrelson realize that he had started a new style trend that would be copied by nearly everyone playing the game in the years to come. The Yankees didn't appreciate the historic significance of the occasion, however. "I was really getting some catcalls from the Yankee dugout," he said. "Back in those days, they had bench jockeys. You can't believe some of the names they were calling me."

As diverting as these "hot dog" antics were, they were scarcely the reason why the Red Sox had acquired him. "The Hawk" could flat out hit and hit with power. In his breakout offensive season of 1965, he connected for 23 homers and 66 RBIs in a cavernous Kansas City ballpark that did not favor right-handed pull hitters like himself. It was not unreasonable then to think he could produce even better numbers within the cozier confines of Fenway. No doubt that was on the minds of team management when they paid top dollar to put him in a Boston uniform. "He gives us another strong bat and definitely a big bench bat," Dick Williams said. "He also gives us more maneuverability."

Despite all the heightened expectations, Harrelson turned out to be an offensive disappointment for the Sox. He hit an anemic .200 with 3 homers and 14 RBIs in 23 games. "The pressure was fantastic—especially on me," he confessed. Where he did make a significant contribution was plugging a big defensive hole in right field, making only 2 errors in 27 chances for a .931 fielding average. Just as important, he fit in well in the Boston clubhouse ("As soon as he joined us, we felt like we had known him all our lives," Rico Petrocelli said) and was able to divert unwanted media attention away from several of his teammates who were trying to cope with the daily strain of a red hot pennant race. For "The Hawk" made colorful copy, which in turn helped sell newspapers and make everyone happy. "That meant [reporters] weren't pestering me," Yaz said. To be sure, Yastrzemski had always found it difficult dealing with the press, particularly now with the national spotlight thrust upon him. "I couldn't be more different from Harrelson," he revealed. "I liked to let my game speak for me. I just wanted to get in there and hit, or play balls off the Wall."

The Red Sox finished August on a tear, winning 14 of their last 19 games to earn sole possession of first place, a half game up on Minnesota and one and one and a half in front of Detroit and Chicago respectively. While there many outstanding individual performances and team highlights during this successful stretch, none stood out more than Boston's rousing 4–3 win over the White Sox in the first game of a doubleheader on the 27th. After jumping out to an early 4–1 lead on a pair of solo homers by Yastrzemski and a two-RBI single by Scott, the host White Sox clawed their way back with two runs in the seventh. That's where matters stood until the bottom of the ninth when Chicago pinch-hitter Duane Josephson faced reliever John Wyatt with teammate Ken Berry on third with one out. Josephson connected on Wyatt's first offering, a knee-high fastball outside the strike zone. "I think [Josephson] was looking for kind of [a] breaking pitch," Wyatt said afterward. "He was bending back from the plate and barely got the bat on it." The ball traveled on a soft liner into short right field where speedy Red Sox backup outfielder Jose Tartabull intercepted it on the fly and threw home after Berry tagged up. "If I make good throw and keep it low, I feel I throw him out," Tartabull recounted. Only this didn't happen. The throw sailed high and Elston Howard had to lunge to catch the ball while still having the presence of mind of blocking the plate. The veteran backstop "grabbed it one-handed, no easy play with the kind of mitt catchers wore in 1967," Yastrzemski remembered. "He came down with the ball while his back was to Berry, who started his slide. Ellie's left foot got to the plate before Berry's shoe, pushing it off to the side." Berry was tagged out to complete the double play and Boston escaped with a hard-earned victory. "That was the turning point for us," Reggie Smith said.

September saw the Red Sox fall out of first place but still maintain their contending status, never being more than a game out in the standings. As he had all season, Carl Yastrzemski led the way. For the most pressure-filled month of his Hall of Fame career, he hit a Ted Williams–like .391 with 9 home runs, 24 RBIs, and a .486 on-base percentage. "[He] was the Sensation of the fall of 1967," wrote Ed Linn of *Sport* magazine. "[He] was right in there with [Robert] Kennedy and the Beatles as the real thing." Ken Harrelson went a step further, arguing his teammate was more productive in the clutch than any player in modern memory. "Now there were guys who had better years numbers-wise than Yaz," he said. "But nobody ever had a better offensive year than he did, as far as when he hit it. Don't tell me what you hit, I don't give (a crap) what you hit. I've played with guys hitting and driving in 100 runs (and it) didn't mean a damn thing. When he hit it, it was phenomenal." The numbers say it all. In bases loaded situations on the season, the Sox team leader went 4-for-5 for an incredible .800 batting average. He was only slightly less impressive with runners in scoring position with two outs, batting .396. "In 1967, [Yaz] had a year that I've never watched a player have, whether he was playing for me or playing against me," Dick Williams later told former Major League Commissioner and author Fay Vincent. "He did everything when he had to do it, and he kept our club afloat." "He never got cheated all year," an awed rival said. "That is, he never got fooled by a pitch. You never saw him take a half swing, a mediocre swing. He was ripping at everything. Every ball he hit, he hit it like a rocket. And he played left field as I've never seen anybody play left field. Making catches and throws and charging the ball. You didn't run on Yaz. You didn't try to take the extra base on him."

In spite of Yaz's heroics, Boston's pennant chances appeared to suffer a mortal blow with four games remaining on the regular schedule. Facing Cleveland in must-win back-to-back contests on September 26 and 27, the visiting Indians swept both games to put the Red Sox on the brink of elimination. The local media had taken to calling them the "Cardiac Kids" for their penchant of coming from behind late in ballgames. But even team members now admitted things had gotten out of reach. "A good year, and it turned into nothing in the last two days," Jerry Adair lamented. Nevertheless, there was a small glimmer of hope. Boston was fortuitously scheduled to close out the season at home with first place Minnesota in a two-game head-to-head matchup and Chicago, which had seemed poised all summer long to take the pennant on the arms of its outstanding pitching staff (a 2.45 team ERA), collapsed down the stretch. They lost all five of their remaining games to drop out of the race. "The whole thing is incredible!" Yastrzemski exclaimed. "Here we are with another great chance to win the pennant." To achieve the latter, however, Boston still had to beat the Twins on Saturday, September 30, and again on Sunday, October 1, while hoping Detroit, which at that point had played two games less than the Sox on the year, would split its remaining four games against the Angels. Due to rainouts, the Tigers would play these games in back-to-back doubleheaders at home over the weekend. A Motor City sweep guaranteed Mayo Smith's club a spot in the World Series regardless of what Boston did. But a combination Sox sweep and a Detroit loss meant the two teams would face each other on Monday, October 2 for a winner-take-all playoff for the AL championship. "The task was clear," wrote Ken Coleman, the team's radio broadcaster that season. "It's either fulfillment or banishment, joy or sorrow."

Going into Fenway for that final weekend showdown, the Twins seemed like a safe bet to win it all. Only two years removed from their first pennant in the "Land of Ten Thousand Lakes," they boasted a powerful lineup of All-Star performers that included Harmon Killebrew, Cesar Tovar, Tony Oliva, Bob Allison, Zoilo Versalles, and a sensational rookie second baseman destined for Cooperstown named Rod Carew. "He amaze[s] me how sure his hands are," said the Cuban-born Versailles, a two-time Gold Glove–winning shortstop and the 1965 AL MVP. "Such sure hands. He charge[s] a ground ball real good. He has everything it takes to be a damn good star." Minnesota's pitching was strong, too, with staff leaders Dean Chance and Jim Kaat notching 20 and 16 wins, respectively. But overall appearances were deceiving. The team was plagued by internal dissension thanks to Minnesota owner Calvin Griffith's firing of manager Sam Mele in June. Mele, the dugout leader of the 1965 pennant winners, had severely divided clubhouse opinion when he dismissed popular pitching coach Johnny Sain following the 1966 season.

"If I were ever in a position of general manager," Kaat fumed, "I'd give Sain a 'name-your-own-figure' contract to handle my pitchers (And, oh yes, I'd hire a manager that could take advantage of his talents.)"

When the Twins convened to vote on the distribution of World Series shares prior to the start of the Boston series, a "minor team riot" broke out. "A bunch of guys didn't want to vote Sam Mele anything, not even a quarter share," revealed Carew, who went on to become the AL Rookie of the Year. "The pro-Mele guys countered that if he wasn't entitled to anything, neither was [new Twins manager Carl Ermer]. . . . The result was Mele got nothing." If this disturbing breach in team unity wasn't cause enough for alarm, the ball club had suffered through an ugly racial incident earlier in the summer. Several black and Latino players had nearly come to blows with their white teammates when Dave Boswell, a dim-witted right-hander who won 14 games in 1967, took out an unloaded handgun aboard the team bus in Detroit and pretended to pull the trigger. "Well, you guys can play with guns in Cuba; why can't we play with guns here," Boswell said. For Carew, an introspective loner who had spent most of his childhood in Panama, the entire episode was disconcerting. "I sat and watched this thing with amazement," he said.

With such luminaries as Vice President Hubert H. Humphrey, Cardinal Richard Cushing and Massachusetts Senators Edward M. Kennedy and Edward Brooke in attendance, the Red Sox rode a fine pitching performance by starter Jose Santiago (two earned runs on seven hits in seven innings] and took the first game, 6–4, before a boisterously loud crowd of 32,209 at Fenway Park. "Destiny's Darlings did it again," the *Boston Herald-Traveler* gushed on its front page. The decisive hit was a three-run homer by Yastrzemski in the bottom of the seventh inning, his 44th and last of the season off Minnesota left-hander Jim Merritt. As Yastrzemski recalled, "I knew [Merritt] liked to throw sliders, but with the longer right field of Fenway, I figured on a fastball. Especially when he took the count to 3–1. *Crack!* I got the sweet spot of the barrel right on it, and the ball sailed into the right field bleachers."

The game had been a relatively close affair until then. The Twins had scored a pair of runs on base hits by Tony Oliva and pinch-hitter Rich Reese. But the Sox had countered with RBI singles from Jerry Adair and

Yaz in the fifth before George Scott put them ahead to stay an inning later with a solo home run blast into the center field bleachers, his 19th of the season. "We were so excited we nearly tore Boomer's uniform off when he got back to the dugout!" Petrocelli said. Santiago, meanwhile, demonstrated a commendable ability to pitch out of jams, especially in the first when he put three men on base and escaped with only one run. "I wasn't bending my back and I was pitching too quick," he said. "In the second inning I got in the groove and had great stuff." Prior to the contest, Dick Williams had received considerable flack from the local press about his selection of the Puerto Rican right-hander as the starter, particularly since he had well-rested staff ace and 21-game winner Jim Lonborg available. The supremely self-confident Sox manager shrugged off such criticism. "I went with Jose Santiago to keep with the regular rotation, giving Lonborg the start in Sunday's final," Williams later maintained. "True, if we didn't win Saturday, there wouldn't be a Sunday. But if you play like you aren't going to win, often you don't."

Santiago, who notched his 12th victory of the season with the win, had had a frustrating career up to that point. Signed by the Kansas City Athletics in 1959, the pride of Juana Diaz, Puerto Rico, had spent five long years in the minors before finally being called up to the bigs at the end of the 1963 season. He appeared in only four games but managed to pick up his first major league victory in relief over the World Series–bound New York Yankees on September 9. "You're going to be a real good pitcher," Mickey Mantle told him afterward. A broken ankle and an extended stay on the disabled list curtailed his development over the next two seasons. "Luck has never been Santiago's long suit," Boston sports columnist Larry Clafflin wrote. "He's the kind of guy to stay away from at the tables in Las Vegas." But Red Sox GM Dick O'Connell was impressed enough by his makeup to purchase his contract from Kansas City in the 1965 offseason. There were no hard feelings. "I liked my time with the A's," Santiago later said. Santiago did fulfill O'Connell's faith in him by posting a credible 12–13 record with Boston in 1966. But this was merely a tune-up for his late season heroics in 1967. Including his gutsy victory over the Twins, Santiago won his last eight decisions, making him second only to Lonborg in terms of being the team's most reliable starter down the stretch. "He's done a lot of good pitching for us this year," Williams said. "When he's right he's mighty tough to bear."

Santiago had not been the only game decision Williams came under fire for on that picture-perfect fall day in New England. With two away in the ninth, Williams flashed a sign from the dugout for Gary Bell, spelling relief for a tiring Santiago, to pitch a fastball to Twins slugger Harmon Killebrew with a runner on second base. Killebrew responded by crushing the offering over the Green Monster in left field, tying him with Yastrzemski for the league lead in homers. "I didn't want Bell walking Killebrew [with the .304 lifetime hitting Oliva following him in the lineup]," Williams said afterward. "I wanted him to earn his way on." Significantly, Yaz did not take issue with the move either, even though it jeopardized his chances of being only the 16th player in major league history to earn "triple crown" honors; that is, leading his respective league in overall batting average, RBIs, and home runs. Entering the game he had established a comfortable lead over his closest competitors in the first two categories (a .319 batting mark with 115 runs driven in), but was tied with Killebrew in homers with 43. "There wasn't any reason to apologize," he said of Williams' call. "If I have my choice between a pennant and a triple crown, I'll take the pennant every time."

The Sox did receive a big break in the third inning when hard throwing Twins starter Jim Katt ("You can't hit Katt for distance when he has his stuff and control, and he had both that day," Yaz remembered) came down with a season-ending injury to his left throwing arm while pitching to Santiago. "I wanted to come in away, low and outside," said Katt, who had struck out four while issuing only one walk in his short outing. "Sometimes I lean back toward third to get a little extra on the pitch, and when I did something just popped. I had never had anything like that before." Making the situation doubly problematic for Minnesota was that Kaat had been the team's most reliable starter during their late season pennant drive, compiling a 7–0 record with a 1.51 ERA for the month of September. He also had Boston's number, boasting a dominating 14–6 career mark against them. But now he was done for the year and the thought frankly sickened him. "I felt really bad because I thought I had good stuff, especially my fastball," he said. "It was moving as it had been all season."

As elated as the Red Sox were by their victory, they felt even better when news arrived from Detroit that the Tigers had ended up splitting their Saturday doubleheader with the Angels. Boston, Minnesota, and Detroit now each had legitimate shots at winning the league title going into the Sunday finale, an unprecedented situation. "All we had accomplished was keeping our chances alive for one more day, but it was impossible not to celebrate in the clubhouse like we'd already won the pennant," noted Rico Petrocelli. "The only thing missing was the champagne." The festive atmosphere even extended to the press box where the normally cynical Harold Kaese of the *Boston Globe* penned not so much a newspaper column, but a love poem. "O, give us the strength of Hercules, the courage of David, the wisdom of Pericles, the luck that has helped bring us this far, to the edge of paradise, to the golden halyard that raises the pennant," he wrote. Not everyone joined in on the fun. "I don't want to feel anything now," said Jim Lonborg, Sunday's scheduled starter. "It can't help me now." His surprisingly dour mood was understandable. He had gone winless in all three of his starts against the Twins that season and was 0–6 against them since reaching the big leagues in 1965. "They're just an unlucky team for me," he confessed.

His luck was about to radically change. Pitching the game of his life, Lonborg went the distance, scattering 12 hits, striking out 5, and giving up 1 earned run in Boston's pulsating come-from-behind 5–3 victory over the Twins on Sunday. "Karl Marx, who said religion was the opium of the people, would have revised himself had he watched the Red Sox unite to throw off their ninth place chains," *Boston Globe* columnist Bud Collins wrote. "The Red Sox are the opium right now, Karl baby, although you might classify them a religion."

The pivotal moment in the contest came in the sixth inning when Lonborg surprised everyone in the ballpark by laying down a textbook bunt single along the third baseline. "When I came up to the plate, nothing was working," said Lonborg who had been the victim of two earlier unearned runs on uncharacteristic errors by Scott and Yastrzemski. "We were down 2–0 and Tovar was back at third base and I looked down and it just seemed like a perfect opportunity. It wasn't something I had previously planned. A little light went off when I went into the batter's box and it just happened." Energized by Lonborg's daring play, the Red Sox loaded the bases for Yastrzemski (4-for-4) who responded by drilling a two-run single off a Dean Chance sinker ball. "I didn't try to kill the ball or pull it," Yaz said. "I just stepped into it, swinging easy but solidly. The ball shot on a line over second base." The Sox piled on three more runs to go up 5–2 before the inning was over as the Twins imploded on a pair of wild pitches and sloppy fielding by Versailles and Killebrew. "When they got a 2–0 lead on us, I thought they'd take charge of the ball game," Yastrzemski admitted. "They didn't. They seemed to lack drive. They didn't seem to want to take the role of aggressor."

The Sox slugger assumed that mantle two innings later when he killed a potential game-tying Minnesota rally with two outs and Killebrew and Oliva on second and first. Next batter Bob Allison hit a screamer into the left field corner that had all the makings of a bases-clearing double. That was until a racing Yastrzemski retrieved the ball backhanded and gunned down a flummoxed Allison at second for the final out of the frame. "I thought I had two," Allison maintained. "I looked at Carl and saw the throw coming, and I had to try and make it. But I didn't. It was just another great play by Yastrzemski." Indeed, Yaz had become determined at the crack of the bat to deny Allison, a notoriously slow runner, extra bases. "I wanted to make it a hard throw and I used that good ole grandstand Wall to set my right foot," he reminisced years later. "The throw went on a line to Andrews at second. Allison was hook sliding but Mike nabbed him with the tag." Although Killebrew managed to scamper home with Minnesota's third run on the play, his team was effectively finished for the season. Yastrzemski had personally seen to that with his bat, glove, and throwing arm. "He did everything," Twins manager Cal Ermer said.

After Minnesota pinch-hitter Rich Rollins popped out to Rico Petrocelli for the game's final out, thousands of deliriously happy Sox fans poured on to the playing field. "These were the zealots," Collins wrote. "They made Mao Tse-tung's gang [of militant Red Guards in China's Cultural Revolution] look like peace marchers, yet this was a frenzy of love, not hate." Lonborg soon became the focus of their attention. "It was fun for a moment-getting lifted onto shoulders, just like in the movies,"

Jim Lonborg celebrates his pulsating pennant-clinching victory over Minnesota with his teammates. PHOTO BY THE BREARLEY COLLECTION/BOSTON RED SOX PHOTO ARCHIVE

he said. "But . . . I was being swept in a direction I didn't want to go, and people were just clawing at you." His uniform was torn to shreds and his initial feelings of elation now turned to dread and alarm. "You can't believe the feeling of being of being swept up in a crowd like that," he said. "It's frightening." If not for the timely intervention of some Boston police officers, the Sox ace pitcher might have been seriously injured—or worse. "Jim could have been hurt bad," confirmed one patrolman. "We barely got him out of there." A relieved Lonborg was extremely thankful they did. "When I got to the dugout, my shoelaces were gone, my belt was gone, my inner jersey was somehow gone, my hat was gone," he said.

The mood inside the home clubhouse was slightly more subdued. Although they had beaten the Twins, there still remained the Tigers who were in the process of losing the second game of their doubleheader with the Angels to officially give the Sox the AL pennant. Once word finally arrived about the outcome of that contest, "all hell broke loose." "It's over! It's over!" Williams exclaimed as his players began to spray each other with bottles of champagne and shaving cream. "I haven't had [a drink] in four years," a beaming Tom Yawkey announced as he surveyed the scene holding a paper cup filled with champagne. "This is the happiest moment of my life." For Carl Yastrzemski, who went a dazzling 7-for-8 in the final two Minnesota games, the moment represented the pinnacle of his professional ball playing life. The soon to be AL MVP finished with a .326 batting average, 44 home runs, and 121 RBIs, good enough to win the Triple Crown in this "Year of the Yaz." But along with this moment of great personal triumph came an overwhelming desire to thank his teammates for helping make it all possible. Brandishing an empty bottle of champagne, he mounted a nearby table to emotionally congratulate them for "not quitting" and giving him "the thrill of my life." Sitting by myself in a corner of the clubhouse, Tony Conigliaro had an entirely different reaction. "I just don't feel part of this," he wept. Making note of the disconsolate state the injured slugger was in, Yawkey made a point of approaching him and offering warm words of encouragement. "Tony, he said, "if it weren't for what you did for us before you got hurt, we wouldn't have been in the fight at all. And if you'd been in there all the way, we'd have won it easier."

Outside the ballpark, the situation was chaotic as exuberant fans took to the streets in what became a spur of the moment Mardi Gras, Boston style. Traffic was stopped, cars were rocked, large quantities of alcohol were consumed, and a rousing chorus of "We're Number One" was raised. Not since the Sox' last pennant-winning year of 1946 had the city experienced such a spontaneous eruption of joy for a sporting event. As one enthusiastic reveler put it, "This is no place for anyone with a bad heart." But far from the maddening crowds, a more poignant moment of commemoration was unfolding. Having recovered from his mauling by the hyper-enthusiastic Fenway crowd, Jim Lonborg was purposely negotiating a warren of dimly lit back hallways inside the ancient stadium to reach Tom Yawkey's office. "It was like the dark rooms from the movie *The Natural* where you walked in those little catacombs or caves," Lonborg recalled. Surprising the 65-year-old Sox owner, who had retired

A winner at last: Carl Yastrzemski signals his jubilation in the clubhouse. PHOTO BY DENNIS BREARLEY/BOSTON RED SOX

there after participating in his team's riotous locker room celebration, Lonborg proceeded to formally present him with the day's game ball he had received from Petrocelli. "I've never seen a man so happy and so joyful to have that ball in his hand," he said. "It was the culmination of a wonderful season for him."

His Cardiac Kids had come through.

# Chapter Seven

# The Series Begins

The Red Sox had not been in a World Series in 21 years and Bostonians were understandably eager to acquire tickets for the October 4 opener at Fenway Park. Massachusetts Governor John Volpe's office reported their phones were ringing off the hook. "Nearly every call represented a demand for tickets," Volpe aide Barry Locke told the *Boston Globe*. "The governor wishes he could oblige them all, but he's lucky to have tickets himself." Indeed, tickets were about as hard to come by as a sit-down interview with famed New England author and recluse J. D. Salinger. But that didn't prevent thousands of Sox fans from trying. "You'd be surprised how many veterans are arriving from Vietnam, just in time for the Series," said Fenway Park usher Mike Picillo in the same *Globe* piece. "Practically every stranger who calls my house tells me their kid is coming home and would like to see the first game. If all these jokers really had kids in Vietnam, there wouldn't be any left over there to do the fighting." Press box steward Tommy McCarthy could relate. "I once worked at the Navy Yard [in nearby Charlestown] with about 14,000 people," he said. "Since Sunday night half of them have called. The others must be dead or dying. Everybody wants tickets."

Former Red Sox radio and television broadcaster Curt Gowdy, now calling baseball games for the NBC-TV network, did not need to stoop to such levels. The upbeat Wyoming native had been assigned to announce the Series alongside Ken Coleman and Harry Caray, the respective voices of the Red Sox and Cardinals. "It's like a dream come true," said Gowdy, whose viewing audience was expected to number over

35 million. "I've seen practically all these kids grow up during my years with the club." Gowdy specifically recalled Carl Yastrzemski's early days in the outfield. "I used to get so mad at [his] rainbow throws," Gowdy said. "And now he's the biggest star in the game. . . . He must have made up his mind to play up to his potential."

Red Sox manager Dick Williams expressed little concern about his ball club playing up to its potential, though many in the sporting press were predicting a performance drop-off against the heavily favored Cardinals. "I don't go for these stories that this Series is anti-climatic," Williams said. "This is something great coming up, and I don't think for a minute that there will be any letdown by our players." Nationally syndicated columnist Milton Gross counted himself among the doubters. "The Red Sox caught lightning in a bottle, but it may be the last thing they catch this year," he wrote. "The Cardinals, rested and ready, are going to whip them badly. St. Louis could do it in the irreducible minimum of four games. The Red Sox are a worn-down team, their pitching reduced to frayed arms, their opposition much too much."

Regardless of whether the Sox were worthy opponents, the visiting Cardinals were disappointed to be playing them at Fenway Park. "Like the rest of our guys," Bob Gibson confessed, "I was hoping that we'd just get a bigger park to play in. We were rooting for Detroit [to win the AL pennant], but only because of the bigger capacity of their park." For sure, Fenway's limited seating meant smaller gate shares for all the participating players and coaches. But the Cardinals ace stopped short of saying the ballpark's modest footprint would alter the way he planned to pitch to the powerful Sox lineup. "I don't care about the size of the park," Gibson said. "It won't make me change my pitching style. I think we'll win it in either five or six games." The reasons for Gibson's optimism came down to talent and experience. "This (Boston) is a young club, and they're going to be so keyed up about this thing that I think it will make them play that much better," Gibson said. "But we have the better club, and I feel we are going to win."

Wednesday's Game 1 before a boisterous Fenway crowd of 34,796 gave Gibson little cause to think otherwise. He dominated through nine innings, fanning 10, and giving up just six hits in a convincing 2–1 Cardinals victory. "Gibson pitched a helluva game," Dick Williams said. "He overpowered our guys." Even Carl Yastrzemski had a bad day. The newly anointed AL Triple Crown winner entered the contest as the hottest hitter in baseball but was easily neutralized by Gibson. He went 0–4 and could manage only a pair of weak fly balls to left field. Gibson could not resist commenting on the underwhelming performance in light of all the pre–Series media hype surrounding Yastrzemski. "You make more of Yastrzemski than I do," he chided reporters in the visitors' clubhouse afterward. "He's a good ball player. That's all."

Yastrzemski was more charitable about Gibson in his postgame remarks. "[Gibson] is everything they said about him," he offered. "He had a good fastball and a good breaking ball." What neither Gibson nor Yastrzemski revealed at the time was the heavy amount of trash talking that went on between them. "Every at-bat he hollered at me, and I'd yell back at him," Yastrzemski recalled. While such heated exchanges were not then considered uncommon, especially in big games, Yastrzemski took them as the backhanded compliments they were intended to be. "I think that Gibson saw me as a one-to-one challenge, and he was going to go with his best against my best, with no distractions," Yaz later said.

Gibson's lone miscue came in the bottom of the third inning. Boston pitcher Jose Santiago, starting in place of team ace Jim Lonborg due to the latter having pitched the pennant clincher three days earlier, received an unexpected gift. On a 0–2 count, Gibson hung him a curve that Santiago sent out of the ballpark. "It was a mistake, a perfect home run pitch," Gibson recalled. "I just got careless and didn't dig down on the ball hard enough and it came up there big as a balloon." Santiago didn't complain. "It was a good breaking ball, and I saw it all the way," he said. "It was a thrill." Santiago had a lot to be thrilled about. Apart from the homer, the second and last of his big-league career, he had hung tough with Gibson most of the game. He gave up 10 hits, but he pitched his way out of several jams while yielding only two runs. "I wanted to win, of course, but I was happy with the way I pitched," Santiago said.

What Santiago, the first Puerto Rican in history to start a World Series game, couldn't account for was Lou Brock. The fleet St. Louis outfielder tied a Series record for most hits in a game by going a perfect

4-for-4 and scoring both Cardinal runs. In the third inning, he singled to center and was moved to third on a Curt Flood double down the left field line. Roger Maris, hitting in the number three spot of the Cardinal batting order, brought him home on a sharp grounder to first. Brock struck again in the top of the seventh. He reached on a one-out single, stole second base (his second theft of the day), and advanced to third when Sox first baseman George Scott fielded a Curt Flood bouncer to the bag. Brock then scored when Maris hit another hard grounder, this time to second with the Sox infield drawn in. "Brock isn't human the way he runs," wrote Tony Conigliaro, who was covering the Series as a special correspondent for the *Boston Record-American*. "That run he scored in the seventh inning to beat us was fantastic. Even a normally fast runner wouldn't have scored. Usually, we're told not break for the plate with the infield in until we see the ball go through for a hit, or unless it's a slowly hit ball." But Brock had other ideas. "[He] was running all the way," Conigliaro said. "He was off as the bat made contact with the ball." Predictably, the low-key Brock took his record-tying day all in stride. "I tell you, they know I'm going to run," he insisted. "I get a jump on the pitcher and so I run. I'm not as fast now as I was in 1960 or 1961, maybe, and I've been clocked, but I know I had good takeoff today."

As he had all year, Brock quietly dedicated his performance on the field to the memory of his younger brother Curtis, who had passed away in the off-season at the age of 25. "To me his death was a tragedy," Brock said. "He was a tremendously talented kid. He could play baseball, football and run track. He could do it all. And then he had to die. He never had a chance." Curtis had been in the service when he was diagnosed with cerebral edema, an acute swelling of the brain. He received a medical discharge but lapsed into a coma the day after Christmas. He remained in that unconscious state until he died three weeks later with Brock by his side. "Sitting there with him was the toughest thing I ever had to do," Brock revealed.

Yastrzemski could not shake the feeling his mechanics were off. He was a creature of habit and it did not sit well that pregame team batting practice had been cut short from the usual 45 minutes to only 20, owing to a scheduling snafu. "In twenty minutes a ball club can't possibly get enough batting practice after a two-day layoff," he argued. "I can't speak for the others, but I was still cold and my timing wasn't right because I couldn't take many swings. Normally, I take about twenty, but this time I had only six or seven. I knew before I left the batting cage that I wasn't ready." To rectify the problem, Yaz arranged a postgame workout with teammates Rico Petrocelli, Joe Foy, and Ken Harrelson, who had gone a collective 0-for-7 against Gibson. "The workout lasted about an hour and a half, with all of us—Foy, Petrocelli, Harrelson and me—taking turns pitching and batting," he said. The results were encouraging. "After forty-five minutes of hitting, my timing was back, my swing was good, and everything was fine," Yaz said. "I got so sharp that I hit six Foy pitches in a row into the right-field bullpen or stands with just a flick of the wrists." Filled with renewed vigor and purpose, Yastrzemski informed team photographer Jerry Buckley back in the clubhouse he would hit two out the next day. "I was only half kidding," he said.

The workout attracted considerable national media attention. "In other years, at other World Series, other superstars have dismissed four hitless times at bat as a bad day, sipped a beer and taken a shower," wrote Dave Anderson of the *New York Times*. "The superstar known as Yaz acknowledged his bad day and sipped a beer, but he took extra batting practice before he took his shower." Yastrzemski was bemused by all the scrutiny. "I didn't think anything of it," he claimed. "Whenever my timing is off in a ball game, I take batting practice later if we're not leaving town right away." The media were not the only ones taking measure. Showered, dressed, and still emotionally high from their victory, the Cardinals silently watched the workout from the stands. They were waiting for the team bus to take them back to their hotel, but the impromptu workout caught them by surprise. They had not expected this kind of professionalism and commitment to improvement that Yaz and his teammates were now displaying. It hadn't been that long ago that the Red Sox were the laughingstocks of the game. "We were all impressed," Tim McCarver said.

Respect was something Carl Michael Yastrzemski had always striven for on the baseball diamond. The son of a potato farmer, Yastrzemski had been raised in a large, tight-knit Polish American community in the Bridgehampton-Southhampton area of Long Island after World War

Yaz takes a big cut. PHOTO BY DENNIS BREARLEY/BOSTON RED SOX

II. While not exactly affluent, his family did well enough to operate a 70-acre spread that made Yaz a charter member of postwar America's exploding middle class. Indeed, daily life was more Norman Rockwell than Grant Wood. "When he was real little, you could find him across the road from the house playing pick up games with the other kids," his father Carl Sr. said. "That's all he did. He used to like to be playing out there all the time. I was working, so I didn't have time to watch him." When he wasn't laboring in the fields, Carl Sr., whose family responsibilities forced him to turn down a chance to play in the low minors for the Brooklyn Dodgers, liked to acclimate his eldest son to the vibrant local baseball scene. Carl Sr. would bring him along to games where the elder Yastrzemski starred as a power-hitting shortstop for the Bridgehampton White Eagles, a semipro team that was comprised mostly of extended family members. "Dad was their founder, manager, general manager, treasurer traveling secretary—everything," recalled Carl Jr. who served as the team's batboy. As he got older and his own skills as a ballplayer developed, Yastrzemski played alongside his father. "Although close to forty, Dad was the guts of the ball club, a good shortstop and the best hitter on the team," he said. "He was sort of a right-handed Ted Williams, for, being a pull hitter, he faced packed defenses to left field, just as Williams faced packed defenses to the right." Later on, when Carl Jr. was being scouted by the Red Sox, their minor league director Johnny Murphy quipped, "I wonder if we're going after the wrong Yastrzemski."

The son gradually eclipsed the father as a ballplayer and by the time he graduated from high school in 1957, the popular multisport athlete [he also played football and basketball], was drawing interest from several big-league clubs, including the Yankees. His favorite team growing up, Yaz was excited at the prospect of batting in the same Bronx Bomber lineup as Mickey Mantle, Yogi Berra, and Tony Kubek. That excitement reached a crescendo when he was invited to work out with the team at Yankee Stadium. "I got into a pair of white pin-striped pants, then put on the shirt with the monogram NY in blue letters on the front," he recounted. "Even though there was no number on the back, it was a thrill to wear the most famous uniform in baseball." The workout went extremely well with Yastrzemski belting two batting practice pitches into the right field seats. "I felt, comfortable, loose and confident," he said. It now seemed a foregone conclusion Yastrzemski would sign with the Yankees, that is until team scout Ray Garland visited his Long Island home. "He sits on the living room with me and my father," Yastrzemski remembered. "They talk for a while, and the scout tells my dad to write a figure on a piece of paper that my dad thought I should get for a bonus. The scout said he would do the same thing. They wrote down the numbers and swapped the pieces of paper." That's when the trouble began. "The scout wrote down $45,000," Yastrzemski said. "My dad wrote down $100,000. When the scout saw my dad's figure, he took the pencil he had in his hand and threw it up in the air and it hit the ceiling." That did it. Yastrzemski's father told Garland "to get the hell out" of his house. "Forget it, he's going to college," Carl Sr. said.

The only remaining question was which college Yastrzemski would attend. A solid B student in high school, he had received scholarship offers from several schools, but his heart was set on only one place. "I always admired Notre Dame," he said. "When they offered me one of the three baseball scholarships they give each year, I felt it was too good an opportunity to pass up." Although initially homesick and overwhelmed by his studies, the former altar boy came to love the Catholic South Bend, Indiana, school. "The people there cared about you," he said. Indeed, when he was in danger of flunking out in his first semester, a supportive college counselor by the name of Father Glenn Boarman stepped in to provide assistance. "If he hadn't been around early in my first term, I probably would have left," Yastrzemski later revealed. "When he knew I was struggling, we would go out and have a few beers and would talk about my dreams and where I had come from and my family." The talking helped and Yastrzemski turned things around academically the next semester, making dean's list and getting elected president of the freshman class. But the desire to become a professional ballplayer proved too strong. After just one season of freshman baseball (undergraduate first year students weren't allowed to play varsity), Yastrzemski made his availability known to major league clubs. There was only one stipulation, as insisted upon by his father. "No West Coast for Carl," Carl Sr. said. He wanted his son to stay close to home and family. That left the Dodgers, now of Los Angeles and hot to secure Carl Jr.'s promising young bat for their aging lineup, in the cold. "If only you were still in Brooklyn," Carl Sr. lamented. This qualification notwithstanding, there was no shortage of suitors for the younger Yastrzemski. The Tigers, Phillies, Reds, and the Red Sox all took turns courting him. "I liked the ballparks I saw—Briggs [later Tiger] stadium in Detroit, Crosley Field in Cincinnati and Connie Mack Stadium in Philadelphia—because they all had short right-field fences," Yaz said. "I had been a pull hitter in high school." That he chose to go with Boston, whose home park dimensions were decidedly not tailored to his left-handed swing, is ironic. It takes nearly 400 feet for a ball to leave the park in deep right center. "Funny, when I first walked into Fenway park in late November after I signed, I couldn't even see right field because of the snow," he said.

So what made Yastrzemski ultimately choose Boston? It was the advice he received from Father Joe Rapkowski, his Long Island pastor and a family confidant. "He had been a close friend of [8-time NL All-Star first baseman] Gil Hodges of Brooklyn, and Hodges had often told him that no owner in baseball treated his players more decently or ran his entire organization—all the way through the minors—with more class than Mr. Yawkey," Yastrzemski said. "Father Joe kept telling us what a fine man Yawkey was, and what a great organization he ran." There were other considerations, too. The Red Sox "were very frank with me," Yastrzemski recalled. "They didn't make any promises, and they told me that I would be better off playing full-time in triple-A ball than part-time with the Sox." Given how bad a ball club Boston then had, his advancement to the majors could not be expected to take long. "I felt I'd have a good chance to make the team in a hurry," he said. The money wasn't bad either. Yastrzemski received a $108,000 signing bonus with a two-year minor league contract worth $5,000 per season. And just to ensure he had something to fall back on if baseball didn't work out, he also insisted on and received a team assurance they would pay for his remaining college education. "So I signed," he said.

Yastrzemski's first stop in pro ball was Raleigh of the Class B Carolina League and it was not an easy transition. "The biggest thing was to get used to playing every day," he said. "In college and semi-pro ball, we played only once or twice a week and got plenty of rest between games. But Raleigh was completely different. We played most of our games at night and that turned our usual schedule inside out." The other major issue was where he would play. Signed as a shortstop, Sox management was not happy with what they saw in the field. "I had a gun for an arm, and I had played the same way for my whole life," he said. "When I threw the ball, I just threw the hell out of it." The problem was the ball wasn't consistently finding the first baseman's glove. A move to second was arranged and the shorter throwing distance across the diamond seemed to help. Yaz settled down defensively and appeared more comfortable overall with his surroundings. "The bus trips were actually enjoyable," he said. "The cities in the league were all together, so we were able to go home every night. The people down there were great, too. But I didn't really learn anything new except how to conserve my energy. Playing every day, of course, gave me a lot of experience." Although he got off to a slow start at the plate [he was batting .240 in his first three weeks in Raleigh), he soon was able to get untracked and finish with a .377 average, tops in the Carolina League. He did receive an unexpected visitor during the season—Carl Sr. had apparently been enjoying himself a little too much after games with his fellow rookies ("We'd get one of the older guys to buy some beer for us and we'd have a few. Sometimes a lot more than a few," he said) and team management made a call to the elder Yastrzemski. "Goddammit, Carl!" he screamed. "How many years did we spend trying to get you here?! Are you going to just piss away your career acting like some punk?!! Now cut this crap out!!" A chastened Yaz did what he was told. "Well, I sure didn't want to go through that again," he said. "And Dad was right. My focus wasn't there. The discipline, the intensity. This was a new life for me, OK, but I still needed to approach it my way."

When Raleigh's season concluded in early September, Yastrzemski was invited to Boston to become acquainted with Fenway Park and to work out for team officials. But the highlight of the trip was getting to meet Ted Williams. The baseball legend was nearing the end of the line as a player and Yastrzemski was awed to be his presence. "Nobody had to introduce us," he said. "He came over from his corner of the room, held out his hand, and said, 'I'm Ted Williams.'" Williams had been one of his favorite players growing up and Yastrzemski was taken aback by the informality of Williams's friendly greeting. He was further surprised that Williams knew who he was. "I know—I know all about you," Williams said. The last of the .400 hitters then proceeded to give him a bit of advice. "Look, kid, don't ever—y'understand me?—don't *ever* let anyone monkey with your swing," he thundered. Having spoken his piece, Williams retreated to his locker and ignored Yastrzemski the rest of his visit. It was just as well. Yastrzemski had to meet with the Boston media for the first time and field questions about whether the 20-year-old was major league–ready to play for the Red Sox. "The press and the public wanted me to stay," he said. But the team was playing it careful. Having learned from years of rushing top prospects to the majors and seeing them flop, the Sox settled on a more prudent course of action. He was sent back to the minors for more seasoning. "We don't want him to get discouraged," said one club official.

Yastrzemski was assigned to play the remainder of the 1959 season for the Minneapolis Millers of the American Association. He could not have arrived in the Land of 10,000 Lakes at a more propitious time. Managed by future major league skipper Gene Mauch, the Millers were in the middle of their league playoffs and Yaz was immediately pressed into service. He hit a scorching .389 (7 for 18 in 6 playoff games) to help the Millers win the championship. Next stop was the Little World Series where the Millers faced the International League champion Havana (Cuba) Sugar Kings. "The first three games of the Series were supposed to be in Minneapolis, but it snowed the day before the first game, and the temperature when we opened was 30 degrees," he recalled. "They had maybe 2,500 out that day, and the next, with the weather no warmer, there were barely a 1,000 people in the stands. Everyone threw in the towel, and by mutual agreement we went to Havana to finish the series." The Millers lost in seven games but Yastrzemski had a brush with history in the third game. To the shouts of "FIDEL! FIDEL!," recently victorious Cuban revolutionary leader Fidel Castro was flown into Havana's packed Gran Stadium by helicopter. The chopper deposited the former left-handed pitcher, who had reportedly failed in two tryouts with the Washington Senators, onto the infield. From there he waved to the crowd with his trademark cigar jutting from his mouth. "You could hardly see in the night lights [the cigar] because his black beard was in the way," Yaz said. Adding to the drama were heavily armed teenage bodyguards in the Minneapolis dugout. They celebrated the occasion by shooting off their guns. "We all jumped," Yastrzemski remembered. "I might have said a Hail Mary or two."

Yastrzemski didn't need the assistance of a higher power the following year in Minneapolis. Tagged by Sox management as the successor to the retiring Ted Williams, the 19-year-old was moved to left field and batted .339 with a league-leading 193 hits. He hit a disappointing seven homers but he attributed that more to lifestyle than anything else. "I just didn't seem to get enough sleep or eat properly," he said. "We had a lot of long plane trips. We'd go from Minneapolis to Houston, then up to Omaha, back to Dallas, and return home. I was never able to set up a schedule for myself, and I'm sure the loss of weight hurt my power. I know I didn't have the strength or snap I had at Raleigh, and the statistics prove it." Still, the parent club was pleased enough to go forward with their original plan of starting him in left field for the team's 1961 home opener. With Williams gone, all eyes were on this skinny, visibly nervous rookie from Long Island who was being heralded as Boston's next baseball superstar. The pressure and expectations "almost broke me," Yastrzemski later told William Nack of *Sports Illustrated*. "I struggled the first 2 1/2 months. You start having doubts: 'Can I play in the big leagues?' I was hitting about .220." Adding to his woes was the quality of pitching he encountered. "In the American Association, you face about two good pitchers every four days" Yaz said. "But in this league you face a good pitcher every day. And when a starter does get into trouble, he gives way to a tough man from the bullpen. All of them seem to have a good, live fastball and a sharp curve."

Desperate to find a way out of his hitting rut, Yastrzemski went to Tom Yawkey with an urgent request. "I wish Ted were here," he told the Sox owner. Yastrzemski had gotten to know and rely on the advice of Williams during spring training, where the emeritus slugger now served as a part-time hitting instructor. Williams arrived at Fenway the next morning. "Dammit, you're using too much body," he told Yaz during an hour-and-a-half batting cage session. "Use your hands, your hands. And hit through the middle." Yastrzemski responded positively to the coaching. "That night I hit two doubles, one off the wall in left center, the other to right center and from then on I was in pretty good shape," he said. He also reached an important determination about himself as a ballplayer. "Finally, I said to myself, 'You're not Ted Williams.' I started hitting the way I could hit. I think that was probably the best thing ever to happen to me over the 23 years [of my career]. It toughened me so mentally." He raised his average to .266 on the season while driving in an impressive 80 runs on 11 homers and 31 doubles. "You could just see he was going to blossom," noted teammate Gene Conley. For sure, Yastrzemski greatly improved in the coming years, winning a batting title in 1963 (.323 average) and hitting 15 or more home runs four times in five years.

Defensively, he proved to be an elite outfielder, playing balls off Fenway's legendary left field wall better than any Sox outfielder since Duffy Lewis. "I learned by trial and error how the ball bounced off each part of it, and how hard, and in what direction," Yastrzemski said. "I learned to tell from the arc of the ball what part of the Wall it was going to hit. I got to know all the holes in the scoreboard, where the rivets were and all the other little nooks and crannies that made life so interesting out there." For his efforts, he received Gold Glove Awards in 1963 and 1964. "He always wanted to do better, to excel," remembered second baseman Chuck Schilling, who broke into the majors with Yastrzemski. "He was always out there out there doing whatever was needed, like taking extra batting practice. He always had this nervous energy he had to use up. Even after a doubleheader, he'd have to go out and hit until he couldn't lift the bat anymore. On the road, he'd get someone to come out to the park and throw to him."

Yaz also showed a less attractive side that alienated teammates and managers. "If we went 0 for 4 or 0 for 7 or something like that, it would affect his fielding," reliever Dick Radatz said. "He'd pout a little. Sometimes a pitcher would tell him in the clubhouse. . . . 'Hey, I want someone out there behind me who's going to help me get the guy out. Come on, get in the game.'" Nor was it uncommon for Yastrzemski to loaf on the bases and take plays off. In 1964 Sox manager Johnny Pesky benched him three games for failing to run hard to first on a routine double-play ball. Yaz was angered by the move, but Pesky felt it was necessary to establish his authority as manager. "My job is to win games, not go around kissing players to make them happy," Pesky said afterward. "Now I've heard that some players were mad at me because I criticized them in front of other players. Well, if they can't take criticism in front of other players, then they shouldn't be in baseball." Only years later did Yastrzemski take any semblance of responsibility for his behavior. "I regret not being able to talk with Johnny back then," he said in 1978. "I was young; I didn't think I could say anything to a manager. I still feel this way. . . . We were losing, we were out of [the pennant race] very quickly, guys did things you might not do. . . . Yeah, not running out grounders was one—although that was always bullshit the way it was blown up. . . . You hit a hard grounder, you don't run hard. It's that simple. But there *were* quite a few misunderstandings between Johnny and myself. When I think back, I see that some conversation could've prevented that kind of thing."

The "moody young outfielder," as *Sport* magazine took to describing Yastrzemski, had done himself no favors by showing up at spring training 20 pounds overweight and having one of the most disappointing years of his career. He hit over 30 points below his previous season's average. "It was a foolish thing to do," he admitted. "We trained in Arizona then, and it's impossible to lose weight there because you don't perspire. No matter how hard I worked, the fat stayed on. When I stepped on the scales opening day, I panicked. The needle went all the way up to 196. All I had taken off in Arizona was four pounds." Such excuses did not cut it with Billy Herman, Yastrzemski's manager in 1965 and 1966. "You can't be a leader, not the way you played [in 1964]," the former Cubs great told him. "You've got to report in shape, then beat your brains out."

Yaz performed slightly better under Herman but he continued to have games where he flat out quit. Herman was forced to bench him twice and even levied a team fine when Yastrzemski failed to hustle on a routine defensive play against Washington during a doubleheader. "Frank Howard hit [a ball] down the left-field line and it barely reached the wall," Herman later revealed to historian Donald Honig. "Yastrzemski trotted after it and Howard got three bases." Herman, not one to be overly demonstrative, made an exception in this case. "After the doubleheader was over, I was so goddamned mad I could hardly see," he said. "I went into my office and told the trainer to send Yastrzemski in." When Yaz arrived, Herman rose from his chair and locked the door. "Then I told him what I thought of his performance that night," he said. "Very frankly, I've never talked like that to any man in my life, before or since. I called him everything. It got to the point where I kind of got on guard because I thought for sure he was going to swing at me at any second." Yastrzemski wisely refrained from taking any such action, but Herman never forgave nor forgot his lackadaisical attitude. "How did I get along with Yastrzemski?" Herman said. "Like everybody else did. By that I mean nobody ever got along with Yastrzemski. Every manager has trouble with him, and some of them had it by the ton. He plays only as hard as he wants to play, and any manager is going to resent that, I don't give a damn who it is, because his job depends upon the players producing."

Yastrzemski's had his own complaints about Herman. Before the start of the 1966 regular season, Yaz's best friend on the team—Chuck Schilling—was traded to the Twins. "That really soured me on Herman," Yastrzemski said. "He had never liked Schilling as a ballplayer, even though Charlie had been a good second baseman who could hit major league pitching, before he hurt his hand. Whether or not that permanently impaired his efficiency I don't know, but I do know that my resentment against Herman was deeper than my feeling against Pesky. Pesky hadn't given Schilling much of a chance either, but at least he had kept the guy. The whole Schilling situation was a very personal thing with me." Yastrzemski's dissatisfaction deepened when Herman installed him as team captain, as befitting his status as the ball club's best player. Yastrzemski felt the added new responsibility was more of a burden than an honor. "I found myself in the middle of every hassle, every disagreement, every beef and gripe and complaint on a ball club which had specialized in hassles, disagreements, beefs, gripes, and complaints for years," he explained. "If a guy needed money, he came to me. If a guy thought he was unfairly fined, he came to me. If a guy wasn't worried about being traded, he came to me. If a guy got out of bed on the wrong side in the morning, he came to me." Besides these obvious headaches, the extroverted personality traits required of a team captain did not fit Yastrzemski's definition of leadership or his reserved personality. "Look at Mantle," he remarked to a writer at the time. "He doesn't talk much, but the rest of the Yankees look up to him as a leader. The same thing was true of DiMaggio. He didn't get up and make speeches, but he was a leader just the same. Take those two men out of the Yankee lineup, and how many pennants might they have won in the last thirty years? That's the kind of leader I'd like to be. That's the kind of help I'd like to give a ballclub. I hope it can be the Red Sox. We're not going to be down forever. The tide has to turn in our favor some time."

Whether Yastrzemski would be around to see this team renaissance became a big question mark. Herman bluntly told him late in the season one of them would not be around in 1967. "I think I'm going to be here and you're not," Herman said. Trade rumors swirled that Yaz would be suiting up for another ball club by Opening Day. "Carl will never be a Frank Robinson, but he could be a great ballplayer with the right team," one anonymous source told *Sport* magazine. "He can run, throw, field and hit .330 or .340. I think he needs a change of scene, though. Some people think he is a clubhouse lawyer. I don't believe it. If I were Buzzie Bavasi of the Dodgers, I'd trade for him in a minute if I had to give up a good young pitcher and something else. A line drive hitter like Yaz would hit a ton in that big (LA) ballpark and the Dodgers speed, hustle and defense, too—which is what that team's made of." Yastrzemski eventually had enough of the speculation and asked Sox general manager Dick O'Connell directly if the rumors were true. "Remember, Yaz, *we're not trading you*," O'Connell said. "Read all you want, listen all you want, but don't worry. All right?" Buoyed by the team's faith in him and Herman's firing in September, Yastrzemski spent the off-season getting into the best physical shape possible for 1967. On the referral of a mutual friend, he turned to a former Hungarian Olympic boxing team coach named Gene Berde for guidance. Berde headed a local health club on Route 1 and ran tough, demanding workouts that belied his upbeat sunny exterior. His first impression of Yaz was that his body was softer than the Pillsbury Doughboy. "You the big athlete," Berde remonstrated. "But you can't even jump rope for half a minute. In Hungary you would be nothing. Weak and lazy . . . flabby waist . . . not enough resistance." He made Yastrzemski his personal makeover project in the months ahead, putting him through a series of grueling workouts involving a combination of weight training, boxing, and calisthenics. "He told me later he didn't think I'd ever be back, but I made it the next day and the day after that and all the other days for the rest of the winter," Yastrzemski said. By the start of spring training, he was in top physical form and open to the suggestion put forward by Ted Williams that he pull the ball more with his added layers of muscle. "Now I tighten up my hips, face the pitcher a little more and wait a little longer on each pitch," he said. "Everything I hit feels better." Rivals made special note of the change. "He seems to get stronger every week," Orioles third baseman Brooks Robinson said. "It's like watching a boy grow into a man."

That hard-won maturity was on display in Game 2. Yastrzemski slugged two home runs off Cardinals starter Dick Hughes to lift the Sox to a resounding 5–0 Sox victory that tied the Series at a game apiece before a home crowd of 35,188. "Not even the shrillest of alarm clocks can wake up the Red Sox and the Red Sox fans in the compelling fashion of Carl Yastrzemski," wrote Arthur Daley of the *New York Times*. "Boston's living legend sounded his clarion call in Fenway Park today and the response was electrifying. The Bosox tumbled out of the cataleptic state in which the Cardinals plunged them yesterday and all of Boston bubbled over once more in ecstatic delight."

Yastrzemski, whose first homer was a solo shot in the fourth inning that put the Sox ahead 1–0, entered the game full of confidence. The previous afternoon's impromptu hitting session with Harrelson, Foy, and Petrocelli had gone so well that Yastrzemski decided he didn't need any additional batting practice. "It wasn't a question of maintaining my confidence, it was maintaining my strength," he said. "I'm no (Harmon) Killebrew." This loose approach also fit his overall game plan. "I was going to be swinging from the heels, against Hughes, a righty," he said. "We needed something to shake us, and to demoralize them, and there's nothing like the long ball to do that." Yastrzemski's strategy almost bore immediate results when he faced Hughes in the bottom of the first. "I swung just in front of the pitch and whacked it out of the park but foul by a few feet," he remembered. Hughes walked him but Yastrzemski had better fortune three innings later. "I didn't expect to see Hughes' slider anymore—that's the pitch I had hit foul but long," he said. "This time he fed me fastballs, and ran the count to 2–1. His next pitch was hard and low, but over the middle." Yastrzemski took advantage, lining a bullet into the Fenway right field grandstand section. Returning to the dugout after the blow, the adrenaline-filled outfielder was so overcome with emotion that he turned to Sox game starter Jim Lonborg and exclaimed, "Go get 'em, big guy, that's all you'll need."

Yastrzemski was dead on in his prediction, for no one was going to touch Lonborg this particular day. The lanky, blue-eyed Californian retired the first 19 Cardinal batters he faced and had a perfect game going until Curt Flood walked on a low outside pitch with one out in the seventh. "He had the best stuff he's had all year," praised Boston pitching coach Sal Maglie. "Lonnie kept his curve ball down and his fast ball high and inside and threw strikes." Lonborg later lost the no-hitter when Julian Javier doubled in the eighth. "It was a hanging slider," Lonborg explained. "When he hit it I just put my left hand in front of my eyes like someone seeing a car wreck. I just didn't make a good pitch." Not that he made many bad pitches. "I was in a zone . . . that very few times you find yourself in as a pitcher," he later said. "It's like a quarterback that doesn't ever miss a pass or like Larry Bird scoring 50 points because every time he shoots the ball it goes into the basket." Coming so tantalizingly close to becoming only the second pitcher in World Series history to throw a no-hitter (New York's Don Larson performed the deed against the Dodgers in 1956) hurt, however. "It was tough to lose it . . . no doubt about it," Lonborg confessed. "But there is so much luck involved in something like that. [Javier] just as easily could have popped up that ball or fouled it off, but he didn't."

Lonborg had come away from the first game with the impression the Cardinals liked to swing the bat. "Therefore," he said, "I decided that I would challenge them and start right away with Brock." By "challenge," Lonborg meant throwing at Cardinal batters' heads. "We'll see how they hit when they have been knocked on their ass," he told teammates. Indeed, Brock, who had abused Jose Santiago the previous day, encountered chin music on the game's very first pitch. "It was Lonborg's only high pitch of the afternoon, and it was fully as effective in its own way as the knee high curves and sinking fastballs he threw the rest of the way," *New Yorker* essayist Roger Angell wrote. Brock's teammates were understandably less appreciative, hurling insults at the pitcher. "You'll get your turn at bat, too," warned Bob Gibson ominously. None of the heated invective seemed to bother Lonborg, though. He remained a picture of poise on the pitcher's mound. "Some of the Cardinals got on me from the dugout," he recalled, "but I could have cared less. I had to let them know I was out to beat them anyway I could. If I must brush them back to do it, then they're going to know it."

Yastrzemski hit his second homer in bottom of the seventh, a three-run blast off reliever Joe Hoerner. "The pitch came in exactly where I expected it," Yaz recalled. "I stuck the bat out front, a nice quick swing, and hit a real shot, a long high belt that landed ten rows up in the right field stands." For Dick Williams, who had been witnessing such awesome displays of power all year, this was nothing new. "As far as I'm concerned, this was a typical (Carl) Yastrzemski performance," he said. "Every time Yaz swings, it's a potential home run. He's having the best over all season I've ever seen. Ted Williams was one of the best hitters I've seen, but I'm talking about Yastrzemski's all-around ability." The opposition could not help being a little impressed either. "[Yaz] swings hard all the time," observed St. Louis hitting coach Dick Sisler. "Most hitters cut down their strokes when they have two strikes, but not this guy. That's why he's an unusual-type hitter—to swing hard all the time."

Yet the game's highlight reel clearly belonged to Lonborg. He had come through again for the Red Sox, delivering yet another clutch performance when the team most needed it. "Lonborg showed the way for all of us," said Lee Stange, who was limited to bullpen duty throughout the Series. "He proved that no team is invincible as long as you pitch the way a major leaguer should pitch." Lonborg did receive a boost from an unexpected source prior to his start. Fellow Sox pitcher Darrel Brandon, who would not make an appearance in the Series, had presented him with a makeshift golden tinfoil horseshoe that a fan named Elaine O'Mara had mailed to the Boston pitching staff. "I threw the envelope away so [I] don't know where the girl lives," Brandon told Tim Horgan of the *Boston Herald-Traveler*. "But I gave the horseshoe to Lonnie before the game." Never a superstitious type, Lonborg was initially reluctant to accept the gift, but Brandon insisted. "Go ahead, it might help," Brandon said. Against his better judgment, Lonborg accepted and tucked the horseshoe in the hip pocket of his uniform pants. "I knew it couldn't be bad luck," he said.

Luck, in many respects, explains James Reynold Lonborg's rapid advancement to the majors. The son of a college professor, Lonborg was raised in the California suburban coastal community of San Luis Obispo in the 1950s. "I know that you probably think I spent my boyhood throwing avacados at fence-posts," he once told an interviewer. "I did, a bit. But I spent hours and hours—particularly through the long summer days—poking and scooping for specimens in the creek that ran through our yard." Lonborg would then view the samples he had gathered—usually parameciums—under his father's microscope back home. His cerebral bent did not preclude playing baseball. "I was pretty skinny, but the baseball field was just a block away from my house," he said. "Little League started in 1950 in San Luis Obispo and I think I was 10-years-old when I first started playing in an organized situation." Ironically, his team was called the Red Sox and when they won their league championship, Lonborg's coach—an affable man named Stub Sweeney—persuaded the big-league Red Sox to send autographed pictures to each of his players. "It was a big thrill for me as a little kid and I still have the picture," Lonborg said.

Lonborg had already taken up pitching by the time he reached high school, as his baseball heroes growing up were Sandy Koufax and Don Newcombe of the Dodgers. But neither Koufax nor Newcombe left the kind of imprint that his high school coach John Dodge did. "[Dodge] brought the game down to brass tacks for me," Lonborg maintained. "He was the first to tell me that baseball is a constant battle between you and the hitter. It took a long time for me to understand exactly what he meant." Unlike many of his peers, however, dreams of a big-league career never crossed Lonborg's thoughts. He wanted to become a surgeon. "As a senior, I was the No. 1 pitcher," Lonborg said. "But my chief interests were academic. I was more interested in reading and studying than I was in baseball practice. And I gained a straight-A record in my studies." Boyhood friend and future Cincinnati Reds pitcher Mel Queen, who went 17–4 in 1967, later confirmed this. "In school, he was just another ballplayer, maybe a little more awkward than most," Queen said. "But he didn't care because he had no burning ambitions for the [majors] the way I did." In fact, baseball wasn't even his primary sport.

When he gained admission to Stanford University on an academic scholarship in 1960, Lonborg, 6'5", set his sights on becoming starting center for the school's basketball team. But the person in front of him on the squad's depth chart was a 6'8", 225-pound bruiser named Tom Dose. Dose would go on to earn All-American honors and be selected by the Los Angeles Lakers in the third round of the 1964 NBA Draft. "I saw that my career at Stanford being on the bench, so I said, 'Well maybe I'll just go try out for the baseball team,'" Lonborg recalled. He never looked back. Making the team as a walk-on, Lonborg earned outstanding results from the mound, leading the ball club in strikeouts and innings pitched in 1962 and 1963. "I had good control and was able to maintain good mechanics," Lonborg said. "All of a sudden, I got stronger and baseball became a priority." Queen, who by this time had married Lonborg's sister, tipped off the Reds about his brother-in-law's burgeoning talent, especially his superior arm strength. But they weren't interested, citing Lonborg's alleged inability to throw a curve. "Curve?" Queen responded. "Anyone can teach him to throw a curve. But a guy has to be born with a fastball like his."

Lonborg honed his pitching skills further when he spent his summers playing for the Basin League, a Midwestern semipro circuit that showcased some the nation's top collegiate talent. "The nice thing about the league was the fact it was similar to the routine in professional ball," he recalled. "We played five or six games a week and had road trips." While pitching for the Wimmer, South Dakota, Pheasants in 1963, Lonborg piqued the interest of the Red Sox and Orioles, who were impressed by his high strikeout totals, including a head-turning 17 in one game. "The Orioles made me an offer and I thought I was going to take it right off the bat," Lonborg recalled. But his father, who was on the scene to advise him, told him to hold off until they heard from the Red Sox. Wiser words were never spoken. The Sox offered $25,000, a substantially higher amount than Baltimore, with the understanding the premed major would devote his energies strictly to baseball after fulfilling his remaining academic requirements to Stanford. Lonborg never got back to the Orioles. "It was strictly a matter of economics," he recalled. "The Red Sox figure was too high to turn down." Veteran Baltimore scout Bruce Hebner believed there was another factor at work. "We would have given him the same money," he contended. "[Lonborg] just figured he could make the Boston pitching staff a lot quicker than most clubs."

As for Lonborg's decision to turn his back on medicine, he was philosophical. "The successes I was starting to experience on the ball field were great builders of self-esteem and I knew I had crossed a line where I was better than I thought I ever could have been [as a pitcher]," he said.

"I thought it was a great opportunity." He also knew that if he washed out as a ballplayer, he had options. "If something happens that finishes me in baseball by the time I'm 30 or 31, I'll go back to [medicine]," he said. "Otherwise, I'll forget it."

Lonborg's stay in the minors was relatively brief. He started the 1964 season with Boston's Single A Winston-Salem franchise in the Carolina League where he recorded a 6–2 record with 61 strikeouts in 59 innings pitched. "I kind of cruised through that league because my stuff so good," he said. His performance earned him a midseason promotion to the Triple AAA Seattle Rainiers of the Pacific Coast League. Here the going got a little bumpier as Lonborg had to adjust to the superior quality of play. "I mean, my God, there were guys that were on their way up to the big leagues or had been in the big leagues and were on their way down," he said. He had some good games and some not so good ones. Fortunately, there were many veterans on the squad with major league experience such as catcher Earl Averill and pitcher Merlin Nippert, who took a shine to Lonborg. "They were all really beneficial providing advice on the way to get guys out [and] the way to present yourself on the mound," he recalled. "They knew I was aggressive. They knew that I loved having a baseball in my hands and they knew that I could throw strikes. So they basically just let me go out and pitch, which I thought was very helpful. I didn't get cluttered with a lot of information."

Though he finished out the Seattle season with only a 5–7 mark, Lonborg showed enough promise to be invited to Red Sox training camp the following spring. The 22-year-old did not waste the opportunity. Described by one newspaper account as a "dark horse bet to win a job on the Red Sox pitching staff," Lonborg caused many a veteran hitter, including second-year man Tony Conigliaro, to shake their heads in frustration after striking them out in practice. "Up and down. In and out. Doesn't he ever throw the ball straight?" Conigliaro grumbled. Sox manager Billy Herman, who was looking to upgrade the team's woeful starting pitching, didn't complain. "Tony, my boy, that's an occupational hazard," he replied.

Lonborg's ranking on the organizational pitching chart soared and he became confident he could make the jump from Triple AAA to the majors. "I was young and fresh and overflowing with enthusiasm," he said. "I threw relentlessly on the sidelines. I listened to everything everybody said. But even then, as a rookie with the Red Sox, I wanted someone to compete with." The person he eventually selected was brawny veteran right-hander Bill Monboquette, a 20-game winner in 1963. "I wanted to be the best-conditioned athlete on the squad," Lonborg said. Monboquette "was supposed to be the Red Sox' hardest worker. I think I got him. I think I worked even harder than Bill." His efforts did not go unrewarded. He was with the team when they broke camp and traveled north to Washington, D.C., to start the 1965 season against the Senators. "Don't let the lack of pro experience fool you," general manager Mike Higgins told the media. "Lonborg has done a lot of pitching in college. He's more mature than most of these kids." His former Seattle manager had also given his seal of approval. "He's got the ability, and he's got it in the clutch," Billy Gardner said. "And, he's a smart kid. His chances are very good."

Lonborg earned his first major league victory—a 3–2 decision over the Yankees at Fenway Park—on May 10. He won despite giving up two solo homers to Yankees outfielder Mickey Mantle. "According to the game pattern, I had to throw Mantle high fastballs," he later told *Sport* magazine. "So I threw one high and fast his first time up and he belted it into the seats. Next time he came up I threw him another high fast one and he bounced it off the wall for a double. His third time up I gave him the high fast one again and he banged that one into the seats. I allowed four hits that day, and Mantle got three of them." His rough treatment by the Yankees slugger notwithstanding, Lonborg was not in any way intimidated by the major league competition he faced. "It seems almost funny to say this but pitching in the big leagues was easier than any league I ever played in," Lonborg claimed. "It seemed you were not really doing anything different from what you did at each successive stage in the minors but conditions were great, the mounds were always immaculate and the defense was better." Yet Lonborg, who went 9–17 with a 4.47 ERA in 1965, was not always the beneficiary of solid defensive play. "On most days, it was just an adventure going out there because our defense, not to slight anyone, wasn't the greatest in the world," he later confessed. To be sure, his infield was one of the worst in Red Sox history with a very green Rico Petrocelli leading the way with 19 errors at shortstop. "Billy Herman would come out and take me out of the game after I gave up ground ball after ground ball and the guys couldn't catch them because it just wasn't a strong infield," Lonborg said. "I mean, they weren't golden glovers."

Lonborg improved to 10–10 with a 3.86 ERA in 1966, but once again he found himself plagued by a lack of support. The Red Sox committed a whopping 155 errors on the season while compiling a league worst .975 fielding average. Given the porous team defense, another five to seven victories could have easily been added to Lonborg's seasonal total. As Lonborg later ruefully observed, "Staying out of the four-out innings can mean the difference between winning and losing." But even when he later profited from the superior glovework of George Scott, Mike Andrews, Joe Foy, and a vastly improved Petrocelli behind him, Lonborg found there was still one opponent he could not get out. Brooks Robinson of the Orioles simply owned him and during one particularly memorable confrontation, the future Hall of Fame infielder tomahawked a low-and-away curve by Lonborg out of the ballpark. "I didn't think there was a right handed batter alive who could lose it, but Robinson just reached out and creamed it," Lonborg remembered. "As he ran around the bases, I cupped my hands and yelled over and over, 'That was a fabulous pitch. You had no *right* to hit it.'"

In the months leading up to the 1967 season, Lonborg traveled to Venezuela to play winter ball and come up with a complementary pitch to his usual repertoire of fastballs and low curves. Inspiration soon struck. "I have a new pitch," Lonborg excitedly told newspaper columnist Larry Clafflin. "Well, not exactly a new one, but it's something I've never done before. I'm using a slider a lot more when I'm behind on the hitters." Lonborg had had almost no confidence in the pitch before. "When I got behind a batter, say a 2–0 count or 3–1, I almost always threw my fastball," he said. "The hitters knew it was coming and they were ready for it. They teed off on it." Now with some extra fine tuning and game time experimentation, Lonborg discovered his slider had become as good as anyone's in the business. "I can honestly say no right handed batter [in

Venezuela] has pulled the slider yet," he informed Clafflin. "They keep looking for the fastball and they can't recover in time to pull my slider. Most of the time the right-handed hitters have been hitting it on the ground to the right side of the infield."

More changes awaited Lonborg when he arrived at the team's Florida training camp that spring. On the advice of Sox pitching coach Sal "The Barber" Maglie, Lonborg added another weapon to his already formidable pitching arsenal. Maglie, who had fashioned a successful 10-year major league career pitching inside to batters, advised Lonborg to do the same. "The more you pitch inside, the farther away that outside of the plate is going to look to the hitter," Maglie said. Intrigued, Lonborg, who had picked up the nickname "Gentleman Jim" for his exceedingly polite behavior in and around the ballpark, decided to give it a try. He was enthused by the results. "What had started off as an experiment, became something [that] allowed me to dominate in games," he later said. "I was able to knock guys down."

Indeed, batters, once comfortable digging in at the plate against him, now backed off out of fear of being hit by one of his bruising fastballs. That guaranteed him ownership of the outer strike zone as hitters were left guessing whether he would be coming inside on them. He was Gentleman Jim no longer. "Jim hit 19 batters [in 1967]," Maglie noted proudly. "He was just protecting the plate, his bread and butter. No pitcher can allow a hitter to dig in on him. Any hitter who hits or fouls off an outside pitch has got to learn he can't stand that close. Making hitters respect you is one of the ways of pitching. Jim learned that." Lonborg also ascertained that pitching inside helped him perform better at his home ballpark, which he had heretofore viewed as a graveyard for right-handers like himself. "Two years ago, I didn't like to pitch in Fenway Park," he admitted to the *Christian Science Monitor*. "That short left-field wall used to bother me. But now I don't care. I know if I've got my stuff and keep the ball down, I can win anywhere." Even when the stakes were as high as a World Series game.

The Series shifted to St. Louis for the next three contests and the city performed the same celebratory embrace of the Cardinals that Boston had for its ball club. "Even Mr. and Mrs. Abner Doubleday's favorite son,

Abner, would marvel at the way his baseball has turned a metropolis into a mass of frenzied excitement as St. Louis Friday got ready to play host at [Game 3] of the 1967 World Series," wrote John Aubel Jr. and Robert Blanchard of the *St. Louis Globe Democrat*. "For miles around, Cardinal fans called friends for a last minute badgering for tickets or made arrangements to watch the historic games on tv. Hotels and restaurants were jammed with out-of-towners who spent the day discussing each team's chances, taxicab drivers and bartenders centered their conversations around the great national pastime and souvenir salesmen got ready for their big days in the shadow of bunting draped Busch Memorial Stadium." Aubel and Blanchard went on to note that several high-profile celebrities had been spotted around town, including movie star Cary Grant, singing cowboy legend Gene Autry, and Hall of Fame baseball manager Casey Stengel. Stengel, who had been a star high school athlete in neighboring Kansas City, admitted he was rooting for the Cardinals even though he held Red Sox owner Tom Yawkey in highest esteem. "Mr. Yawkey treated me the best of all the teams I played against," he said. "He was my toughest customer; with men like [Bobby] Doerr and [Ted] Williams."

Stengal could have praised Yawkey in person as the famously reclusive multimillionaire flew with his team to St. Louis—his first trip with the ball club in 17 years. "This is wonderful," Yawkey said. "I've never enjoyed myself more in my life." Yawkey remained upbeat when he arrived at Busch Memorial Stadium to see his team go through pregame practice and warm-up drills. "Lovely ballpark," he said. "This would be nice in Boston." His players were less sanguine, as much of the multipurpose stadium's grass playing surface had been torn up the previous Sunday. The city's "other" Cardinals had played host to the Detroit Lions in a regular season National Football League matchup. "It's really slow out there," Reggie Smith observed. "We'll have to charge everything and get to the ball real quick because this field is going to slow the ball down." Although clearly concerned, Dick Williams did his best to downplay the shoddy field conditions. "This field will be the same for both teams," he said. "It all depends on who will get the lucky bounce in his favor. . . . I don't think one team will benefit more than the other."

Nelson Briles received the starting nod for Saturday's Game 3 and the former reliever responded with a gem. Briles held the Red Sox to two earned runs on seven hits in a "controversial" 5–2 win that gave the Cardinals a 2–1 Series advantage before a record home crowd of 54,575. The victory was controversial because Briles hit Carl Yastrzemski in the left calf on his first pitch to the slugger in the first inning. Yastrzemski proceeded to go hitless, not getting a ball out of the infield the entire game. "Briles is nowhere near the pitcher Gibson is, but he eliminated me as a factor," Yastrzemski fumed. "I was so sore I kept trying to pull the ball instead of hitting it down the middle, and I grounded out to second three times."

The beaning was in retaliation for Lonborg's brush back of Lou Brock in the second game. Briles denied any connection, claiming he wanted to challenge Yastrzemski and the ball sailed "a little inside." Yastrzemski didn't buy a word of Briles explanation. "I was mad," he recalled. "I felt he tried to hit me [due to] those two home runs in Boston." Dick Williams thought likewise and stormed out of the Boston dugout in protest. "What's going on? Is this the way it's going to be?" Williams yelled at home plate umpire Frank Umont. Fearing the onset of a beanball war, Umont prudently summoned Red Schoendienst to join them for an on-field discussion. "I told them, 'Look, fellows, I'm going to take charge!'" Umont revealed to reporters afterward. "I said that I'd make sure that the commissioner get a report if there was any more trouble. I guess I also said something about being sure the commissioner would see that money would be deducted from their World Series shares." The mention of potential fines appeared to have had the desired effect. There were no further brushback pitches thrown on either side. "I have to have control of the game," Umont said. "That the only way it's going to be. If things had continued, I'm sure someone would have been fined. However, Dick and Red were great about it. There was no question about any pitches after that." Williams, though, was not happy. "The St. Louis Cardinals are as bush as the name of the beer company that owns them," he said.

While the first inning contretemps appeared to douse the competitive fires of the Red Sox, the Cardinals became energized. Case in point: Boston starting pitcher Gary Bell couldn't make it out of the second

The speedy Lou Brock is safe at second as Boston's Mike Andrews and Rico Petrocelli helplessly look on. PHOTO BY DENNIS BREARLEY/ BOSTON RED SOX

inning as St. Louis bats bludgeoned him for five hits and three runs. "I had a good fast ball," Bell said. "I felt real good, but every time I threw my curve, those guys hit it solidly for base hits. I just couldn't do anything about it." Brock began the hitting barrage with a lead-off triple in the home half of the first that careened off the wall in left-center. Flood then followed with a single to drive him home, his first RBI of the Series. The Cardinals were up by a run and Mike Shannon increased the lead to 3–0 the next inning with a two-run blast into the left field grandstand seats. "A World Series homer has to be something special, but you know it's easier to play in this park than Fenway," Shannon said. "You're more relaxed because you don't have that big wall staring you in the eye. The park here is really a better one for hitters. At Fenway all you think about [is] the wall and the left fielder can play you shorter and catch balls you can't catch here."

Shannon's blow turned out to be the game-winner as Briles tamed the Sox for the remainder of the contest. The lone exceptions were a run-scoring single by Mike Andrews in the sixth that drove in Dalton Jones and a Reggie Smith homer in the seventh. Briles otherwise coasted on his deceptive no windup delivery and steady diet of fastballs and off-speed pitches to the heart of the Boston batting order. "I was a little nervous at the start," Briles admitted. "But I'm a little nervous at the start of every game. My adrenalin kept pumping and I tried to slow down." Withal the adrenalin levels, Sox hitters were loath to give Briles any credit. Not only were they mad at the stocky Californian for hitting Yastrzemski, they were also furious at some earlier comments he had made in the newspapers about the Sox being "a weak hitting team." "The guy talks like he's Sandy Koufax—he's a big mouth," Andrews said. "I think we were so mad at him that we were overanxious at the plate and couldn't hit. He really isn't a good pitcher. In fact, I think he's the weak link in their pitching staff." Jerry Adair, hitless in four plate appearances against Briles, agreed with his teammate's comments. "We got all fouled up," he said. "Everyone was . . . not waiting for good pitches. I just hope we get another shot at the bush-leaguer." Briles, who appeared in 452 games during his 14-year big-league career, was not without his own grievances. The Sox "made us sound [in the media] like our pitching staff was Bob Gibson and a bunch of guys named Harry," he claimed. "My name isn't Harry. They'd better bring lunch if they think that." Despite all the back and forth bickering, long time *Boston Globe* sportswriter Harold Kaese found a silver lining. "It may be a good thing for baseball," Kaese posited. "Recent World Series have been marked by more decorum than an opera buffet. . . . As a result the World Series has become more and more of a baseball social event, almost acquiring an All Star Game conviviality. But in these games the Cardinals and Red Sox were all about one another's threats and the Cardinals must have been better at it than the other side."

The Cardinals were even more dominant in Game 4. They blanked the Sox 6–0 to edge within a victory of the championship on the basis of yet another lights out performance by Bob Gibson. "I thought he was just a thrower in that first game," a humbled Yastrzemski said afterward. "But today he proved to me he's a great pitcher. He didn't challenge me like he did in the game before. He kept turning the ball over, pitching me low and away this time. He made some great pitches and the way he can move the ball around really made a believer out of me, even though I was able to get a couple of hits off him." Gibson, working on three days' rest for the first time all season, struck out five and scattered five hits in a complete game effort representing his fourth straight victory in World Series competition dating back to 1964. "He threw 130 pitches, the most he's thrown since coming back from his injury," Red Schoendienst noted. "He tossed 122 against Atlanta in one game but he did it with more rest than he had for today's game." The lack of recovery time showed. "I wasn't as sharp as I was in the opening game," Gibson said. "I wasn't strong and I knew it. So I threw many more sliders and curves than fastballs today. Even so, I was real tired in the eighth and ninth. I had to force myself."

The Redbird offense gave Gibson all the run support he needed, sprinting out to a 4–0 lead in the first inning against Boston's Jose Santiago. Santiago had pitched well enough to win the first game, but he was no mystery on this damp, blustery day where many of the 54,575 in attendance could be seen wearing heavy outer coats and earmuffs. A two-run double to left by Roger Maris and RBI singles by Tim McCarver and Dal Maxvill forced Santiago's departure before the inning's third out had even been recorded. "I had better stuff than I had the other day and felt better," Santiago said afterward. "And I feel I was keeping the ball down better. But I guess you got to be lucky in this game." Maris, picking up his fourth and fifth RBIs in the Series, was more matter-of-fact about his own contribution. "It's just another game and you have to win it, so you bust your gut trying to do that, as you do all season," he commented.

Dick Williams replaced Santiago with Gary Bell—the previous day's losing pitcher—to stop the bleeding. And while the right-hander did his job by inducing Gibson to fly out to end the inning, the Cardinal offense was not finished. They erupted for two additional runs in the bottom of the third off Jerry Stephenson, Bell's successor and the third Boston pitcher Williams used up to that point. (Dave Morehead and 19-year-old rookie Ken Brett, the older brother of future Kansas City Royals Hall of Famer George Brett, would later make game appearances as well.) McCarver drove in the first run and his second of the game on a sacrifice fly to center after Orlando Cepeda had doubled and advanced to third on a wild pitch. Next batter Mike Shannon, reaching on a one-out walk, completed the successful run when Javier doubled into the left field corner to plate him. Gibson took over from there. "With that lead the fellows gave me," Gibson said, "I just wanted to throw strikes." He did that and much more. "I recall most the surgical precision he had," Nelson Briles told author Peter Golenbock years later. "He had his 'A' game, with everything together. His pitch selection was good, and he was able to make his pitches. Just the whole thought process and physical execution were together at one time. And when you see an athlete do that, sometimes it's just for one moment or one game. When you see the mastery, that's special. When you see that, that's a special moment." Reggie Smith experienced his own "special moment" during the contest. After hitting a long foul ball off Gibson, Smith received a threatening glare from the pitcher that froze him in his tracks. "It scared me to death," Smith remembered. "He sent a stare right through me, like, 'Who do you think you are?' I thought for sure there was a knockout coming, but he fooled me with a slider that I tapped out in front of the plate. McCarver picked it up and tagged me." Smith, known for his own fiery competitiveness, later claimed the moment represented "the closest I ever came to being intimidated."

Equally eyebrow raising was Yastrzemski's all out sprint to third on a fly ball to right in the ninth. He had led off the inning with a double. Irate St. Louis fans believed he was deliberately trying to sabotage Gibson's chances of recording the first World Series shutout of his career. "Certainly I did," Yastrzemski said. "I wanted him to earn the shutout and besides, why shouldn't I do everything possible to get a run even at that stage of the ball game. Who knows what could happen. I heard the fans giving me the business and it didn't bother me a bit." What was troublesome was how close to the brink of elimination the Red Sox were. As Al Hirshberg of the *Boston Herald-Traveler* wrote, "You thought of 1951, the year of the little miracle of Coogan's Bluff-Bobby Thomson's home run that clinched the pennant for the New York Giants. The Giants lost the World Series. You wondered what difference that made. Nobody remembers that series, and everybody remembers Bobby Thomson. And, unless the Red Sox win it with more fireworks, nobody will remember this series. They will remember 1967 as the year of the Red Sox, the year of the Yaz. Which really made you feel pretty good as you sat watching Gibson shut the Red Sox out Sunday." Yastrzemski, still smarting from Briles's painful drilling from Saturday's game, wasn't willing to throw in the towel. "It still takes four games to win it," he said. "We are going to come back, believe me. It's going to be tough but we can do it—and we will do it."

## Chapter Eight

# Lonborg and Champagne

Apart from Gibson, no Cardinal had contributed more to St. Louis's commanding 3–1 Series lead than Lou Brock. Through four games he was batting a team leading .500 with eight base hits, three stolen bases, and five runs scored. Of those eight hits, three were for extra bases—a triple and two doubles. His bat was hotter than Yastrzemski's and he would add four more hits and a homer before the postseason was over. "People were beginning to believe that Brock was ten feet tall and that he could run the 90 feet between the bases in nothing flat and that he was able to hit 450-foot home runs whenever necessary," wrote nationally syndicated columnist Milton Gross. As Red Schoendienst would muse after the Series, "What is there he can't do? He can hit with power. He can steal. He can take the extra base and turn singles into doubles. He *has* to be the most exciting player in the league." Yet the road to baseball superstardom had been far from a smooth one for the All-Star outfielder.

Raised in poverty in Collinston, a small rural village in northern Louisiana that strictly adhered to the segregationist mores of the pre–civil rights era, Louis Clark Brock learned early the corrosive effects racism and bigotry had on the soul. It was not uncommon to have local white kids express their contempt for Brock and his friends by spitting on them. "It was just a struggle to be a decent human being," he remembered. But Brock and his eight siblings always had the love and devotion of their single mother Paralee, a domestic worker, to fall back on. "I knew she gave a damn and wanted me to grow up to be respectable," he said. It wasn't easy. He'd often get into fights and once savagely beat a classmate who had been bullying him. "Well, we got into it, and I finally fetched him a good one, and he went down like a pole-axed steer. I mean he was out cold," Brock remembered. Not even a few well applied sprinkles of water could revive him. "I'd never seen anybody like that before," he said. "I was afraid I'd kill him. I can't recall ever being so scared. He finally came to, but I never tangled with anybody after that." The entire frightening episode did teach him an important life lesson, however. "Sometimes winning something costs you, and you have to learn that," he said.

Baseball entered his life by way of more personal misbehavior. Aiming a spitball at a little girl in his class one day, Brock missed and ended up hitting his fourth grade teacher. "You can believe me she was mad," Brock recalled. Instead of employing corporal punishment, which was all too common for the day, the teacher ordered him to go to the local library and find out all he could on ballplayers like Joe DiMaggio and Don Newcombe and report back his findings. After some poking around in the stacks, Brock discovered to his astonishment that it was common for major leaguers to collect up to eight dollars a day in meal money. "Now what in the world, I said to myself, were they making a *week*?" Henceforward, baseball became the preferred means by which he would escape the privations of Collinston. Of course, it helped that he had the raw ability to play the game. Hitting came naturally to him and he possessed a throwing arm that was strong and accurate. He also displayed a ferocious inner drive to succeed; he didn't as much play games as attack them. "Hustle's my creed," he once explained. "That's what I live by. I have to."

Brock used the same approach in his studies. "I was always academically oriented," he pointed out. "It was a matter of pride and self-esteem. You don't want to be the dumbest kid in the school. Not the smartest necessarily, but not the dumbest. . . . I wanted to be able to hold my own in a crowd." This is not to say there were moments when he felt overwhelmed by the odds then stacked against a young black man seeking to better himself. "In my sophomore year, I felt like stopping," he confessed. "I'd seen so many [friends] who had graduated, but they fell right back [into poverty and destitution]. What was the sense of going to school where there just weren't any jobs open to us and there were no places to live?" These doubts, however, dissolved with Brock's increasing confidence in himself. After all, Jackie Robinson, one of his boyhood heroes, had faced similar obstacles and still prevailed. "If a man is motivated, he'll do anything, regardless of what it costs," Brock said.

While he earned top academic honors and represented his high school in math and science competitions, his main focus remained on the baseball diamond. "All I ever wanted was a bat in my hands," he said. After wrapping up an outstanding senior season in which he batted .535, Brock looked forward to attending college on a baseball scholarship. But no avalanche of recruitment offers followed. In fact, things were looking downright bleak until the historically black Southern University in nearby Baton Rouge came through with an academic scholarship. Majoring in mathematics, Brock experienced a rough transition to college life. Away from home and his supportive family for the first time, his grades suffered and he saw his scholarship revoked. He faired a little better on the playing field, making the school's varsity baseball squad as a walk-on freshman. During tryouts he had first caught his coaches' attention when he passed out shagging flies in the outfield on a particularly warm day. Taking pity on him after he regained consciousness through the aid of some smelling salts, they let him take batting practice and were astonished by the results. "I took five swings and hit four out of the ballpark," Brock said. The performance led to an athletic scholarship but a tepid .140 batting average invoked no comparisons to Willie Mays or Stan Musial. "I kept the air around home plate cool," he said.

That same air heated up the following season when Brock rediscovered his swing and batted over .500 with 13 homers in 27 games. "That first year, you never know (what you're doing)," Brock claimed. "I was a freshman. You're running around with your head cut off. The second year, I knew what a fastball was, and could distinguish it from a curveball." Making that sophomore year extra special was his selection by the United States Olympic Committee to play in the 1959 Pan-American Games in Chicago. There he met a brash young boxer from Louisville, Kentucky, destined to become the heavyweight champion of the world. "I was walking into the U.S. camp, carrying a suitcase in each hand and looking at the ground," Brock recalled. "I heard somebody say, 'If you're a boxer, I'll take you on right now. That's how I met Cassius Clay [now

Muhammad Ali]." Brock would also cross paths with another great athletic talent who would win a silver medal at the games as a steeplechase runner—Deacon Jones. The future All-Pro defensive end and NFL Hall of Famer impressed upon Brock the importance of technique and preparation when it came to running. "Lou learned [these things] from Deacon, by watching him on the track, taking off from the blocks, accelerating, hitting full stride," maintained Franz Schulze, Brock's biographer. "Lou studied Deacon day after day and decided there were important things a ballplayer could learn from [a track athlete]. He filed what he saw, stashed it away in his head, where it stayed securely, waiting to be utilized at some later date."

Major league scouts now flocked to Baton Rouge to take a close look at the lanky, free-swinging undergrad. And nothing they saw dissuaded them from the belief they were witnessing a future star. Although his overall offensive numbers dipped somewhat his junior year ("I didn't think the pitchers would throw strikes to me. But they did—and it taught me a lesson," he explained), Brock remained a highly rated prospect. His rising stock had received a further lift when he accepted an invitation to work out at Wrigley Field. "I weighed about 180 pounds then—I always go about 165 now—and was hitting quite a few balls out," he told *The Sporting News* in 1964. "The scouts and front-office brass came out and they couldn't believe me at first." Cubs field boss Lou Boudreau, a Hall of Famer who had piloted the Cleveland Indians to their last World Series championship in 1948, was especially taken aback. He "told me that I had a very quick bat and said I had everything it took to succeed in the major leagues," Brock said.

Deciding against returning to Southern University for his senior year, Brock opted to join the Cubs in 1961 for a reported $30,000 signing bonus. "Sports, I decided, was a young man's game, so I took the chance," he recalled. "I knew I had something to fall back on. I had only one year to go in school, so if I fell flat on my face in baseball, the other was still attainable." Shipped to Chicago's Class C minor league franchise in St. Cloud, Minnesota, Brock overcame a major case of jitters during his first professional at-bat. "The ball seemed to get small, but I made up my mind to be sure to get my rips, from the moment I left the dugout, and I hit the first pitch for a home run," he said. More big hits followed as he closed out the season with a .361 average and 117 runs scored. Though St. Cloud was only one step removed from the bottom of the Cubs' minor league system, the parent club showed no hesitation in promoting him permanently to their big-league roster the following spring. They really couldn't afford not to given how poorly the team was performing.

Despite being graced with the Hall of Fame talents of shortstop Ernie "Mister Cub" Banks, Chicago's best showing over the previous decade and a half had been a pair of fifth-place finishes. Making matters worse was a lack of overall leadership and direction at the top. After removing Boudreau from the dugout following the 1960 season, eccentric Cubs owner and chewing gum magnate P. K. Wrigley settled on the bizarre idea of replacing him with a rotation of different managers called the "College of Coaches." "We certainly cannot do much worse trying a new system than we have done for many years under the old," Wrigley said. The team became the butt of jokes around the circuit but Brock was not amused. "It was like being in a prison yard with everyone waiting for you to do something wrong," he remembered. As expected, the Cubs did not improve under the new system and continued to flounder deep in the standings. "Manager?" a flustered Brock later vented to Rick Talley of the *Chicago Tribune*. "We didn't have one. Just 14 Indians and 14 chiefs. And you couldn't believe the jealously among the coaches. One would come to me and say 'you're my man.' Then another would say 'you'll just hit against right handers because you can't hit left handed pitching.' Then another would say 'you're not gonna mess up my two weeks as head coach.'"

Brock's development as a player suffered from the surrounding turmoil. He received minimal instruction and maximum frustration. It showed in his on-field performance. In his two full seasons with the Cubs, he put up pedestrian numbers at the plate (.263 in 1962 and .258 in 1963) and was considered a defensive liability. "He was not a good outfielder in Chicago," confirmed general manager Bing Devine, Brock's future boss in St. Louis. "He made a lot of mistakes. But he was under a lot of pressure out there. He was young and everybody was saying how great he'd be." Cubs pitcher Larry Jackson observed close up what toll that pressure was taking. "He'd break out in a big sweat just putting on a uniform," Jackson said. "His desire was so intense that he made things tough for himself." Brock concurred: "There I was, in the outfield at Wrigley Field—and I still believe right field in Chicago is the toughest in baseball because of the varying shades of light that come from behind home plate—and it was trial and error." Nor did Brock receive any confidence boost when the team elected to shift him to the top of the batting order. "All through sandlot, high school, and college ball, I'd been an RBI hitter," he said. "Always batted two, three, or four in the lineup. Now, all of a sudden, I'm hitting leadoff and they're telling me to choke up on the bat. I didn't know how. It took me two years to make that adjustment." Fortunately, veteran teammate and two-time NL MVP Ernie Banks was around to offer constructive words of support and advice. "Ernie was my roommate for two years," Brock later told *Sport* magazine. "He was real good for me, I used to worry about how good the pitchers were. He told me never to think that way. He said I should go to bed every night thinking I could hit everybody. I used to fall asleep at night with Ernie asking me if I could hit Koufax, Drysdale, Podres. . . . I'd keep saying yes until I fell asleep."

Impatient with Brock's progress and in desperate need of quality starting pitching, the Cubs traded him to the Cardinals in June 1964 for what they judged to be an excellent return—18-game winning right-hander Ernie Broglio. "If you want to hit the bull's eye, you have to take a shot at it," Wrigley said. Only this shot fell wide of the mark as Broglio had a sore pitching arm. He won only 7 games against 13 losses for Chicago over the next three seasons before finally calling it a career in 1966. "Nowadays, they'd have you go in and get checked out by a doctor before making a trade, but that wasn't how things were done back then," Broglio later told baseball historian Ed Attanasio. "The Cardinals knew. They were keeping it quiet. In 1961, I took 20 cortisone shots in my shoulder—before every other start. They thought they were getting away with something." Though Devine always denied having any knowledge of Broglio being damaged goods, he and Redbird manager Johnny Keane had kept close tabs on Brock. "I remembered two things," Keane recalled. "I remembered watching the Cubs play Philadelphia one night. Lou hit a line drive 450 feet to center field that never went more than 20 feet off the ground. And I remembered him beating out a bang-bang grounder to Ken Boyer at third base. Kenny said there was no way Brock could do that—and Kenny was right."

Once it became obvious that Brock could be acquired in a trade, Devine and Keane knew they had to pull the trigger. "We liked his speed and, I might add, his power," Devine said. "But we had no way of knowing then that he'd become one of the all-time record-breakers, a Cardinal in the class of Bob Gibson and Stan Musial." Interestingly, the Cardinal locker room was not enthusiastic about the move. Off to a disappointing start, the team thought the addition of an underachieving lead-off hitter from one of the worst teams in the majors would have little effect. "None of us liked the deal," Bill White said. "We lie and say we did, but we didn't like the deal. In my opinion Lou had a lot of talent, but he didn't know anything about baseball." Curt Flood sarcastically wondered aloud if White would be the next teammate to go on the trading block "for two broken bats and a bag of peanuts." Brock had his own doubts. "When I heard the Cards gave up Broglio to get me, I asked myself why they did it," he admitted.

All the same, Brock felt liberated. "The beauty of my being traded from the Cubs to the Cardinals was not the moving from one club to another—but the change in attitude," he said. Indeed, the Cardinals were all about winning and getting results. "Among the first things I noticed with St. Louis . . . was that the club was run on the principle of individual independence. If you wanted to do something, you did it; you didn't have to fill out forms," Brock said. It was like he had moved from the dull grayness of Kansas as depicted in the 1939 movie classic *Wizard of Oz* to the vibrant Technicolor of Emerald City. "You couldn't do everything, of course," Brock went on. "You didn't spit in Johnny Keane's eye, for instance. Furthermore, there was a full system of signals from the coaches, as with any other ballclub. Nevertheless, if you felt like taking extra batting practice on a given day, you took it. In Chicago, somebody told you to take it. If *he* didn't, *you* didn't." Brock appreciated the honesty and forthrightness shown by Keane as well. The Cardinals manager didn't play mind games and told Brock in their first meeting after the trade he would be the team's starting left fielder no matter what. "We know you can do it all," he told Brock. "We're going to stay with you all the way."

Heartened by these words of encouragement, Brock responded with the finest season of his young career. He hit a robust .348 with 12 homers, 21 doubles, 9 triples, and 44 RBIs in 103 games for the Cards. Equally striking was his performance on the base paths as he stole 33 bases. If you add the 10 bags he swiped in 52 games for the Cubs earlier in the year, Brock almost doubled his previous seasonal high in the majors. "When Lou gets a base on balls, that's a two-base walk," Mike Shannon joked. All of this was not achieved by chance. Keane had given him a green light and he relished the opportunity of taking on opposing defenses. "Running is a challenge," he said. "It adds spice to the game for me. It's a little cat-and-mouse game that can upset the pitcher and an entire infield if you play it right." Given the Cards propensity to play for one run and not the big inning, this was an ideal match between player and ball club. "The Cardinals were a scrambling team," Brock said. "They were built for speed and daring." With Brock leading off and constantly getting on base, the St. Louis offense began to click, winning 28 of their remaining 39 contests. "Presto," Bob Gibson said. "We were transformed." But a holdout skeptic like Philadelphia Phillies manager Gene Mauch, whose slumping team the Cardinals overtook for the pennant at the close the 1964 regular season, refused to give credit. He chose instead to target the one aspect of Brock's game that still needed improvement: defense. "Gene Mauch said we couldn't win the pennant with that double-dribbler in left field," complained Brock, who committed 11 errors on the year. "When we got to Philadelphia in September, I looked all around the ballpark for a basketball. If I could have found one, I would have dribbled out to left field in practice, just to show Gene Mauch that I wasn't bothered by what he said any more." As the seasons progressed, Brock developed into a better than average defender, using his superior foot speed to get to balls others couldn't reach. As the author and journalist Ray Robinson noted, "In the field Brock is no Curt Flood—but he still covers his position as well as most of them."

During the 1964 World Series, Brock gave further proof of his emerging greatness. Although he didn't steal any bases and suffered an uncharacteristic 0-for-14 hitless spell midway through, Brock still managed to produce when it counted against the heavily favored Yankees.

In Game 7, for example, he blasted a solo shot over everything in right field that led to a three-run St. Louis explosion in the fifth inning. This sealed the victory and the Series for the Cardinals. His final Series stat line read 9 for 30 for a .300 average, second only to Tim McCarver on the team. "He turned a corner overnight," Keane said. "He was not a great ballplayer in Chicago but he suddenly became a great ballplayer for us—much better than we thought he'd be, much sooner. And we thought he'd be very good for us." Proving 1964 was no fluke, Brock continued to perform at a high level the next two seasons. He hit for high average and demonstrated he was a serious long-ball threat with 30 homers.

But where he really earned a reputation was as the game's most feared baserunner, surpassing even the legendary Maury Wills of the Dodgers, a six-time league stolen base champion battling injuries and getting on in years. Brock earned the crown outright in 1966 by leading the NL in steals (74), the first of four consecutive seasons he finished first in that category. "This guy has an inner conceit, an arrogance," observed television broadcaster and former Cardinals receiver Joe Garagiola. "There are probably other players who can lick him in a straight race. But on those bases he's the best. I guess the only way to stop him is to sneak into the clubhouse and burn his spikes."

Brock would not have argued the point. "I don't believe that I can be thrown out stealing second base if I get the proper jump on the pitcher," he said. "If they pitch out on me, most of the time I can anticipate the pitchout." Brock acquired his base-stealing acumen through an intense study of pitchers and their individual flaws, often using a stopwatch to time how long it took for their throws to reach home plate. He also made innovative use of an eight-millimeter handheld movie camera during spring training games to capture the idiosyncrasies of opponents like Cy Young Award–winner Don Drysdale. "I could spend every night with [Drysdale] and his motion stuck in a frame so I could study it. And there was nothing he could do about it," he revealed to Ira Berkow of the *New York Times*.

This wealth of data all added up in the end. "Pitchers can be put in categories," Brock maintained. "It's like keeping a card file in the back of your head. When you learn to read a pitcher, you wait until you know he's going to the plate, then call upon your technique to set you in motion." And a big part of his technique involved using a shorter lead. "By taking a shorter lead and looking relaxed, my body is telling the pitcher I'm not going to run," Brock explained. "Standing there, relaxed, up right, I'm causing doubts. All people who sprint start from a low position. The pitcher associates a low stance with running. He's conditioned to believe it's impossible to run from a straight-up position. I do."

The Cardinals required no subterfuge in determining Boston's chances of coming back from a 3–1 deficit in the Series. They felt they were the same as The Beatles getting crewcuts. But their certitude was about to be rudely put to the test, for starting on the mound for Boston in Game 5 was a grimly determined Jim Lonborg. Coming off a near no-hitter in the second game, the "Stanford slinger" was only slightly less brilliant this time around before a crowd of 54,575 anxious St. Louisans. He held the Cardinals to three hits and a single earned run in a 3–1 complete game victory to stave off Series elimination for the Sox. "I think I was meaner psychologically that morning than at any time in my career," Lonborg commented afterward. "That's why I waited until just before game time to come to Busch Stadium. I was walking through the streets with my own thoughts."

Whatever those thoughts were, the Cardinals didn't have an answer—or a prayer. "I could pick the ball up better, but he was a lot tougher to handle than in Boston," said Mike Shannon, who went hitless in his second consecutive game against Lonborg. "He threw me four fast balls. I got only one the first time but [in Busch Stadium], he seemed to change. I guess he realizes you can pick up that big curve of his better than in Fenway." Lonborg, despite suffering from a nasty head cold, shut them out through eight innings before giving up a booming homer to Roger Maris over the fence in right with two outs in the bottom of the ninth. It marked the Cardinal outfielder's sixth career Series home run. Orlando Cepeda, who had entered the game with only 2 hits in his previous 15 plate appearances, followed with a weak groundout. "Maris hit a change-up, and I'd have thrown him the change even if I did have only a 1–0 lead," Lonborg said. "I've been getting him out with the change all year." Then the right-hander stopped himself. "All year? I mean in the Series. It seems like a year."

Lonborg had readied himself for the contest the previous Sunday evening by holing up in his hotel room and watching the hit television spy series "Mission: Impossible." "That is what a lot of people here said the Red Sox were embarking upon Monday against the St. Louis Cardinals," Lonborg claimed. He added he found it noteworthy the episode's storyline didn't end but carried over to the following week: "That's the way things turned out Monday—we still are going and the next act [Game 6] is to be played Wednesday [October 11] at Fenway Park." Sox bats secured the outcome by squeezing out three runs on six hits and an error. The first run came in the third when Ken Harrelson punched a base hit through the left side of the St. Louis infield with two out. The hit drove in Joe Foy, who had singled and advanced on a sacrifice by Andrews. "I just knew I was going to hit the ball hard," Harrelson said of his RBI single. "In fact, I felt pretty certain that I would get it between short and third because they were playing me straight away and left a big hole in that spot." The Sox sealed the victory with two more tallies in the top of the ninth.

With the bases loaded, Elston Howard hit a "dying quail" before a charging Maris in short right field to bring home George Scott, the lead runner. "What a smash!" Howard sarcastically remarked afterward. Reggie Smith, who had earlier doubled, came round to score from second on the same play when Maris's hurried throw to the plate sailed over McCarver's head. The Cardinals receiver managed to get a glove on the ball, but lost the handle when he attempted a sweeping tag. Smith easily slid in for the final Boston tally of the game. "I knew Maris couldn't get the ball and Scott played it right because he could have tagged up if Maris did make it," Smith explained. "It's tough to make a shoe-string catch and make a throw to the plate when you're off-balance. But I was running because I was certain the ball was going to fall in and I was right on Scott's heels." Maris was charged with an error. "I was going from the plate toward the line and when I got the ball, I had to let go in a hurry," he explained. Rookie Cardinals starter Steve Carlton was pegged with the loss, even though he had pitched fairly effectively. "He just had no luck," Gibson later said. Even with luck, it probably would not have made a difference. "Let's face it," Red Schoendienst said. "Lonborg did another great job. He just had us off balance all day. We swung at a lot of bad pitches and we didn't have many good swings." Lonborg could not have put it any better. "I felt great out there," he said. "I went with a fast ball most of the way, hitting the outside corners. Then when they seemed to start getting good rips at it, I started to rely more on my breaking ball."

Lonborg and his teammates had received all the motivation they needed when Dick Williams posted a scathing Jim Murray piece on the team's locker room bulletin board prior to the game. "The Boston Red Sox are now the Boston Dead Sox," the acerbic California columnist had written following Sunday's one-sided loss. "The Hose have holes in them. The only thing they lead the Cardinals in is long names. They are the Boston Sad Sox. Put them on the Boston & Albany and ice them down good. Run the statehouse flag to half-mast, lay a wreath on Plymouth Rock." Yastrzemski, who went 1-for-3 in the game, couldn't believe the piece's harsh tone. "It was like a guy kicking a crippled kid because he was down like we [were], 3–1," the AL MVP said.

The Red Sox completed their comeback two days later when they returned to what syndicated columnist Red Smith called their "seedy little playpen on Boston's Jersey street" for Game 6. Paced by a record-setting home run performance and the superb pitching of surprise rookie starter Gary Waslewski, the Sox downed the Cardinals, 8–4, to force a winner-take-all seventh game. "The Red Sox, a gung-ho ball club if there ever was one, continue to pile one incredibility atop the another," wrote *New York Times* columnist Arthur Daley. "Insuperable obstacles faze them not a whit." Waslewski, who had been acquired in the 1965 minor league draft, exemplified this defiant spirit. He had once been considered a so-so prospect, but Dick Williams selected him over veterans Gary Bell and Jose Santiago to start the crucial sixth game. "I have every confidence in the world [in] him if he throws as well as he's capable of doing," Williams said. But then, the tall right-hander of mixed Polish and Native American heritage had always been a bit of a mystery to the Boston manager. "Most guys I can figure," Williams told the *Christian*

*Science Monitor*. "But Waslewski never gives you any emotion. You talk to him and he just stands there and looks at you." Indeed, Waslewski didn't flinch when Williams informed him of his pitching assignment two days earlier. "A lot of guys would have taken that message home with them and thought about it every minute," Williams said. "They'd have driven themselves crazy trying to live with it. But I knew Gary wouldn't do that."

It was Waslewski's ability to respond well under pressure that had endeared him to Williams. Back when Williams was still managing Toronto in the International League, Waslewski had been his ace after his skipper offered some helpful advice. "I told him to stop trying to be a Thomas Edison," Williams said. "I told him to stop experimenting. Finally, he got rid of his slow curve and stuck to the fast ball." Williams did not politely ask Waslewski to change his pitch selection so much as demand it in his usual inimitable way. "I had to insult the devil out of him," Williams confessed. While Waslewski didn't appreciate all the "hollering and yelling," there was no disputing the results. He won a league-leading 18 games in 1966 while pitching the Maple Leafs to the IL championship. "I was the guy he put on the mound against the teams we had to beat, which back then would have been Rochester and Richmond," Waslewski said. "Dick said I was a big-game pitcher. Little did I know, back then, what that would lead to." But the 26-year-old University of Connecticut product, whose repertoire included a fastball, a hard slider, and a fork ball, had developed shoulder problems during spring training and pitched in only 12 games during the 1967 regular season. He compiled a 2–2 record with 20 strikeouts and a 3.21 ERA. As unremarkable as these numbers were, Williams never lost faith in him, especially after he came in and threw three innings of shutout relief against the Cards in the third game. "I remember saying to myself, if I screw up, everybody in the world is going to see it!" Waslewski later said. "You screw up and, it's not just a local thing anymore!" Regardless of the fine outing, Williams was well aware of the gamble he was taking. "I knew I was going out on a limb by picking Waz," he acknowledged. "If we lost, I'd have been second-guessed."

Waslewski exceeded all expectations. He allowed just two runs on four hits in 5 1/3 innings. The Cardinal runs came on run scoring singles by Brock and Flood in the top of the third. "If he'd been pitching regularly, and maybe his legs were in better shape, I think he might have gone nine innings," Elston Howard said. "Actually, he started to tire in the fifth. He wasn't pushing off the mound as he did earlier in the game. He stopped pitching and started to aim the ball. But while he had it, his stuff was as good as Lonborg's." Waslewski confirmed his catcher's analysis. "I got tired," he said afterward. "I could feel it in my legs. I just ran out of gas." As for failing to qualify for the victory (that honor went instead to reliever John Wyatt), Waslewski professed not to care. He had given his team an opportunity to play for the championship the next day. That's all that mattered. "There were stories in the newspapers comparing my chances with General Custer's but I didn't let it bother me," Waslewski told the writer Jack Lautier. "I had pitched in 'must' games before and if I had my stuff, I figured I could win."

The Cardinals tacked on two more runs in the seventh on a Brock two-run homer to deep right center. But it would be Boston bats that made the loudest noise. They cranked out 11 hits and 4 home runs, including a Series record three round-trippers against St. Louis starter Dick Hughes in the fourth inning. "I didn't have my good stuff at all," Hughes said. "It's nothing mental at all. No, this park has nothing to do with it. I tried to reach back for something extra—and didn't have it." That was an understatement. Petrocelli touched the bespectacled right-hander for the first homer in the bottom of the second, hitting a long solo blast that cleared the Green Monster. "I think the wind blowing out to left carried [the ball] into the screen," he said. Petrocelli, who had gone hitless in his previous 10 at-bats entering the game, hit his second homer of the day two innings later on a Hughes fastball that also ended up in the left field screen. "I was really surprised when they gave me another fastball, and I tore into it," he said. Preceding Petrocelli's homer were long bombs by Yastrzemski and Reggie Smith. "Each drive shook Fenway," Yastrzemski recalled of the thunderous fan response. "In the dugout, you could feel the benches swaying, your teeth chattering." Yaz, who had singled in the first, took particular satisfaction from correctly guessing Hughes's pitch selection. "I thought [Hughes] was going to keep it away from me when I led off the fourth," he explained. "I saw one on the outside corner and I went with it, crushing it hard enough to land into the screen in left center."

Smith, notching his second homer of the Series, also guessed right. "I was waiting for a breaking pitch because I figured I'd been set up with two fast balls," he said. "That's what I got." The rest of the Boston's game offense came in the bottom of the seventh when a Jerry Adair sacrifice fly and singles by Jones, Andrews, and Smith added up to four runs. "It really helps being home," Yastrzemski said in the loose Boston clubhouse afterward. "The crowd gives us a big boost."

For Smith, his performance on the day represented the capstone to an exceptional rookie campaign. After a slow start, in which the *Christian Science Monitor*'s Phil Elderkin wrote, it was "almost impossible to say enough bad things about Reggie Smith's first 100 at-bats," the speedy switch-hitter found his stroke. Though he averaged only .246, Smith hit 15 homers while driving in 61 in 565 at-bats. The performance came as no surprise to Williams who had coached Smith in Toronto. "He was an improving ball player with me each year I had him," Williams said. "The man's a super athlete, really super." Smith, who later starred for the Los Angeles Dodgers in the late 1970s, blamed his early season batting troubles on his own worrisome nature. "I was a rookie and I figured I had to prove myself quickly," he said. "A couple of times I caught myself bailing out at the plate—you know, pulling away from pitches I should have been hitting. I wondered if my slump would ever end. And then I got a couple of bloop hits in the same game late in June—real cheap singles—and since then I've been all right."

Having just witnessed his team dramatically even up the Series at three games apiece, the Red Sox manager Dick Williams now faced the daunting task of deciding who should start Game 7 on Thursday afternoon. Despite it being Santiago's scheduled turn in the rotation, Williams decided to go with Lonborg on two days' rest. Santiago had been terrific in a losing cause during the Series opener, but he had been roughed up badly in his next start and Williams was unwilling to risk a repeat performance. "I'll be damned if I lose a Game Seven with anybody but my ace," he said. Besides, Lonborg had already pitched on two days' rest twice before during the regular season, earning a solid if unspectacular split of the decisions. Williams wasn't afraid to roll the dice again as he had complete confidence in the Stanford graduate's ability to tame the Cards' offense, if only for a few critical innings. "I was praying for one last miracle," he admitted.

Although he was facing his fourth critical start in 11 days, Lonborg was confident. "I felt I could win anyway," he later said. "Even if I didn't have my best stuff. I always felt I could compensate with location and by tricking the batters. That's the difference between a pitcher who wins 15 and a pitcher who wins 20—being able to compensate to get by when he has poor stuff." The fact it would be St. Louis batters he would be facing made the task all the more easier in his mind. "The Cardinals are mostly all free swingers," he had told the *Christian Science Monitor* following his pulsating Game 5 victory. "Hitters like that are easier to set up than those who wait and try to punch the ball. I don't mean the Cardinals aren't good hitters. They are. But I figured I could beat 'em with the kind of stuff I throw."

On the Cardinals side, there was no doubt concerning whom Red Schoendienst would tap as his Game 7 starter. But in selecting Bob Gibson, who had won the deciding game of the 1964 World Series, the Redbirds manager was not without his detractors. "It is none of my business," a concerned St. Louis fan telegrammed Schoendienst, "[but] I cannot understand your reasoning for pitching Gibson tomorrow. If the Cards have lost today [in St. Louis] I would understand your pitching choice. Busch Stadium is not like Fenway Park [with its short fences]. Why take the chance and use Gibson after only [three] days' rest? It seems to me the Boston pitchers are all worn out." The truth of the matter was the Cardinals staff was not all that well rested either. "The only pitchers who didn't pitch for us in game six were Carlton, who had started the day before, and me," Gibson pointed out. "Red hadn't hesitated to use [Nelson] Briles, [Ray] Washburn, and [Larry] Jaster in relief because he knew all along that I would be pitching the seventh game, if there was one."

To get himself prepared mentally for the biggest game of the year and possibly his entire career, Gibson tried to purge his mind of all thoughts baseball the night before. "I'd been thinking about the Red Sox for ten days and there wasn't much left to think about," he said. He went to see his friend, the legendary Jazz pianist Les McCann, perform at a Boston nightclub before returning to his room at the Sheraton Motor Inn in suburban Quincy, where the Cards were staying. There he hoped to turn in early and catch a few winks. Only it didn't work out that way. Bothered by an aching tooth that required dental attention and a mysterious lack of air conditioning throughout the hotel, Gibson tossed and turned all evening. As he recalled, "I got as much rest as I could expect under the conditions and the next morning left myself about an hour to have some breakfast downstairs and catch the bus for the ballpark." Ordering scrambled eggs, ham, toast, and coffee, Gibson looked forward to eating a hearty meal before settling down to the serious business of the day. But after 45 minutes had elapsed, the food had still not arrived. "The waitress said that my order had somehow been lost," Gibson explained. Offered a plate of burnt toast instead, an irritated Gibson told the server to take

A fearsome sight to all batters: Bob Gibson on the mound. BASEBALL HALL OF FAME PHOTO ARCHIVE

it away. "We'll take *you* away," she responded. Maintaining his cool, Gibson concluded it wasn't worth engaging any further with the obviously aroused Red Sox fan. He calmly got up from his table and boarded the team bus waiting outside to take him to Fenway Park. "The bus had been delayed for me on the premise that it might useful for the starting pitcher to have something in his stomach, but after the toast episode I got the hell out of there," he said.

Gibson's edgy teammates, who were predisposed to thinking this incident was all part of an elaborate "New England plot" to derail the Cardinals' chances, were left incredulous. "We're going to the World Series, Game 7, and you haven't eaten breakfast?" Nelson Briles asked in amazement. Thinking fast, Bob Broeg of the *St. Louis Post Dispatch*, a fellow passenger on the bus, ordered the driver to pull over at the nearest red light. "I'll get off and get Hoot a couple of sandwiches," Broeg said. The longtime Cardinals beat writer flagged down a cab and proceeded to a nearby greasy spoon where he procured a pair of ham and egg sandwiches in a dripping brown takeout bag. Broeg triumphantly presented the bag to Gibson when he stopped by the visitors' clubhouse at Fenway a short time afterward. An appreciative Gibson greedily devoured one of the sandwiches on the spot but he downplayed the significance of the gesture. "Broeg has always been very proud of the role he played in the 1967 World Series and was crushed to find out years later that I often pitched on an empty stomach," he said. "In some ways, it helped to stay hungry."

Robert Gibson knew all about hunger. The youngest of seven children to a millworker and a laundress, Gibson experienced extreme hardship and privation while coming of age in the black ghetto of Omaha, Nebraska, in the late 1930s and 1940s. "They tell me my father died three months before I was born," he told author Roger Kahn. "We were poor people. Not only didn't I know my father, I've never seen his picture. There were no cameras in the four-room shack where I grew up." There were also few items of furniture as Gibson was forced to sleep on an old Army cot, which offered scant protection from the rats that regularly came out at night. "I was bitten on the ear," he said of one particularly unsettling encounter. But that was the least of his concerns. Getting him and his siblings enough food to eat proved a major challenge for his widowed mother Victoria. Yet somehow she managed to scrape by with the few dollars she earned working at a local laundry and cleaning houses on the side. "Maybe we didn't eat good, but we ate," Gibson said. "After Mom went to work in the morning, we would have to get ourselves ready for school. The only milk I remember having was evaporated milk and we added water to it to pour over our cereal." Ensuring the children were all properly clothed proved more problematic. Through many a bitterly cold Nebraskan winter, Gibson had to wear the same threadbare coat regardless of whether it fit or not. "It was a hand-me-down from one of my brothers and I wore it until it had too many holes in it," he said. His footwear options were equally limited: "I had one pair of shoes. No Sunday shoes, just one pair for every day of the week, and I wore them until they practically fell off my feet. When they got holes in the bottom, I put a piece of cardboard in them so the water would not seep through when it rained."

Gibson's family eventually improved their living situation by moving to a nearby housing project that provided heat and electricity, material comforts they heretofore had been unable to afford. But young Bob had a rude awakening when he arrived there. "The housing project was segregated," he later said. "The first thing I noticed was that the Negroes lived on one side of the project and the whites lived on the other side. At first it was something I took for granted and accepted the natural order of things. But when they start calling you names you begin noticing it, and you realize the reason they are calling you names is that you are a different color." It didn't help that there were precious few positive images of blacks in the broader American culture at the time. "All blacks had in those days was Stepin Fetchit, the [African American] movie clown," he said. "And I remember he embarrassed me, sitting right there in the theater, because he was making a fool of himself and others were making a fool out of him." Gibson refused to play a shuffling, Fetchit-like fool himself by responding to all racial taunts with his fists. "The fights were part of our daily life," he explained.

As much as he engaged in them, he was usually at a physical disadvantage. He suffered from a variety of ailments, including asthma, hay fever, rickets, a rheumatic heart, and pneumonia. "I hardly let him out of the house until he was 4 years old," his mother said. The bout with pneumonia had been the most serious, requiring Gibson to be hospitalized amid concerns for his life. "No, Robert, you're not going to die," his eldest brother Josh Gibson assured him. "And when you're well, I'm going to buy you a ball and glove." Josh, a college graduate who acted as a father figure and mentor to Gibson, was as good as his word. Gibson received his ball and glove and began playing the game in earnest under Josh's watchful supervision. "He's the one responsible for me learning all the fundamentals of the game and by God did he teach me fundamentals," Gibson said. "I never thought we were ever going to get a chance to really play in a ball game. And it wasn't just baseball. He had a knack of getting me involved in baseball, basketball, track or whatever else and he taught me the fundamentals of all the games to a point that I was always a little bit ahead of kids my own age, so I would never play with those kids, I would always play with the older kids."

His brother's relentless prodding eventually paid off as Gibson developed into a top three-sport athlete at Omaha Technical High School. And while he enjoyed competing as a record-breaking high jumper in track and starring on the baseball diamond, his first love was basketball. Filling out at a rugged 6 feet, 180 pounds his senior year, Gibson dominated the local hardwoods, leading his team to the state tournament and earning all-city honors as a small forward. "He's the boy with springs in his toes and basketball magic in his fingertips," raved the local newspaper. So proficient were his talents that he came under serious consideration for a full basketball scholarship to the University of Indiana. "I waited on pins and needles for their reply," Gibson said. Alas, he was destined to be disappointed. The eventual reply, which was addressed to his high school coach, read as follows, "Your request for an athletic scholarship for Bob Gibson has been denied because we already have filled our quota of Negroes." Heartbroken, Gibson did his best to put the sorry episode behind him, accepting a scholarship offer to attend the less prestigious Creighton University in Omaha. But the humiliation of being denied admission to Indiana on account of his race never left him. "*Quota of Negroes*!" he fumed in his autobiography. "That was a new one on me."

The transition to undergraduate life proved less traumatic though Gibson was noticeably unenthusiastic about Creighton. "It's a Jesuit school," he explained. "I'm not Catholic. You have your choice—take either religion or philosophy. I took philosophy. It turned out the philosophy was Jesuit philosophy. If you wanted to do well you had to indicate you thought the way they wanted you to think." Gibson, a sociology major, was given freer license to express himself athletically—he averaged over 20 points a game for the varsity basketball squad while earning additional kudos as a standout outfielder and pitcher. "We played only twelve or thirteen games a year, so I didn't get to pitch much," he said. "When I did I racked up a lot of strikeouts. I could always throw hard and I was a little wild and hitters were afraid to dig in up there. They just stood there and kind of waved at the ball." His raw pitching talent attracted big league attention and led Gibson to make a life-altering decision at age 22 in 1957. Only a few credits shy of a bachelor's degree, he opted to drop out of Creighton and sign a $4,000 contract to pitch for the Cardinals' Triple A affiliate in Omaha. "It was not $30,000 [the amount he initially sought], but to a kid out of the ghetto it seemed like a fortune," he said. As to why he chose to focus his energies on the pitcher's mound rather than the outfield where he hit conference-leading .340 as a senior, Gibson was characteristically pragmatic. "I felt I could get to the majors fastest as a pitcher," he said. "Outfielders are a dime a dozen, unless you're a Willie Mays."

Gibson's professional baseball career did not get off to a flying start. He spent most of his time on the bench in Omaha and when he was put into games, he experienced difficulty throwing strikes. "Gibson can throw a ball through the side of a barn if he could hit the barn," one team official commented. Gibson didn't disagree with this assessment. "All I had then was a fastball and a slider," he remembered. "No real curve, and no control." Dissatisfied with his performance, the Cards demoted him to their Class A franchise in Columbus, Georgia, the lowest rung of their minor league system. Gibson was devastated. "The last place in the world I wanted to go was Columbus, Georgia," he said. The emotional reaction went beyond his failure to pitch at a higher level. As he later told the writer Arnold Hano of *Sport* magazine, "In the North, you're segregated, but you don't know it. In Columbus, I knew it. I got a lot of static from the fans. One man called me 'Alligator Bait.' I laughed. I had no idea what he meant." He soon found out. "Negro kids used to be tied to the end of a rope and dragged through the swamps, to attract alligators," Gibson explained. "The Negro kid would be pulled out of the water and onto the shore, and the alligator would come out of the water after him. Then they'd catch the alligator. Alligator bait. That was what Negroes were good for, in Columbus." Despite the oppressive racial climate, Gibson pitched more frequently in Columbus and work out his control problems. By the end of the season, he had turned things around, compiling a respectable 4–3 record in 43 innings of work. "The need for long minor league experience often is overrated," Gibson said. "It's all a matter of getting to pitch. A guy could be in the minors 10 years and he wouldn't get here if he just pitched now and then."

Following in the footsteps of then All-Star Milwaukee Braves pitcher Gene Conley, who had been a power forward with the Boston Celtics in 1952 and who would resume his NBA career in 1958, Gibson chose to play professional basketball that off-season. He had recently married his high school sweetheart and was in need of the extra cash. Yet suiting up for the Harlem Globetrotters, a legendary touring outfit that staged theatrical hoop exhibitions around the country, had its own special rewards. "I did a lot of creative ball-handling for the Globetrotters, and as the shortest guy on the team, I was the one who broke out of the warm-up circle—where we spun the ball on our fingers and bounded it off each other's backsides—and started the dunking parade," he recalled. While dunking particularly captured Gibson's fancy (he specialized in a crowd-pleasing two-handed backward jam), other aspects of the Globetrotters style turned him off. "I never went too much for the clowning," he said of the team's emphasis on staging set comedy routines rather than seriously competing. "I enjoy playing basketball, period, and I always enjoyed the second and third periods most because that was when we usually played it straight. I was more amused than amusing." Unfortunately for Gibson, the Cardinals were not laughing, fearing he would seriously injure himself on the basketball court. He was advised to give up basketball, which he reluctantly agreed to do. "Really, it's hard to get hurt with the Globetrotters," he told the *Sporting News*. "I was mostly a straight man with them, but I could dribble behind my back and between my legs."

In 1958 Gibson received an invitation to pitch at the Cardinals major league spring training camp in St. Petersburg, Florida. "This was my big chance," he said. "I had less than a year's experience in professional baseball and I was being given an opportunity to train with the big team." He made enough of a good impression to be reassigned to Triple A ball in Omaha and Rochester, New York, during the regular season, where he went a combined 8–9 with a sparkling 2.84 ERA. Gibson took off from there, making the parent club the following summer and meeting Stan Musial for the first time. "I found Stan to be a friendly, talkative guy," said Gibson of the Hall of Fame great. "He was the same with everybody, whether you were a rookie or a ten-year veteran. He used to sit down and talk to me a lot. Not about anything in particular, just small talk, and he wasn't going out of his way to be especially nice to me. He talked with everyone, that's the kind of guy he is." Gibson had less kind words for Solly Hemus, his first big-league manager. "I was up and down [with Hemus]," Gibson said. "I'd start for a while, then I'd miss a turn. I never knew where I stood. I don't think Hemus had confidence in me. I couldn't have confidence in myself. I pitched once every 15 or 20 days. The result was my control was bad. . . . Hemus didn't care for me." Indeed, Hemus, a lifetime .273 hitting infielder with the Cards and Phillies, thought Gibson would never amount to much as a pitcher. "He had a lot to learn," Hemus contended. "He has great speed and great ability but he was putting the ball over the middle of the plate, I don't care who you are, you can't get away with that in the majors. If you get jocked, often enough, you learn something."

But Gibson believed then and later that Hemus's skepticism of his pitching ability had less to do with on-field performance and more with personal prejudice. "Either he disliked [black players] deeply or he genuinely believed that the way to motivate us was with insults," Gibson said. "The result was the same regardless. He would goad us, ridicule us, bench us—anything he could think of to make us feel inept." Gibson was backed up in this assessment by several of his black teammates, including outfielder Curt Flood. "Hemus acted as if I smelled bad," Flood claimed. "He avoided my presence and when he could not do that he avoided my eye." Hemus later strenuously denied these allegations, but his credibility on the issue was suspect due to an ugly incident that occurred in the second game of a doubleheader against Pittsburgh in 1959. Hemus, still playing in the field, was batting against an African American pitcher named Bennie Daniels when the tall right-hander from Compton, California, hit him on the leg. Accounts vary, but Hemus seems to have called Daniels either "a black son of a bitch" or a "black bastard" during a team meeting afterward. His comment understandably upset Gibson and other blacks on the roster. "We had been wondering how the manager really felt about us, and now we knew," Flood said.

Gibson developed a far more positive relationship with Johnny Keane, Hemus's successor. "I felt as if I had been let out of jail," Gibson remembered. "The day it happened, Keane came over to me and handed me the ball." The message was clear—Gibson would be in the starting rotation "come hell or high water." Gibson did his best to reward Keane's faith in him, averaging 17 wins, 14 complete games, and 206 strikeouts over the next two seasons. He also made the first of nine eventual All-Star Game appearances. "They don't like to hit against Gibson," Keane said. "He throws a heavy ball. He knocks the bats right out of their hands." For sure, the big right-hander was now being mentioned in the same breath as Sandy Koufax of the Los Angeles Dodgers, another flamethrower who had struggled with control issues early in his career before turning things around. In both cases, they had developed outstanding off-speed pitches to set up their fastballs and were not afraid to move around the strike zone. "My general plan was to stay on the outside corner and break up the [pitching] pattern now and then by coming inside to drive the batter away from the plate," Gibson said. Critics accused him of being a head-hunter, but statistics indicate Gibson hit only 0.83 percent of the batters he faced during his 17-year big-league career.

Still, this figure does not take into account the number of times Gibson brushed backed batters during the course of a contest. "The way he saw it," writes Josh Benjamin of the *Bleacher Report*, "he was the boss when he was on the mound, and if you crowded the plate, you were trespassing on his property. Even if the guy up at bat was a friend, he would go ahead and throw at him if he felt the need." Bill White was one such friend. After being traded to the Phillies in 1966, the All-Star first baseman leaned in on a pitch against Gibson one day and suffered the consequences. His elbow became ground zero for one of Gibson's patented fastballs. "I warned you, you-son-of-a-bitch," Gibson yelled. For his part, Gibson played down this controversial part of his game. "You hear about knockdowns, and to protect Cardinal hitters, I've thrown my share," he admitted. "But with the years, I throw at batters less and less. . . . I've come to realize that not everyone is bothered by knockdowns and some of them are afraid of my fastball, whether I throw at them or not."

Things only got better for Gibson in 1964. He upped his strikeout total to 245 and won a team-leading 19 games as he paced the Cardinals to the NL pennant, their first since 1946. "That was a wild pennant race that year, and toward the end of it the Cardinals had pushed me up to three days of rest instead of the four we usually got," Gibson said. Not that it mattered. Gibson became an unstoppable force down the stretch, winning 9 out of his last 11 decisions while providing four innings of relief in the pennant clincher. "He'd be exhausted at the end of the game," Keane said of his 1964 performance. "But I wanted to leave him in every game. I felt that he would do better for me, as tired as he was, than anybody in the bullpen. I had the feeling that he'd reach back and find one more pitch. There was no holding back with him. Another pitcher, you might not be sure he could reach back. You knew it with Gibson." In the World Series against the Yankees, Gibson's star shone even brighter. He took home Series MVP honors by setting a new postseason record with 31 strikeouts and winning two games, including a memorable Game 7 showdown at Yankee Stadium. Pitching on just two days' rest, a visibly exhausted Gibson held on to a 7–5 complete game victory, despite giving up homers to Mickey Mantle, Clete Boyer, and Phil Linz. "I still had good control," Gibson said. "I wanted to throw hard and I wasn't worrying about corners. I was trying to put 'em right down the middle. . . . I did—and you see what happened." In perhaps one of the greatest compliments ever paid to a ballplayer by a manager, Johnny Keane told reporters afterward that at no point did he have any intention of pulling him. "I had a commitment to his heart," he said.

His heroics in the 1964 World Series transformed Gibson into a major national celebrity, a status he was reluctant to embrace. Whereas before he could quietly keep to himself and meld into the background after performing in a ballgame, he wasn't afforded that opportunity now. Everyone wanted a piece of him and his reserved nature recoiled at all the unsolicited attention. "One of the worst things about being in the limelight is trying to go somewhere and enjoy yourself for just a little while without being bothered," he complained. "Your steak gets cold and your drink gets flat and you can't even go to the rest room without someone asking for an autograph." Keeping up with the deluge of interview requests was likewise taxing. "Writers," he once said. "Aw, I can take 'em or leave 'em. I've met some good ones, I've met some bad ones. Some of them think they can make or break you. Well, they can't make or break me unless they're pretty good fastball hitters. But most writers aren't that bad. There's always just one or two guys who'll try to stir up a little stuff." As tolerant as Gibson could be of these demands on his time, there were occasions when his impatience with members of the fourth estate and their intrusive questioning got the best of him. A case in point was the broken ankle injury he suffered in 1967. Tired of media inquiries pertaining to when his leg cast would come off and when he would be physically able to return to action, Gibson found a succinct, if unconventional way to address them without uttering a single sentence. He wore a homemade sign taped to the front of his shirt which read as follows:

*1-Yes, it's off!!! (the cast).*
*2-No, it doesn't hurt!*
*3-I'm not supposed to walk on it for one week!!*
*4-I don't know how much longer!*
*5-Ask Doc Bauman!*
*6-Ask Doc Middleman!*

While many reporters on the scene did not appreciate the sarcastic edge, Gibson professed not to care. "It wasn't in my nature to put on a happy face when I hadn't won a ballgame in over a month," he said.

Nor did he attempt to downplay issues of racial injustice that he and his fellow blacks were facing in American society in the 1960s. "In the past," he said, "not enough people were willing to voice their opinion. Now the young Negroes are concerned. They're not afraid to speak out. They have no jobs, no families to support, nothing to lose by speaking out. Their parents don't like what's going on, either, so now they're speaking out, following the kids. They've got to speak out." Still smarting from the memory of being told as a rookie that he could not stay at the same hotel as his white teammates when the Cardinals trained in Florida, Gibson demanded equal treatment and respect for himself and his family, even if that meant challenging the segregationist mores of the Jim Crow South. "One time we stopped at a filling station for gas," he recalled. "The attendant, a white Southern 'gentleman,' had no objection to selling me gasoline. But when I asked if my girls might use the ladies' room, he directed them to a room in the back of the station. The sign above the door said *Colored Only*. Angry and humiliated, I told him, 'Forget the gas,' and drove off." By 1967, landmark civil rights legislation had largely banned such overt discriminatory practices. But sadly, formidable barriers of economic and social inequality still persisted. Gibson knew this well. Although a certified World Series star and one of the premier pitchers in baseball, he had a hard time securing lucrative commercial product endorsements like pitching peers Don Drysdale, Whitey Ford, and an up-and-coming Tom Seaver. "I did an ad for one car agency," Gibson said. "That was it. I've got to assume it's because I'm a Negro. White players get their share of advertisements." White players also had their pick of housing without encountering the same kind of petty resistance Gibson and other black teammates did. As he observed, "A Negro buys a house in an otherwise all-white neighborhood. Instantly you hear the cry 'Here they come! Here come the Negroes!' What I want to know is, how are the Negroes going to come if the whites don't move out? It's stupid."

Likewise insipid was a headline-grabbing comment Dick Williams had made following Boston's scintillating Game 6 victory. The Red Sox manager, who should have known better, boasted to reporters he was expecting "Lonborg and Champagne" the next day. George Scott added more fuel to the fire by claiming Gibson wouldn't make it passed the fifth inning. "Gibson wasn't as tough in the fourth game as he was in the first," Scott said. "He figures to be even less effective now. Also, Gibson labors harder than Jim Lonborg does and figures to tire more easily at this point." That's all Gibson needed to hear. He never entered a contest expecting to lose, but now, thanks to Williams and Scott, he had all the extra motivation he needed. "My state of mind before the seventh game pretty much reflected the way the team felt," he said. "As long as I was with the Cardinals, I don't think we ever wanted to win a game as badly." It showed as he and his teammates readied themselves in front of a raucous Fenway Park gathering on Thursday, October 12. Resplendent in their red-trimmed road uniforms, which stood out against an overcast gray afternoon sky, the Cardinals had a determined air about them. Game 7 or no Game 7, they were still El Birdos, a unique fusion of talent, drive, and attitude that had few peers in the history of baseball. The Red Sox had been lucky to have made it this far, they felt. Now it was time to pull the plug on Boston's aptly named Impossible Dream. "It would have taken something monumental to stop us that day," Gibson later mused.

Jim Lonborg was far from monumental. Starting his second game in three days, Lonborg got roughed up for 7 runs on 10 hits in a 7–2 shellacking by the Cardinals. "Lonborg and Champagne, Hey!" the Cardinals chanted in their wild locker room celebration afterward. "They shouldn't have had all that jazz in the newspapers," Curt Flood said. "I've never seen anything like that in my life. Everybody had something to say. They could have finished fourth on the last day [of the regular season], they forget that." Mike Shannon agreed. "We didn't like it at all—them saying how they were going to win—things like 'We'll win in six or seven,' and 'We'll get Gibson in five,'" he said. "I know we wouldn't do it. We wouldn't say anything like that. To me, that's putting yourself out on a limb. And you better damn sure be able to back it up. They couldn't back it up." Even the usually circumspect Dal Maxvill couldn't resist taking a potshot. "Give this champagne to Lonborg," the Cardinals shortstop joked while brandishing an empty bottle of the bubbly at reporters. "I have respect for Lonborg. He's a pretty good pitcher, and he's got it right here in the belly, too. But Superman couldn't have beaten us today."

Gibson appeared as lethal as kryptonite to Red Sox batters. Though his fastball lacked its customary zip due to growing personal fatigue as the game wore on, Gibson still had enough left in the tank to ring up 10 strikeouts while allowing just three hits. He went the distance to record his third victory of the Series and second championship in four seasons. "It's nice to do so well in the Series, but I was honestly more excited about the 1964 Series," reflected Gibson, who also earned Series MVP honors. "The first time you're in a World Series, you think you have to win. But after you've been through it, you know that if you don't make it, you're not going to die." If Gibson seemed almost nonchalant about his standout performance, his batterymate wasn't. "Listen, Gibson's got some kind of vicious desire, hasn't he?" Tim McCarver exclaimed between mouthfuls of victory champagne. "Tenacious. That's what he is. Tenacious. He pitches on guts. You can see it. He challenges anybody. Hell, he'd challenge Michael the Archangel, if he had to." The Red Sox were equally impressed, even a now chastened George Scott. "He never lets up," the Boston first baseman said. "Never. He challenges you on every pitch. Everybody lets up once in a while, but not him. There are a lot of guys with talent but his attitude is unique. It's him and you, every pitch. It's like he's telling you, 'Here it is; if you can hit it, go ahead.' It's his best, all the time."

The contest started as a pitching duel. Lonborg gave up two harmless singles through the first two innings, while Gibson didn't allow a hit. But Lonborg appeared far from his usual commanding self, a fact Cardinals pitching coach Billy Muffett made note of when he closely monitored Lonborg's pregame warm-up tosses in the bullpen. "I don't think he's nearly as quick as the two other times he pitched," Muffett informed Red Schoendienst in the St. Louis dugout. Lonborg did not dispute this observation. "My arm was loose when I came to the ball park, but not really strong," he said. "I guess I was a little more tired than I thought I was. I know this: I made some bad pitches." One of them bounced off the center-field wall in the third when Dal Maxvill led off with a triple. He scored two outs later when Flood singled. "It was a low fastball and [Flood] just stuck out his bat and went with the pitch and stroked it to center field," Lonborg said. Flood advanced to third when George Scott couldn't make the play on a routine Maris grounder to his right that skipped through the Sox infield. "George usually handles that ball very well," the *Globe* said. Next batter Orlando Cepeda, who ended up hitting a disappointing .103 for the Series, didn't need a base hit to bring Flood home. Lonborg did it for him by bouncing a curve off home plate that got by Elston Howard, allowing Flood to score St. Louis's second run. "I knew I was struggling," Lonborg said. "That's the thing about pitching. The spirit is always willing, but the arm isn't at times. Today was one of those times." His teammates knew it from the first inning. "When you're looking over a man's shoulder all year you can tell right away when he's going to be good," Reggie Smith said. "Lonborg's at his best when he really has the mustard on his pitches. Today he didn't. His stuff wasn't sharp and he had to battle them with what he had."

Running out of gas: Lonborg in Game 7. PHOTO BY DENNIS BREARLEY/BOSTON RED SOX

The Sox were down only 2–0, but the score might as well have been 10–0 given how imposing Gibson looked. He fanned 7 of the first 12 batters he faced. "It wasn't that [Lonborg] was that bad," Howard said. "It was the other guy just wouldn't let us into the game. [Gibson] overpowered the Red Sox. He's big and he's strong." Gibson's strength was not limited to the pitching mound. He crushed a Lonborg slider over everything in center field when he came to bat with one out in the fifth. The homer represented the Redbirds third run of the game. "I can still see Lonborg's hanging slider," he recalled nearly three decades later. Lou Brock followed with a single and steals of second and third to tie an all-time postseason stolen base record with seven thefts. Roger Maris plated him with a sacrifice fly to make it 4–0. It was the eighth and final run that Brock would score in the Series to lead all hitters. "I felt looser on the bases than I had in a long, long time," he told *Sports Illustrated* afterward. "Not just in stealing, but freedom in running them. I found that with this looseness I could go four, four and a half, five steps off first base and get back to it on a pickoff throw fairly easily."

The Sox responded to the St. Louis outburst with a run in the bottom frame. Scott tripled and scored on a botched relay throw by Cardinal second baseman Julian Javier. But a "silence of foreboding," as the great baseball writer Roger Angell described it, had settled onto the proceedings. Sox fans were sensing, even with Lonborg pitching courageously if imperfectly, that the Series and season were slipping away. Clif Keane of the *Globe* captured the mood in his game story the following day. "The glass slipper that everyone thought belonged to Cinderella wound up on her step-sister's foot," he wrote. The Cardinals ensured this outcome in the sixth. Javier, making up for his earlier miscue, slammed a sidearm Lonborg curve into the left field screen for a three-run homer. "Dick [Williams] wanted to take me out before the home run," Lonborg said later. "But I wanted to pitch. I guess it's like the politician running for office time after time even though he knows he'll be beaten. He just thinks he'll eventually be successful. That's the way I felt. I knew I wasn't right, but you don't always have to be right to get batters out." Blinking aside tears, a physically and emotionally spent Lonborg departed the contest to a standing ovation that caught him off-guard. "I think it was the first time I realized that they are sensitive fans where a lot of places they could be animals, just hungering for the winning and the glory of winning," he commented. "But . . . they were sensitive and they were hurting with us." The timing of Lonborg's exit infuriated at least one member of the Boston coaching staff. Sal Maglie, who had clashed with Williams all season over communication and personality issues, believed the manager had messed up. "You just don't let a guy who pitched as Lonborg had get pounded like that," he said. "I should know. I had pitched. I had been a damn good pitcher." Williams swatted aside such criticism. "I didn't want Lonny to take a pounding, but tired or not, he's my best," he said. Unsurprisingly, Maglie was not invited back as pitching coach for the 1968 season.

There were still three innings left to play but Javier's home run blast had taken the heart and soul out of the Red Sox. The Sox did scratch out another run in the eighth but it was strictly perfunctory. "You try not to let it happen, but lopsided games affect a hitter's concentration. He's so eager to get those runs back that he starts swinging at bad balls," admitted Yastrzemski, who ended what had personally been a magnificent Series (a team-leading .400 average with three homers and five RBIs) with a meaningless single in the ninth. Concentration had not been a problem for Gibson. Still nursing a bad tooth and feeling completely exhausted, Gibson adamantly refused to hand the ball over to a reliever. He had started the game and he felt duty-bound to finish it. "Over the last four innings," McCarver maintained, "no one could have taken Gibson out of there. If they tried, he would have punched somebody." Schoendienst did gingerly broach the subject in a short mound visit in the ninth but Gibson waved him off. "I told him I wanted to stay and finish," Gibson said. "Red said he knew it and gave me a pat on the pack. The rest helped." Only when Gibson recorded the final out—a Scott strikeout—did he allow himself the luxury of smiling and relaxing. His jubilant teammates rushed to his side to congratulate him. "Helluva game, Hoot," McCarver said as he hugged him.

The on-field celebration soon moved to the visitors' clubhouse where Gibson and a number of other Cardinals held court with the media. "I couldn't have pitched another inning," Gibson revealed. "I had good stuff for six innings, then I had to go to breaking pitches, trying to trick them. I was laboring from the start of the game. I threw fastballs and sliders and I can't remember throwing a curve. Oh yeah, I do, I guess I threw two or three." Roger Maris, a veteran of five World Series with the Yankees, told reporters what a privilege it had been to play with Gibson a full season instead of against him. "Playing behind Gibson is like playing behind Whitey Ford," Maris said. "They're the same type of guys. You know they've got to win if you get them some runs." Maris had extra reason to celebrate given how many people both inside and outside the game had written him off as a has-been. In the postseason, he upped his average to .385 while driving in a Series-leading seven runs, most of them critical. "The Series finally returned Roger Maris to the company of gifted athletes he belongs with," wrote Shirley Povich of the *Washington Post*. "The Cardinals had an edge at several positions, but their edge in right field was the widest of all." Another key performer who had been playing with something to prove was also now basking in the championship glory. Although Orlando Cepeda's Series performance rated as a major bust (3 hits in 29 at-bats), his gargantuan contributions on and off the field during the regular season were not forgotten. "Orlando carried us all summer," McCarver stressed. "Don't forget that if he hadn't been great all year, we wouldn't be here now." McCarver's supportive words could have easily applied to Brock. He also had had a great year, but unlike Cha-Cha, he hit .414 to carry the Cardinal offense in the Series. "The Boston strangler turned out to be Louis Clark Brock," wrote Jim Murray. "His fingerprints are all over the Red Sox throat. He got 12 hits, stole 7 bases, hit a home run. The Red Sox strategy was to keep him off the bases, but the only guy who succeeded was the one who gave him the home run." Nevertheless, in Series MVP talk, Brock became an afterthought to Gibson or as he liked to say "the third man in a two man act." He didn't mind. "Look what he did," Brock later said. "He's a money pitcher. If you want one game and you want it worse than anything—in other words, if you want the last game of the World Series—you go to Gibbie before you go to anybody else. That's why he deserved that award."

The mood was understandably downcast in the Red Sox clubhouse. More than a few tears were being shed as Tom Yawkey moved from locker to locker trying to console his players. "I don't care whether it's a regular season game or a World Series game," the Red Sox owner said. "Any time you play, you want to win. When you don't, you're disappointed. But—we had a great year and I have a lot of wonderful memories." Elston Howard was touched by Yawkey's warm gesture. This was not something that would have happened on his old Yankee ballclubs, where losing was deemed unacceptable. "I'm sorry we couldn't have won it all for you," Howard told his boss. When Yawkey replied he hoped Howard would be back with the team the next season, the veteran catcher, who had been contemplating retirement, did not bat an eye. "I sure will," he said. "I promise you that."

Carl Yastrzemski, still absorbing the loss, tipped his hat to the opposition. "Gibson was great," he told a group of reporters huddled around his locker. "All the Cardinals were. It was a 25-man effort. I'm only sorry Lonborg didn't have one more day's rest. But this gives us something to shoot for next year. And it'll give the Cardinals something to think about. It won't surprise me if we do this all over again next October." Yastrzemski had delayed speaking to the media for 20 minutes while he and several distraught teammates, including Lonborg, holed up in the trainer's room, which was off limits to reporters. "We just wanted time to regain our composure," Lonborg said afterward. "There wasn't much to it. We swapped small talk and that was about it. Yaz and I are supposed to be on a TV show this week-end, so I told him, 'Now they won't want us.'" Rico Petrocelli tried to mask his own disappointment with praise for Gibson. "I'm glad there aren't too many Bob Gibsons around," he said. "The guy is just great. He wasn't as good today as he was in the first game, but he was still great. Anytime a pitcher can throw like that when he's tired, he has to be great." Petrocelli's manager, whose "Lonborg and Champagne" comment had done so much to rile the Cards, now did his best to sound equally gracious. "It was just a matter of Gibson being superior today," Dick Williams said. "When you're beaten by a club like the Cardinals, there's no reason to hang your head." Jim Lonborg had been hanging his head since being pulled from the game in the sixth inning, but he perked up when trying to summarize the eventful season just passed. "We've given a lot of people a lot of happiness, including ourselves," he said. He added that the full magnitude of what the Sox had accomplished would not personally register until the New England snows piled up over the coming winter months.

The Cardinals did not have to wait that long. Returning to St. Louis, the team was greeted as conquering heroes. Over 15,000 fans showed up at Lambert–St. Louis Municipal Airport when they deplaned from their chartered Boston flight. "If there are any lobsters left in Boston, Lou Brock will go back and get them," a beaming Red Schoendienst told the crowd. "He's stolen everything else in the town." Brock could only smile in amazement at all the adulation. "How did you get so many people out there?" he asked. Bob Gibson, at ease and enjoying the moment, was momentarily startled when a fan stepped forward to pump his hand. The interloper told him he had made "some money" off the pitcher's performance in the Series. "I won some money, too," Gibson responded. Earlier in the day, throngs of other enthusiastic fans shut down large sections of the downtown area to automobile traffic. "The celebration began as soon as [Gibson] struck out George Scott, the final Boston batter," the *St. Louis Post Dispatch* reported. "It went into the night. Tons of scrap paper, ticker tape, and torn telephone books were tossed from the windows, and the long awaited revelry started in the streets." The rowdy party atmosphere resulted in eight arrests, most of them for public drunkenness, and extensive property damage. Somehow it all seemed worth it to Cardinal fans. "They are the greatest, the absolute greatest," maintained one elated team supporter.

For Gibson, the long whirlwind of victory celebrations that followed did not end until the middle of November when he accepted a White House invitation to meet President Lyndon Johnson and attend an elegant state dinner in honor of Japanese Premier Sato Eisaku. While Johnson appeared aloof and distracted during the event, Gibson drew a more favorable impression of Vice President Hubert H. Humphrey. The genial Minnesotan was wearing a similar blue dress shirt to his under their tuxedos. "We're the only ones here who dress with any class," Humphrey joked. Gibson and his wife Charline spent the remainder of the evening dancing with Hollywood movie star Kirk Douglas and his wife before a live orchestra in the East Room. "It seemed like we closed the doors of the White House," he said. Gibson felt on top on the world. He was a two-time World Series champion, a national celebrity, and the greatest pitcher in baseball. Several more seasons of greatness still awaited him. But not everyone was eager to acknowledge his accomplishments. "I guess [the White House visit] will make you and your swollen head several times larger," a Florida man wrote Gibson not long afterward. "Why don't you and the other blackbirds on the Cardinals move to Africa where you belong? If you and the other darkies can't read this because of your low mentality, get one of the white players to do it." While the hateful message was clearly meant to provoke a negative emotional response, the proud and sensitive Gibson refused to take the bait. His indomitable character and the warm afterglow from his recently earned championship saw to that.

The Spirit of '67 lived on.

## Chapter Nine

# Twilight Years

Life would never be the same for Carl Yastrzemski. The 1967 AL MVP and Triple Crown winner earned a raft of additional awards and honors that off-season, including *Sports Illustrated*'s Sportsman of the Year. He became a national celebrity, appearing on the popular television variety show *Kraft Music Hall* with comedian Don Rickles and writer George Plimpton. He even had his own bread—*Big Yaz Bread*—stocked on supermarket shelves throughout New England. Such was the quality of the product that one teammate declared, "We should feed this to the Orioles. Then we'd win the fucking pennant!" All humor aside, fame exacted a steep price on Yastrzemski. "He crisscrossed the nation like an airline pilot from October to February, speaking, signing autographs, accepting awards, and doing everything but getting ready for the season to come," noted Al Hirshberg. The longtime Boston journalist had a point. Slacking off from the rigorous off-season workouts with fitness guru Gene Berde that had made him such an imposing physical force in 1967, Yaz appeared off his game in 1968.

His power numbers decreased and he had trouble coping with a nagging wrist injury. Only a late season hitting surge allowed him to top the .300 level, the lone player in the league to do so. It was enough to earn him his third and final AL batting crown in what became known as the Year of the Pitcher. "The pitchers overpowered the hitters," Yastrzemski said.

The 1968 Red Sox still had pop in their lineup. Rebounding from a dismal World Series performance in which he recorded only one base hit in 13 plate appearances, Ken Harrelson submitted the finest season of his baseball career. Driving in 109 runs on 35 homers to lead the majors, Harrelson became the *Sporting News* choice for AL Player of the Year. "He's done everything I've been unable to do," Yastrzemski said. Harrelson became an instant fan favorite as Bostonians admired not only the 13 game-winning home runs he smashed that season, but the charismatic way in which he carried himself on and off the field. "The Hawk Flies High" screamed the headline to one flattering magazine profile. "I had the world by the ears," Harrelson confessed. And unlike his days with Charlie Finley's Athletics, Harrelson had plenty of opportunities to earn extra cash outside the ballpark from lucrative commercial endorsement deals. "In Kansas City I had to duck guys trying to collect what I owed them," he said. "In Boston I had to take the phone off the hook to duck the guys trying to dump money into my lap."

Harrelson's outstanding performance was not enough to make Boston a repeat pennant winner. The team dropped to fourth place in the standings with an 86–76 record. "The magic was gone," Rico Petrocelli said. Everything that had gone right the previous season, now seemingly went sour, especially the pitching. Jim Lonborg, fresh off winning the Cy Young Award and notching two World Series victories, fell apart. He posted a 6–10 record with a 4.29 ERA in 113 innings of work. The decline was mostly attributable to injury. A couple of months after the 1967 season ended, Lonborg seriously injured his left knee while skiing down a slope in Vale, Colorado. "The bindings then were less sophisticated," he explained. "If it had been earlier in the day, and I were less tired, I could have gotten them to release. But it was late in the day, and, as I recall, the night before I hadn't gotten much sleep." Rumor had it he was trying to catch the eye of a famous Hollywood movie actress. "Some people said it was Jill St. John," Gerry Moses said. "I wasn't there, but if it had been Jill St. John, I would have been chasing her down the mountain too. I don't blame him." Moses might have been the only Red Sox to hold this view. "I just couldn't believe it," Yastrzemski fumed. "My next reaction was anger. I was ticked off. We won a pennant by one game with a 22-game winner—and now we had lost him. You don't know before a season that you're going to win, but dammit, you want to compete. And when I heard about it, I didn't think we could even compete. It hit me: *The season's gone.*" Lonborg had torn two knee ligaments that required surgery at a Boston hospital. When he finally made it back to the mound during the regular season, he encountered more trouble. "My knee was completely healed but I over-compensated for the injury and hurt my arm," Lonborg said. "I came back throwing too hard." The Red Sox were thin in the pitching department even before the injury. But what happened next completely derailed the team. Jose Santiago—the other pillar of the 1967 rotation—was coasting along with a 9–4 record and 2.25 ERA when he developed elbow problems. He went on the disabled list in July after 18 starts and never threw another pitch for the rest of the season. His big-league career was over two years later. "We were through," Dick Williams said.

The 1967 AL Manager of the Year would soon be through himself in Boston. Despite improving the team's record by one game in 1969 and moving up the standings to third place, Williams was given his walking papers at the end of the season. "It wasn't just a firing, it was more like a shooting," Williams said. The precipitating cause was his deteriorating relationship with Tom Yawkey. The Red Sox owner had maintained a cordial but distant relationship with Williams. Always a friend of the players, Yawkey was increasingly turned off by Williams's dictatorial approach in the clubhouse. "He said, 'Williams has a communication gap with the players,'" Williams later remarked. "I don't know, maybe I stepped on a few toes." One particularly sensitive set of toes belonged to Carl Yastrzemski. Williams fined him $500 for failing to hustle in a game against Oakland that August. Yaz became incensed. "I was already ticked off at the guy for the way he treated guys in his doghouse," he said. "The more I thought about it all, the madder I got." He burst into Williams's office after the game and challenged him to a fight. "All right, Dick. Let's go. You and me, right now! Come on!!" he yelled. Williams declined the invitation and calmly instructed his superstar to "cool off." Yastrzemski did as he was told, but not before firing a cup of beer he was holding in his hand against a nearby wall. Yawkey had seen enough and instructed Dick O'Connell, the team executive who had pushed the hardest for Williams's hiring, to sack the manager. Williams took the news remarkably well. O'Connell "was extremely apologetic about it, even though this was obviously not his decision" he recalled later. "So I couldn't get mad. Not at first. Maybe I was too stunned. Maybe it was because I didn't hear it from Yawkey, who had gone to his vacation place in South Carolina to avoid dirtying his hands."

The firing of Williams did little to improve the team's prospects. "The Red Sox continued to play better than .500 ball and draw fans, but from 1969 to 1971 they were no match for the minidynasty in Baltimore," Dan Shaughnessy writes. Indeed, the hard-hitting and pitching-rich Orioles of Frank Robinson, Boog Powell, and Jim Palmer crushed their opposition, averaging over 100 victories a season and winning three straight AL pennants. It wasn't until 1975 that a new core of young homegrown stars such as Jim Rice, Fred Lynn, Carlton Fisk, and Rick Burleson joined '67 holdovers Yastrzemski and Petrocelli in leading the Sox back to the World Series. To get there, they swept the defending three-time world champion Oakland Athletics in the AL Championship Series. "We were cooking," said pitcher Bill Lee, a 17-game winner.

As was the case in 1967, the Sox lost in seven games to a superior opponent. The Cincinnati Reds, winners of 108 regular season games, boasted a powerful lineup that included three future Baseball Hall of Famers: Johnny Bench, Tony Perez, and Joe Morgan. If not for his later gambling difficulties, third baseman Pete Rose would have represented the fourth team member to make it to Cooperstown. Even though they fell to the Big Red Machine, the Sox could take comfort in winning an electrifying come-from-behind victory in Game 6 on a homer by Fisk in the twelfth inning. "When anybody thinks about the 1975 World Series, they think about Game 6," Yastrzemski said. "A lot of times things get bigger the farther away you get from them, but when people say Game 6 was the greatest game ever played, I wouldn't argue. And I was there."

The future seemed bright for these Sox but the team was never able to return to championship form. "We had the best talent on the field," 1975 AL MVP and Rookie of the Year Fred Lynn told writer George Castle. "We might not have had it on the mound. That's where we lost the division championships. We averaged like 95 wins in four, five years that I was there. That's a lot of wins without winning anything." Poor team morale became another contributing factor. It was the dawning of the modern free agent era and several younger Sox, namely Lynn, Fisk, and Burleson, roiled the waters by holding out for more money. "Guys were worrying about their contracts, whether they were reaching incentives, why they weren't making as much as other guys," Yaz said. "You could hardly call it a baseball club anymore. It was more like a business." And Tom Yawkey, that most generous of owners when it came to paying his players, grew disillusioned. He had earlier told Dick O'Connell he was thinking of leaving the game. "I'm disturbed at what's going on [with player-management relations]," he said. Now this. He passed away from leukemia in July 1976. He was 73.

The team compiled a mixed record over the next two decades under the principal ownership of Yawkey's widow, former Manhattan fashion model Jean Remington Hollander. The Sox did make another memorable World Series appearance against the New York Mets in 1986. But they lost again, after blowing a substantial series lead and being "one strike away" from a championship in Game 6 at Shea Stadium. First baseman Bill Buckner wore the goat horns for this one as he booted an easy grounder in the bottom of the tenth inning allowing the winning New York run to score. The Mets took Game 7 the next day. "One fucking out," Sox manager John McNamera said. "That's all we needed was one fuckin' out." The stunning loss coupled with a litany of other historic Boston postseason collapses led many baseball fans to conclude the franchise was "cursed" for having sold Babe Ruth to the Yankees decades earlier. "The Red Sox truly are the boys of summer; it's always been the fall that's given them trouble," noted Dan Shaughnessy, who did more than anyone to popularize the "Curse of the Bambino" myth.

The Sox finally ended talk of supernatural hexes by sweeping the Cardinals in the 2004 World Series. "This is like an alternate reality," said new Boston owner John Henry, the publicity-shy billionaire who purchased the team from the Yawkey estate two years earlier. "All our fans waited their entire lives for this." It almost didn't happen. Down 0–3 in games to the Yankees in a best-of-seven ALCS, the Sox mounted "the Greatest Comeback in Sports History" by taking the next four contests. "We were our own team," said Johnny Damon, the club's All-Star center fielder and leader. "People kept talking about the Curse of the Bambino.

Well, shit, we weren't even around. Why do we feel this pressure? That's why I was like, 'We're a bunch of idiots, we don't care about any of the stuff that's happened before.' We knew then that our job was to win right now."

The Sox would win two more World Series (2007 and 2013) in the new century. But as scintillating and cherished as these victories are, they take a back seat to what was accomplished in 1967. After years of losing and organizational drift, the team suddenly became a big winner and, in the process, recaptured a disaffected fan base that had all but written them off. "The fans were proud of us," Gary Bell later said. Proud and supportive. Home attendance soared to a league-leading 1,727,832, eclipsing the previous season's mark by almost a million. A ticket to Fenway suddenly became a hot commodity and by 2015 almost three million fans were lining up for the privilege. "It was not always the way it is now; and it might never have been but '67," veteran Boston baseball writer Peter Gammons has concluded. Yaz agreed. "The whole attitude of the organization changed after that year," he said. "It even changed things all the way down to the minors. I remember when I was in the minors, you'd look up and see the big team was a loser and it affected you."

While the Impossible Dream Red Sox are rightly celebrated for their collective deeds, less examined is how they ultimately fared individually. After sitting out the 1968 season due to his damaged left eye, Tony Conigliaro made a spectacular return to the Sox lineup the next season, hitting 20 homers and driving in 82 runs. To the surprise of no one, Conigliaro was named the Comeback Player of the Year. "Talk about the Comeback Player of the Year Award. They ought to give him the Comeback of the Century Award," Reggie Smith said. But the feel-good story turned sour by the end of the 1970 season. That off-season Conigliaro was the centerpiece of a trade that sent him to the California Angels for reliever Ken Tatum and two lesser talents. Driving the transaction was internal clubhouse dissension. According to many reports, Conigliaro and Yastrzemski were feuding. Conigliaro lasted only 74 games with the Angels. He batted a weak .222. Forced to announce his retirement at 26, he cited his deteriorating vision as the main reason.

The years that followed were not especially kind to Conigliaro. Following an unsuccessful comeback attempt with the Red Sox in 1975, he bounced around at a few sports casting gigs until he appeared tantalizingly close to landing his dream job—broadcasting Sox games on a local Boston television station. Then tragedy struck again. In 1982 he was felled by a heart attack that left him permanently disabled. Death finally claimed him in 1990, prompting many fans and former teammates to ponder what might have been. "Tony C was going to Cooperstown the night he was hit [by Jack Hamilton's pitch], and he wasn't going to have any need to buy a ticket when he got there, if you know what I mean," veteran Boston sports columnist Bob Ryan wrote.

The fates also had a special surprise in store for Conigliaro's popular successor in right field. Despite having a career year in 1968, Ken Harrelson received word at the start of the next season he had been traded to Cleveland for two pitchers and a backup catcher. Harrelson didn't take the news well and considered quitting rather than report to the Indians. But with the careful prodding of new baseball commissioner Bowie Kuhn ("The loss of Ken Harrelson would be a tragedy for baseball," he said) and a fat new contract offer, the Georgia native changed his mind and signed on with Cleveland. Although his offensive numbers tailed off some, Harrelson still managed to finish with 30 homers and 92 RBIs in 1969. He seemed destined for many more productive seasons but lingering arm and leg injuries and a general distaste for playing in Cleveland led him to formally retire in 1971. Harrelson returned to baseball and Boston as a popular color man for Red Sox TV broadcasts in the late 1970s following a failed attempt to become a professional golfer. He greatly enjoyed his second time around in Boston. "It's my town and these are my people," he said. But his "people" could not save him when he publicly criticized team management in 1981. He was summarily let go and landed on his feet in Chicago where he has broadcast White Sox games for most of the last 35 years, excepting brief stints as team general manager and as a Yankees announcer. Through all the ups and downs, Harrelson never lost sight of his deep appreciation for the game. As he once told *Sports Illustrated*, "Everybody knows I'm a fan."

Dick Williams did not remain unemployed for long. In 1971 he became manager of the Oakland A's, major league baseball's version of *The Bad News Bears*. Consisting of young emerging stars such as Reggie Jackson, Jim "Catfish" Hunter, Rollie Fingers, Sal Bando, Vida Blue, Joe Rudi, and Gene Tenace, the team acquired a well-deserved reputation for drinking to excess, partying to all hours, and brawling. They were loaded with talent but they had finished a disappointing second in the AL West the previous two years under the new divisional format. What they needed was the kind of discipline and single-minded devotion to winning that had put the Red Sox over the top in 1967. Williams provided that and more. Under his intense leadership, the A's won three straight divisional titles and back-to-back World Series championships in 1972–1973. "We happened to become what may be baseball's last true dynasty," Williams later said. "We also became baseball's last team that didn't hate having Dick Williams as manager." After a public falling out with meddling Oakland owner Charlie Finley, Williams left the A's and helmed clubs in Anaheim, Montreal, Seattle, and San Diego, where he won his last pennant in 1998. As much as Williams is known for being the only manager to win league championships for three different franchises, he is best remembered for ending Boston's long pennant drought in 1967. "The players probably thought I was crazy as a loon," Williams said. "But hell, I had a one-year contract. So if I were crazy, I was going to be crazy all year and give it the best I had." Williams passed away in 2011 from an aneurysm.

Rico Petrocelli set the American League record for homers by a shortstop (40) in 1969. He also hit a career-high .297 and drove in 97 runs. "What a year—everything went right, every ball I hit," he said. "I hit pitches that were good pitchers' pitches, low and away, up and in. It was amazing—I wasn't doing anything different; it all just seemed to come together for that year." Petrocelli remained a productive fixture in the Red Sox infield well into the next decade. Ever the team player, he agreed to move over to third base when the Sox acquired Hall of Fame shortstop Luis Aparicio in 1971. Petrocelli started in all seven games of the 1975 World Series and batted a robust .308 against Cincinnati pitching. It turned out to be his swan song. The lingering aftereffects from a beaning and a slow bat forced the Red Sox to release him during spring training camp in 1977. In the years since, Petrocelli has maintained close ties to the ball club, serving as a radio and television broadcaster, minor league manager, and director of sports programs for the Jimmy Fund, a team affiliated charity that supports children's cancer research and treatment efforts. "My dreams from when I was a kid actually came true," he said.

Elston Howard did return behind the plate for one final season with Boston in 1968. He played in only 71 games and hit .241. His lack of playing time stemmed from a major falling out he had with Dick Williams in August. In a game against Baltimore, Howard inadvertently allowed Baltimore baserunner Don Buford to steal second base when he argued a called ball with the plate umpire. "That's the first time in my life I've ever done that," Howard said. Williams was unsympathetic. He immediately put Howard in his personal doghouse, where he would languish for the rest of the year. It was a sad epilogue to what had been a meritorious 14-year career. But Howard refused to complain. "My father taught me a long time ago in St. Louis to respect authority," he said. "Whatever I think, I keep to myself. I just don't understand why things are the way they are." Howard returned to New York as a Yankees coach, but his long-term ambition to become a major league manager was never realized. Howard was passed over repeatedly for dugout jobs due to MLB's long-established resistance to hiring African Americans for such positions. "There is no reason he couldn't have been a manager," his friend and ex-Cardinal Bill White said. "He was quiet, not an extremist in any way. He did his job, didn't rattle cages. His private life was exemplary. Lots of times when they talked about blacks as managers, they'd find something off the field to rip apart. Elston had the perfect marriage and the perfect family. No reason he couldn't have been chosen as a manager." Howard died from a cardiac arrest at 51 in 1980.

Jim Lonborg struggled to regain his 1967 Cy Young pitching form after his skiing accident. He posted losing records in 1968 and 1969 and had to be sent down to the minors for a time. "I began to feel sorry for myself," Lonborg said. The team's patience finally ran out in 1972. In a multiplayer deal with the Milwaukee Brewers, the Red Sox sent Lonborg along with George Scott and Ken Brett to Milwaukee for All-Star base-stealing outfielder Tommy Harper and pitcher Marty Pattin. Lonborg had the lowest ERA (2.83) of his 15-year career and won 14 games for a last place Brewers club. He was traded to the Philadelphia Phillies the next season and picked up where he left off in Milwaukee. Although he never attained elite status again, Lonborg won 17 games in 1974 and started two National League Championship Series games in 1976 and 1977. He slipped to 8–10 in 1978 and was released by the team the following season. Returning to Boston, Lonborg went to Tufts University Dental School for three years and upon graduation opened a successful practice in the suburbs. The game and the Red Sox were never far from his thoughts. "I don't know if there is a better way to live a life in America than to be a professional athlete, especially a baseball player," he said.

George "Boomer" Scott flourished in Milwaukee. His best season was 1975 when he led the AL in homers (36) and RBIs (109). He also added a fifth straight Gold Glove to his growing personal collection. In 1976 Scott was traded back to the Red Sox for Cecil Cooper, ironically the man who had replaced him in Boston. "I sat in Milwaukee the last five years, watching the Red Sox come in, and trying to figure out how to get back with them," he said. "I'm happier right now than I've ever been in my whole baseball career." His happiness was short-lived. After hitting 33 homers and driving in 95 runs in 1977, an aging Scott saw his hitting numbers drop through the floor the next two seasons. In 1979 the Sox traded him to the Kansas City Royals, who then flipped him to the Yankees. But he was never able to recapture his old batting stroke. He was out of the majors the following year. He fell upon hard financial times in retirement and was forced to sell two of his prized Gold Gloves. Scott passed away at 69 in 2013. Despite his later setbacks, Scott always kept a warm spot in his heart for Boston. "I still love the Red Sox," he told an interviewer in 2012. "When they play great, I feel great. When they play bad, I feel bad."

Carl Yastrzemski was never able to replicate his magical 1967 performance. Boos greeted him everywhere at Fenway Park and forced him to stuff cotton in his ears to shut out the noise. "I knew they'd hold it against me for not having another year like '67," he said. The public razzing stopped in the mid-1970s when Rice, Lynn, and Fisk arrived to dislodge

Yaz appeared in another World Series in 1975 but dropped a seven-game heartbreaker to Cincinnati. BASEBALL HALL OF FAME PHOTO ARCHIVE

him as the team's main star. Yastrzemski didn't mind. In fact, he loved the idea of no longer having to carry the team on his broad shoulders. The pressure was off and he could just kick back and enjoy the game and his teammates. "I couldn't believe the change in the guy," George Scott said. "Used to be you couldn't say anything to him. Then I saw him giving hotfoots, throwing water around, instigating. Usually, this wouldn't mean shit to me—but it was Yaz doing it, a guy who'd rather ignore everybody in here. He was saying he cared about the team." With his body banged up by assorted injuries and his batting reflexes slowed by age, Yastrzemski retired at 44 at the conclusion of the 1983 season. It was not a difficult decision. "My intensity left me," he confessed. Yastrzemski gained induction to the Hall of Fame in 1989 and has since spent his retirement fishing and closely following the career of his grandson Mike Yastrzemski, a Vanderbilt University product and outfielder in the Orioles minor league system. "It means a lot," Yaz said. So does the memory of his prodigious accomplishments in 1967.

The Cardinals continued to function like a well-oiled machine. In 1968 they won their third NL pennant of the decade with a 97–65 record. The final gap between them and San Francisco—their closest challenger—was nine games. But this time around the team's offense—so potent a force in 1967—went into tailspin. Lou Brock, Roger Maris, Tim McCarver, and Orlando Cepeda had subpar seasons, especially Cepeda. The reigning league MVP hit 77 points below his previous season's average. "What no one seemed to know was that 1968 would be the year of the pitcher, a season quite unlike any other in recent memory," Cepeda said. Indeed, batting averages fell to modern historic lows across the board, prompting baseball's ruling powers that be to compensate by lowering the pitcher's mound and decreasing the size of the umpire's strike zone the following season. They "started screwing with the game on the premise that the only way to fix it . . . was to manipulate conditions in a way that could offer new hope to hitters," Bob Gibson said.

Gibson offered precious little hope to hitters in 1968. He went 22–9 with 263 strikeouts and 13 shutouts. Even more impressive was the historically low ERA he posted. In 304 innings, he averaged a miniscule 1.12 earned runs per game. "As a player, I was always concerned with consistency and consistency is what I had in 1968," Gibson said. "I can't remember having a bad start—I just seemed to do everything right. It seemed that every pitch was knee high on the corner. It was a once-in-a-lifetime year and a season I cherish." So dominant was Gibson that teammate Mike Shannon joked about being reduced to a bored spectator when

Gibson pitched. "I hardly paid any attention at all unless there was a man on first base and less than two outs," the third baseman said. "Otherwise, all I did was catch the ball from the catcher after strikeouts." With Gibson leading the way, the Cardinal pitching staff recorded a league-leading 2.49 ERA that more than compensated for the club's offensive drop off. "We had a great team," Cepeda said. "No one could deny that." What also couldn't be denied was the soaring popular interest Gibson engendered. Simply put, St. Louis fans could not get enough of the 1968 NL MVP and Cy Young Award Winner. "I'd frankly never considered myself a gate attraction," Gibson admitted. But the team averaged 2,500 more fans on the days he took the mound. "The additional ticket receipts alone would have covered my salary for the season," he said.

Gibson saved his best performance for Game 1 of the 1968 World Series. He set a new single-game postseason strikeout record by fanning 17 Detroit Tigers in a 4–0 St. Louis triumph. "It made for memorable watching—not just the last three batters [Gibson] whiffed in the ninth but a whole lineup of fine hitters utterly dominated and destroyed by the man on the mound," book author Roger Angell wrote. "Gibson worked so fast that I was constantly falling behind the actual ball-and-strike count. His concentration was total. Not once, it seemed, did he look at his outfielders, tug at his cap, twitch his sleeve; he didn't even rub up the new ball after a foul. The instant he got his sign, he rocked, flailed, threw, staggered, put up his glove for the catcher's throw back, and was ready again." Gibson would notch another victory in Game 4, a 10–1 thrashing of Detroit in which Gibson whiffed 10 more Tigers. But all the strikeouts were taking a toll on his already overworked arm. "His stuff was terrible," Tim McCarver confessed to Peter Golenbock. "When you crank it up that many times over a seven-month period, you wear down. There was no question he was hurting during the Series." Still, confidence remained high when Gibson received the starting assignment for Game 7 after the Tigers rallied from a 3–1 Series deficit. He had been in a similar situation against the Red Sox the previous fall and dominated. And there was no reason to think he couldn't do the same again.

Gibson looked strong through six innings in a scoreless pitching duel with Detroit's Mickey Lolich. He allowed only one Tiger to reach base. But in the top of the seventh inning, Gibson gave up three runs on four hits, including a two-run smash to center by Jim Northrup that the usually reliable Curt Flood misplayed into a triple. Gibson didn't make any excuses. "What is often forgotten about that play is the fact that Northrup hit the damn ball four hundred feet," he said. Gibson remained in the game and allowed an additional Tiger run to score in the ninth. His St. Louis teammates rallied for a score in the bottom half of the inning but Lolich held on for a Series clinching 4–1 Tigers victory. "We had back-to-back world championships within our reach, and it slipped through our fingers," Nelson Briles said afterward.

As crushing as the loss was, Cardinal prospects moving forward appeared excellent. The only major contributor not coming back was the retiring Roger Maris. Other than that, the club retained a solid veteran core that looked to win several more championships. Gussie Busch reached a different conclusion, however. After the Cardinals slumped to fourth place in 1969, their famously impatient owner decided to break up the team. "St. Louis was never an organization that stayed put a long time—if you look at their history," Briles explained. "So that wasn't anything out of the ordinary." Orlando Cepeda had already been sent packing to Atlanta in March when he showed up at spring training out of shape. "I'm thirty-one," Cepeda told a reporter. "Maybe they figure I'm over the hill." Other Cardinal stars such as Briles, Flood, McCarver, and Steve Carlton were also traded in the coming seasons. "Management was messing in a major way with a club that had run away with two straight pennants," Gibson complained. Yet one of his former teammates was not willing to go quietly.

Curt Flood had accomplished much during his Hall of Fame worthy playing career (.293 batting average with six Gold Gloves and 1,861 hits in 15 seasons), but what he was about to do would rock the legal and financial foundations of baseball. After being traded to the Philadelphia Phillies along with Tim McCarver for slugger Dick Allen and second baseman Cookie Rojas, Flood refused to report on legal and moral grounds. He formally asked baseball commissioner Bowie Kuhn to declare him a free agent. "After twelve years in the Major Leagues, I do not feel that I am a piece of property to be bought and sold irrespective of my wishes," he solemnly informed Kuhn in a December 24, 1969, letter. "I believe that any system which produces that result violates my basic rights as a citizen and is inconsistent with the laws of the United States and of several other states." He went on to say that even though the Phillies tendered him a contract offer, he had the right to entertain offers from other teams. "I, therefore, request that you make known to all Major League Clubs my feelings in this matter, and advise them of my availability for the 1970 season," he concluded.

In taking this bold stance, Flood was challenging the way the game had been conducting business for almost a century. Under the reigning reserve clause system, players were contractually bound to the ball club that had initially signed them for perpetuity or until said ball club decided to trade them to another team or grant them their outright unconditional release. Kuhn rejected Flood's free agency request in a tersely worded December 30 response letter. "I certainly agree with you that you, as a human being, are not a piece of property to be bought and sold," Kuhn wrote. "This is fundamental in our society and I think obvious. However, I cannot see its application to the situation at hand." Undaunted, Flood sued on the grounds Major League Baseball was acting like a business monopoly and therefore in violation of federal antitrust laws. "I think the owners are underestimating me," Flood said. But he was under no illusions. "He knew what a million-to-one-shot this was, winning this case. Because if he lost, then he'd never play again," said Major League Players Association Executive Director Marvin Miller, whose organization provided Flood with key legal and financial assistance. The case eventually reached the US Supreme Court, where in a 5–3 decision the high court upheld the sport's reserve clause system. Flood fell short, but his legal challenge emboldened other players to take on the baseball establishment in the coming years. By 1975, the reserve clause was finally overturned by an independent arbitrator named Peter Seitz. He ruled the owners had no right or power to retain a player's services "beyond the 'renewal year' in the contracts which those players had heretofore signed with their clubs." The modern free agency era had begun. For Flood's trailblazing efforts, noted conservative columnist and baseball fan George Will dubbed him "Dred Scott in Spikes." "The national pastime is clearly better because of [Flood's cause]," Will wrote. "But more important, so is the nation because it has learned one more lesson about the foolishness of fearing freedom."

As Flood was establishing his historic legacy, the Cardinals were on their way down as a franchise. The team compiled an underwhelming 800–813 record in the 1970s, despite the presence of All-Star performers such as Joe Torre, Rick Wise, Dick Allen, and Ted Simmons. The problem was chemistry. The "El Birdos" years had never been about amassing individual honors. They were about putting the team first in pursuit of championships. Torre, Wise, Allen, and Simmons couldn't replicate that winning formula. "I loved the Cardinals, was proud to be one, and recognized that Curt Flood and Tim McCarver [and their selfless attitudes] were two of the biggest reasons why," Gibson later explained. "With them gone, being a Cardinal would never mean quite the same thing." The club bottomed out in 1978 with a 69–93 record, the lowest winning percentage (.426) for a Cardinals team since 1924.

It was not until the hiring of future Hall of Fame manager Dorrel "Whitey" Herzog by an aging Gussie Busch two years later that the team climbed back into contention. It marked one of the last important baseball decisions Busch ever made. He died from pneumonia following a brief hospitalization at age 90 in 1989. Herzog harnessed the diverse talents of Ozzie Smith, Keith Hernandez, Joaquin Andujar, and Bruce Sutter to build a team around pitching, tight defense, and line-drive hitting. The latter had been mandated by the installation of artificial turf in Busch Stadium in the 1970s, which deemphasized the importance of the long ball in favor of speed on the base pads. Critics "seemed to think there was something wrong with the way we played baseball," Herzog wrote in his autobiography *White Rat: A Life in Baseball*. "They called it 'Whitey-ball' and said it couldn't last." The naysayers turned out to be dead wrong. The Cardinals won three NL pennants in the 1980s, including a World Series upset victory over the power-laden Milwaukee Brewers in 1982. "We just came in there, well, what are we going to do against these guys?" Smith said. "But we proved that David and Goliath theory, you find a way to make it happen." The team raised two more World Series banners (2006 and 2011) under new team owner William O. DeWitt Jr., putting them in elite company with 11 titles. Only the

Yankees as a franchise have won more championships. The closest a NL team has come to this record of accomplishment are the Giants with a combined eight titles from their days in New York and San Francisco. Yet the memories of "El Birdos" endure. "It was a very intelligent, talented group of people," Tim McCarver later said. "What gets lost in the discussion of how good of baseball players they were is the overall success they achieved after they finished playing."

McCarver knew this from personal experience. Following his trade to the Phillies, McCarver played several more seasons, primarily as a backup. Upon his retirement in 1979, he accepted a job broadcasting Phillies games. Such was his talent behind the mike that he was tapped to become a network color commentator and called his first World Series in 1985. "I was nervous, very nervous," he said of the experience. "From a player's standpoint you think you know about 85 percent of the game.

Historic game changer—Curt Flood at bat. BASEBALL HALL OF FAME PHOTO ARCHIVE

Then you go upstairs and find out you're wrong about that." McCarver would broadcast a record 23 other World Series, but he was not averse to taking on other assignments. In 1992, he was one of the prime time co-anchors of the Winter Olympics in Albertville, Canada. Always a witty raconteur and keen observer of human foibles, McCarver also hosted his own talk show, which is still syndicated nationwide in several large television markets. Yet, McCarver never strayed too far away from his first love—baseball. Stepping down from his network duties in 2013, he became a part-time announcer for the Cardinals. "My experience has been made richer by running into all these smart people, and the thrill and the memories I have of the World Series and the big moments is what I've taken away from the game," McCarver said.

Unlike most of his 1967 teammates, Lou Brock finished out his career in a St. Louis uniform. Following the Cards' heartbreaking loss in the 1968 World Series—in which he hit a dazzling .464 with two homers, seven stolen bases, and five RBIs—Brock's importance to the team only increased. He became the face of the franchise, just as Stan Musial had been in the 1940s and 1950s. "When you start out playing, you can't see that far," confessed Brock, who amassed 3,023 hits and 938 stolen bases during his illustrious 19-year career. Brock set the all-time season stolen base record (later broken by Ricky Henderson) in 1974 with 117 steals. "The amazing thing about Brock is that he did it when he was 35 years old," Bob Gibson said. The old mark of 104 held by Maury Mills was passed in a September home game before a crowd yelling "Lou! Lou! Lou!" Play had to be temporarily halted for a special on-field ceremony in which former Negro League star James "Cool Papa" Bell, no slouch himself on the base paths, handed Brock the record-setting bag. "If I didn't, you'd steal it anyway," Bell said. In 2015, a now frail Brock experienced the biggest challenge of his life. Owing to an infection brought on by Type-2 diabetes, the 76-year-old Hall of Famer had to have surgery to amputate his lower right leg. Demonstrating the kind of resilience and determination that made him baseball's premier stolen base king, Brock made rapid progress during his physical rehabilitation and could walk again with the aid of a fitted prosthetic leg. He also threw out the first pitch for the 2016 Cardinals home opener. "Somebody said—I don't know who it was—they said, 'Finally Lou, after all these years, you hit the cutoff man,'" Brock said. More gratifying was the emotional reception Brock received from Bob Gibson and other Cardinal veterans who were on hand to provide moral support. "That was special," Brock said.

Although he enjoyed three productive seasons in Atlanta, Orlando Cepeda was never enamored with his new home. Much of Atlanta's white community still adhered to the old Jim Crow attitudes, despite the significant advances made during the civil rights era. "They called [my son] a nigger, a Puerto Rican monkey," Cepeda said. "He had never heard these words before. I had to explain what they meant what they meant when they called him nigger. It was not easy. Atlanta was not my favorite city. The Blacks, Latins, and white players did not get along so hot when I was playing for the Braves." In 1973, Cepeda signed on as a free agent with the Red Sox to become the team's first designated hitter—an innovative change the American League had introduced to generate more offense in games. "I've always wanted to play in Boston since Ted Williams was my idol," Cepeda told reporters. "Now I have my chance." While he had lost appreciable pop in his bat since his glory days with the Cardinals and Giants, Cepeda still managed to drive in 86 runs and hit 20 homers in 142 games. His oft-injured knees made him a liability on the base paths, however, and the Sox gave him his unconditional release the next season. Cepeda hooked on briefly with the Kansas City Royals before opting to retire with a career .297 average and 379 home runs. These numbers normally would have made him an easy lock for the Hall of Fame. But in 1975 Cepeda was arrested and convicted on marijuana possession charges in Puerto Rico. He served 10 months of a 5-year prison sentence behind bars before finally being paroled. But he was dropped from serious consideration for Cooperstown in the process. "I made a huge mistake," Cepeda later said. "Bad judgment. Bad friends. Stupidity." By 1999, though, the Hall's Veterans Committee had come around to the opinion that Cepeda's overall body of work merited induction. "They saw me play, and they know what I did in the field," the Baby Bull said.

There were no similar happy endings for Curt Flood. After losing his high-profile Supreme Court case against baseball, Flood fled the country and became a bar owner on the Spanish island of Majorca in the

Mediterranean Sea. He claimed to be happy. "My ulcer has healed," he said. "I smoke only one pack of cigarettes a day instead of three. I'm a whole person again, you dig?" But this outward bravado was all for show. Flood was undergoing financial difficulties and drinking heavily. He also reportedly spent some time in a mental hospital. Flood eventually returned to the states, but finding personal peace was illusive. He went through a series of unfulfilling jobs and struggled to achieve sobriety. "There was nothing fair about what happened," Tim McCarver observed. "It was hideous that Curt had to go through what all he went through." For his part, Flood expressed no regrets. "People try to make a Greek tragedy out of my life and they can't do it," he said. "I have never felt I gave up too much. All the things I got from [challenging baseball], they're all intangibles. They're all inside me. Yes, I sacrificed a lot—the money, maybe even the Hall of Fame—and you weigh that against all the things that are really and truly important that are deep inside you, and I think I succeeded." Flood died from throat cancer at 59 in 1997.

Red Schoendienst remained Cardinals manager until he was dismissed at the end of the 1976 season. Just two years before, *Los Angeles Times* sports writer Bill Christine had described Schoendienst as having one of the safest jobs in baseball. "The day Schoendienst gets fired by the Cardinals," Christine wrote, "the Gateway Arch will keel into the Mississippi . . . and Gussie Busch will endorse scotch." But two consecutive mediocre finishes convinced the St. Louis brass that a change in the dugout was needed. "This move was discussed carefully within our organization, and the decision was based on the recommendations of several people, including the general manager," Busch said in a released statement. Schoendienst was disappointed but took solace from the fact he was leaving as the longest serving Cardinals manager in club history—12 full seasons with two NL pennants and a World Series championship. "I thought I did a good job," Schoendienst said. The former second baseman moved on to the Oakland A's where he coached a couple of seasons before returning to St. Louis as a hitting instructor. He was glad to get away from A's owner Charlie Finley. "People say Gussie Busch was a very hand-on owner, getting involved in a lot of decisions that he should have left to his baseball people," Schoendienst recalled. "Compared to Finley, Gussie was a saint." In 1989 he received a phone call at his Florida condo telling him of his induction into the Hall of Fame. "I was standing up," Schoendienst said. "Then I had to sit down." He was still attending Cardinals spring training camp at the ripe old age of 93 in 2016. "I'm just hanging around," he told a reporter. After 70 years of service to baseball, most of them with the Cardinals, Schoendienst had certainly earned that right.

Roger Maris got to own and operate the beer distributorship Gussie Busch had promised him. Although a novice, he quickly learned the ropes of the business, which was located in Gainesville, Florida. "I'm usually out of the house at eight-thirty in the morning and sometimes don't get home until one in the morning," Maris said. The experience was satisfying. Maris claimed he preferred it to his days swinging a bat for a living. "I couldn't get away from [the game] fast enough," Maris said. Still, he never failed to keep in touch with old teammates or attend baseball events. He was on hand in Atlanta in 1973 when Braves slugger Henry Aaron was closing in on Babe Ruth's all-time career home run record of 714. "I thought the pressure on Roger [to break Ruth's single season homer mark] was tougher on Roger than the pressure on me," said Aaron, who received multiple death threats in his pursuit of Ruth. "He had to get his 61 homers in a set time. I felt it was a matter of my staying healthy. If I couldn't do it that year, there was always next year." Diagnosed with lymphoma cancer in 1983, Maris spent the remaining two years of his life battling the disease. He finally succumbed at 51. "Other than my health problems, I feel very good about my life," he said shortly before his death.

Nelson Briles still had a lot of baseball left in his right arm after the Cardinals unwisely traded him to Pittsburgh in 1971. He went 8–4 as a spot starter and reliever with the Pirates that regular season. But he made an even bigger splash in the World Series against the defending champion Baltimore Orioles. In the pivotal fifth game, Briles threw a complete game, two-hit shutout. "It was 1967 all over again," he said afterward. His new Pittsburgh teammates appreciated his cool professionalism and ability to respond under pressure. "The postseason experience he brought to us was tremendous," said pitcher Steve Blass. Briles posted consecutive 14-win seasons over the next two seasons and he also earned headlines for his budding side career as a nightclub singer. "I have always enjoyed show business," he confessed. "I knew I had a pleasant voice and I thought I could do something with it." Briles became a popular Pirates television broadcaster following his retirement in 1978 and later moved into the team's front office as a director of corporate sales. "He was the perfect ambassador for the club," said a fellow employee. Briles was fatally struck down by a heart attack while competing in a team golf tournament in 2005. He was 61.

Bob Gibson remained a dominant and feared presence on the mound for several more seasons. He notched back-to-back 20-game seasons in 1969 and 1970 and consistently gave up less than three runs a game. "He works just as hard as he ever did," Red Schoendienst said. "The only difference in him now is that he's not able to come quite as hard on every pitch near the end." Gibson also maintained an aloof attitude toward individuals not wearing a Cardinals uniform. "He hated everyone," claimed Dodgers pitcher Don Sutton. "He even hated Santa Claus." Gibson did not argue the point. "I don't warm up very easily to a lot of people," he said. "Why? Why should I? . . . All a person has to do is say one or two wrong words to me and he's on my a---- list and I won't spend any more time with him because I'm wasting my time." Gibson's hard-bitten competitiveness began to wane as he headed into the sunset of his 17-year career. "I'm 36 now and not quite as bad as I used to be," he confessed. "Success hasn't changed me. It's just that I'm older. You don't fight quite as much as when you're younger. It's easier to live with things now." He retired after the 1975 season with a lifetime 251–174 record. "An athlete reaches a point where the physical and mental stresses begin to work against him," he explained. Gibson remained active in the game as a network television broadcaster and as a major league pitching coach with the Braves and Mets. But the true climax of his celebrated life and work occurred in 1981 when he stepped up to the podium in Cooperstown to deliver his induction speech into the Hall of Fame. "Sometimes I wasn't too good," Gibson said, "but nobody could ever accuse me of cheating them out of what they paid to see."

None of the other Red Sox or Cardinals who competed against or alongside Gibson during that memorable 1967 season would have disagreed.

# Selected Bibliography

The following books, interviews, and materials provided major sources of information for *The Spirit of '67*.

## Books


Aaron, Hank, with Lonnie Wheeler. *If I Had a Hammer: The Hank Aaron Story*. New York: HarperPaperbacks, 1991.

Abdul-Jabbar, Kareem, and Peter Knobler. *Giant Steps: The Autobiography of Kareem Abdul-Jabbar*. Toronto: Bantam Books, 1983.

Abrams, Roger I. *The First World Series and the Baseball Fanatics of 1903*. Boston: Northeastern University Press, 2003.

Ali, Muhammad, with Richard Durham. *The Greatest: My Own Story*. New York: Random House, 1975.

Anderson, Dave. *Pennant Races: Baseball at Its Best*. New York: Doubleday, 1994.

Anderson, Ron. *Long Taters: A Baseball Biography of George "Boomer" Scott*. Jefferson, NC: McFarland, 2012.

Andrews, William L., ed. *From Fugitive Slave to Free Man: The Autobiography of William Wells Brown*. Columbia: University of Missouri Press, 2003.

Angell, Roger. *The Summer Game*. New York: Popular Library, 1972.

Appel, Marty. *Pinstripe Empire: The New York Yankees from Before the Babe to After the Boss*. New York: Bloomsbury, 2012.

Armour, Mark. *Joe Cronin: A Life in Baseball*. Lincoln: University of Nebraska Press, 2010.

Ballou, Bill. *Behind the Green Monster: Red Sox Myths, Legends and Lore*. Chicago: Triumph Books, 2009.

Belth, Alex. *Stepping Up: The Story of Curt Flood and His Fight for Baseball Players' Rights*. New York: Persea Books, 2006.

Berry, Henry. *Boston Red Sox*. New York: Routledge, 1975.

Bradlee, Ben, Jr. *The Kid: The Immortal Life of Ted Williams*. New York: Little, Brown, 2013.

Brennan, Charles. *Amazing St. Louis: 250 Years of Great Tales and Curiosities*. St. Louis, MO: Reedy Press, 2013.

Breslin, Jimmy. *Branch Rickey: A Life*. New York: Penguin Books, 2011.
Brock, Lou, and Franz Schulze. *Stealing Is My Game*. Englewood Cliffs, NJ: Prentice-Hall, 1976.
Brown, William Wells. "The American Slave-Trade." In *The Liberty Bell, by Friends of Freedom*, Boston, MA, 1848.
Brokaw, Tom. *Boom!: Voices of the Sixties—Personal Reflections on the 60s and Today*. New York: Random House, 2007.
Brooks, Victor D. *Boomers: The Cold-War Generation Grows Up*. Chicago: Ivan R. Dee, 2009.
Browne, Ian. *Idiots Revisited: Catching Up with the Red Sox Who Won the 2004 World Series*. Thomaston, ME: Tilbury House Publishers, 2014.
Bryant, Howard. *Shut Out: A Story of Race and Baseball in Boston*. New York: Routledge, 2002.
Buck, Jack, with Rob Rains and Bob Broeg. *Jack Buck: "That's a Winner!"* New York: Sports Publishing, 2014.
Buckley, Steve. *Boston Red Sox: Where Have You Gone?* Champaign, IL: Sports Publishing, 2005.
Califano, Joseph A., Jr. *The Triumph and Tragedy of Lyndon Johnson: The White House Years*. New York: Simon and Schuster, 1991.
Cantor, George. *The Tigers of '68: Baseball's Last Real Champions*. Dallas, TX: Taylor Publishing, 1997.
Carew, Rodney, with Ira Berkow. *Carew*. New York: Simon and Schuster, 1979.
Cataneo, David. *Peanuts and Crackerjack: A Treasury of Baseball Legends and Lore*. San Diego, CA: Harcourt Brace & Company, 1991.
———. *Tony C: The Triumph and Tragedy of Tony Conigliaro*. Nashville, TN: Rutledge Hill Press, 1997.
Cepeda, Orlando, with Herb Fagen. *Baby Bull: From Hardball to Hard Time and Back*. Dallas, TX: Taylor Publishing, 1998.
Clavin, Tom, and Danny Peary. *Roger Maris: Baseball's Reluctant Hero*. New York: Touchstone, 2010.
Cohen, Robert W. *The 50 Greatest Players in St. Louis Cardinals History*. Lanham, MD: Taylor Trade Publishing, 2013.
Coleman, Ken, and Dan Valenti. *The 1967 Red Sox: The Impossible Dream Remembered*. Lexington, MA: Stephen Greene Press, 1987.
Conigliaro, Tony, with Jack Zanger. *Seeing It Through: The Story of a Comeback*. New York: Macmillan, 1970.
Creamer, Robert. *Babe: The Legend Comes to Life*. New York: Simon and Schuster, 1992.
Deane, Bill. *Baseball Legends: Bob Gibson*. New York: Chelsea House, 1994.
Delaplaine, Andrew, ed. *The Delaplaine Bob Gibson: His Essential Quotations*. New York: Gramercy Park Press, 2016.
Devine, Bing, with Tom Wheatley. *The Memoirs of Bing Devine: Stealing Lou Brock and Other Moves by a Master GM*. Champaign, IL: Sports Publishing, 2004.
Dewey, Donald, and Nicholas Acocella. *The Ball Clubs: Every Franchise, Past and Present, Officially Recognized by Major League Baseball*. New York: HarperCollins, 1996.

DiMaggio, Dom, with Bill Gilbert. *Real Grass, Real Heroes: Baseball's Historic 1941 Season*. New York: Zebra Books, 1990.
Durocher, Leo, with Ed Linn. *Nice Guys Finish Last*. New York: Simon and Schuster, 1975.
Editors of Esquire. *Smiling Through the Apocalypse: Esquire's History of the Sixties*. New York: Crown, 1987.
Eig, Jonathan. *Opening Day: The Story of Jackie Robinson's First Season*. New York: Simon and Schuster, 2007.
Einstein, Charles, ed. *The Fireside Book of Baseball*. New York: Simon and Schuster, 1956.
Eskenazi, Gerald. Lip: *A Biography of Leo Durocher*. New York: William Morrow, 1993.
Feldmann, Doug. *El Birdos: The 1967 and 1968 St. Louis Cardinals*. Jefferson, NC: McFarland, 2007.
———. *Gibson's Last Stand: The Rise, Fall, and Near Misses of the St. Louis Cardinals, 1969–1975*. Columbia, MO: University of Missouri Press, 2011.
Fetter, Henry D. *Taking on the Yankees: Winning and Losing in the Business of Baseball, 1903–2003*. New York: W.W. Norton, 2005.
Flood, Curt, with Richard Carter. *The Way It Is*. New York: Trident Press, 1971.
Ford, Whitey, with Phil Pepe. *Slick: My Life In and Around Baseball*. New York: William Morrow, 1987.
Frommer, Harvey. *Where Have All Our Red Sox Gone?* Lanham, MD: Taylor Trade Publishing, 2006.
Gibson, Bob, and Reggie Jackson. *Sixty Feet, Six Inches: A Hall of Fame Pitcher and A Hall of Fame Hitter Talk about How the Game Is Played*. New York: Doubleday, 2009.
Gibson, Bob, with Phil Pepe. *From Ghetto to Glory: The Story of Bob Gibson*. New York: Popular Library, 1968.
Gibson, Bob, with Lonnie Wheeler. *Stranger to the Game: The Autobiography of Bob Gibson*. New York: Viking, 1994.
Gillette, Gary, and Eric Enders, with Stuart Shea and Matthew Silverman. *Big League Ballparks: The Complete Illustrated History*. New York: Metro Books, 2009.
Golenbock, Peter. *Dynasty: The New York Yankees, 1949–1964*. Chicago: Contemporary Books, 2000.
———. *Fenway: An Unexpurgated History of the Boston Red Sox*. New York: G.P. Putnam's Sons, 1992.
———. *The Spirit of St. Louis: A History of the St. Louis Cardinals and Browns*. New York: itbooks, 2000.
Goodwin, Doris Kearns. *Lyndon Johnson and the American Dream*. New York: St. Martin's Griffin, 1976.
Green, G. Michael, and Roger D. Launius. *Charlie Finley: The Outrageous Story of Baseball's Showman*. New York: Walker & Company, 2010.
Gutlon, Jerry M. *It Was Never About the Babe: The Red Sox, Racism, Mismanagement, and the Curse of the Bambino*. New York: Skyhorse Publishing, 2009.
Halberstam, David. *October 1964*. New York: Villard Books, 1994.

———. *Summer of '49*. New York: William Morrow, 1989.
Harrelson, Ken, with Al Hirshberg. *Hawk*. New York: Viking Press, 1969.
Harris, Mark. *Pictures of a Revolution: Five Months and the Birth of the New Hollywood.* New York: Penguin Press, 2008.
Harwood, Richard, and Haynes Johnson. *Lyndon*. New York: Praeger, 1973.
Heidenry, John. *The Gashouse Gang: How Dizzy Dean, Leo Durocher, Branch Rickey, Pepper Martin, and Their Colorful Come-from-Behind Ball Club Won the World Series—and America's Heart—During the Great Depression*. New York: Public Affairs, 2007.
Heidenry, John, and Brett Topel. *The Boys Who Were Left Behind: The 1944 World Series between the Hapless St. Louis Brows and the Legendary St. Louis Cardinals*. Lincoln: University of Nebraska Press, 2006.
Herman, Bruce. *St. Louis Cardinals Yesterday and Today*. Lincolnwood, IL: West Side Publishing, 2008.
Hirsch, James S. *Willie Mays: The Life, The Legend.* New York: Scribner, 2010.
Hirshberg, Al. *What's the Matter with the Red Sox?* New York: Dodd, Mead, 1973.
Holland, Gini. *A Cultural History Through the Decades: The 1960s*. San Diego, CA: Lucent Books, 1999.
Hollander, Phyllis, and Zander Hollander, eds. *The Masked Marvels: Baseball's Great Catchers*. New York: Random House, 1982.
Honig, Donald. *Baseball Between the Lines: Baseball in the '40s and '50s as Told by the Men Who Played It*. New York: Coward, McCann and Geogheagan, 1976.
———. *Baseball When the Grass Was Real: Baseball from the Twenties to the Forties Told by the Men Who Played It*. Lincoln: University of Nebraska Press, 1975.
———. *The Boston Red Sox: An Illustrated History*. New York: Prentice-Hall, 1990.
———. *The Man in the Dugout: Fifteen Big League Managers Speak Their Mind.* Chicago: Follett Publishing, 1977.
———. *The October Heroes: Great World Series Games Remembered by the Men Who Played Them*. Lincoln: University of Nebraska Press, 1979.
———. *The St. Louis Cardinals: An Illustrated History.* New York: Prentice-Hall, 1991.
Houk, Ralph, and Robert W. Creamer. *Season of Glory: The Amazing Saga of the 1961 New York Yankees*. New York: G.P. Putnam's Sons, 1988.
Howard, Arlene. *Elston and Me: The Story of the First Black Yankee*. Columbia: University of Missouri Press, 2001.
Jackson, Robert. *"Let's Go, Yaz": The Story of Carl Yastrzemski*. New York: Henry Z. Walck, 1968.
Johnson, Dick, and Glenn Stout. *Ted Williams: A Portrait in Words and Pictures*. New York: Walker and Company, 1991.
Johnson, Lyndon Baines. *The Vantage Point: Perspectives of the Presidency 1963–1969*. New York: Holt, Rinehart and Winston, 1971.
Kahn, Roger. *The Boys of Summer*. New York: Harper Perennial, 1998.
———. *The Head Game: Baseball Seen from the Pitcher's Mound*. Orlando, FL: Harcourt, 2000.
———. *Rickey and Robinson: The True, Untold Story of the Integration of Baseball.* New York: Rodale, 2014.
———. *A Season in the Sun*. New York: Harper and Row, 1977.

Kashatus, William C. *Jackie and Campy: The Untold Story of Their Rocky Relationship and the Breaking of Baseball's Color Line.* Lincoln: University of Nebraska Press, 2014.

Klima, John. *Bushville Wins! The Wild Saga of the 1957 Milwaukee Braves and the Screwballs, Sluggers, and Beer Swiggers Who Canned the New York Yankees and Changed Baseball.* New York: Thomas Dunne Books, 2012.

———. *The Game Must Go On: Hank Greenberg, Pete Gray, and the Great Days of Baseball on the Home Front in WWII.* New York: Thomas Dunne Books, 2015.

Kronenwetter, Michael. *America in the 1960s.* San Diego: Lucent Books, 1998.

Kubek, Tony, and Terry Pluto. *Sixty-One: The Team, The Record, The Men.* New York: Macmillan, 1986.

Kuenster, John, ed. *The Best of Baseball Digest.* Chicago: Ivan R. Dee, 2006.

Lautier, Jack. *Fenway Voices: From Smoky Joe to Rocket Roger.* Camden, ME: Yankee Books, 1990.

Lee, Bill, with Dick Lally. *The Wrong Stuff.* New York: Viking Press, 1984.

Leonard, Candy. *Beatleness: How the Beatles and Their Fans Remade the World.* New York: Arcade Publishing, 2014.

Lieb, Frederick G. *The Boston Red Sox.* Carbondale: Southern Illinois University Press, 2003.

———. *The St. Louis Cardinals: The Story of a Great Baseball Club.* New York: G.P. Putnam's Sons, 1944.

Linn, Ed. *The Great Rivalry: The Yankees and the Red Sox 1901–1990.* New York: Ticknor and Fields, 1991.

———. *Hitter: The Life and Turmoils of Ted Williams.* San Diego, CA: Harcourt Brace and Company, 1993.

Liss, Howard. *The Boston Red Sox: The Complete History.* New York: Simon and Schuster, 1982.

Lowenfish, Lee. *Branch Rickey: Baseball's Ferocious Gentleman.* Lincoln: University of Nebraska Press, 2007.

Lowry, Philip J. *Green Cathedrals: The Ultimate Celebration of Major League and Negro League Ballparks.* New York: Walker and Company, 2006.

Lyle, Sparky, and Peter Golenbock. *The Bronx Zoo.* New York: Crown, 1979.

Madden, Bill. *1954: The Year Willie Mays and the First Generation of Black Superstars Changed Major League Baseball.* New York: Da Capo Press, 2014.

———. *Pride of October: What It Was to Be Young and a Yankee.* New York: Warner Books, 2003.

Mailer, Norman. *The Armies of the Night.* New York: Plume, 1967.

Mantle, Mickey. *All My Octobers: My Memories of 12 World Series When the Yankees Ruled Baseball.* New York: HarperCollins, 1994.

———. *The Quality of Courage.* Garden City, NY: Doubleday, 1964.

Mantle, Mickey, with Herb Gluck. *The Mick.* New York: Doubleday, 1985.

Markusen, Bruce. *The Orlando Cepeda Story.* Houston, TX: Pinata Books, 2001.

———. *The Team That Changed Baseball: Roberto Clemente and the 1971 Pittsburgh Pirates.* Yardley: Westholme, 2006.

McCarver, Tim, with Danny Peary. *Tim McCarver's Baseball for Brain Surgeons and Other Fans.* New York: Villard, 1998.

McCarver, Tim, with Ray Robinson. *Oh, Baby, I Love It! Baseball Summers, Hot Pennant Races, Grand Salamis, Jellylegs, El Swervos, Dingers and Dunkers, Etc, Etc, Etc.* New York: Villard Books, 1987.
McMane, Fred, with Stuart Shea. *The 3,000 Hit Club: Stories of Baseball's Greatest Hitters.* New York: Skyhorse Publishing, 2012.
McSweeny, Bill. *The Impossible Dream: The Story of the Miracle Boston Red Sox.* New York: Coward-McCann, 1968.
Meany, Tom. *Baseball's Greatest Players.* New York: Grosset & Dunlap, 1953.
Michelson, Herbert. *Charlie O: Charles Oscar Finley vs. the Baseball Establishment.* Indianapolis, IN: Bobbs-Merrill Company, 1975.
Miller, Jeff. *Down the Wire: The Thrilling Inside Story of the Greatest Pennant Chase Ever—The 1967 American League Race.* Dallas, TX: Taylor Publishing, 1992.
Miller, Marvin. *A Whole Different Ballgame: The Sport and Business of Baseball.* Secaucus, NJ: Carol Publishing Group, 1991.
Montville, Leigh. *The Big Bam: The Life and Times of Babe Ruth.* New York: Broadway Books, 2006.
———. *Ted Williams: The Biography of an American Hero.* New York: Doubleday, 2004.
Mullen, Maureen. *"Yogi Was Up with a Guy on Third . . .": Hall of Famers Recall Their Favorite Baseball Games Ever.* Chicago: Triumph Books, 2009.
Neyer, Rob. *Rob Neyer's Big Book of Baseball Legends: The Truth, the Lies and Everything Else.* New York: Fireside, 2008.
Norman, Philip. *Shout!: The Beatles in Their Generation.* New York: Warner Books, 1981.
Norwood, Kimberly Jade, ed. *Ferguson's Fault Lines: The Race Quake That Rocked a Nation.* Chicago: American Bar Association, 2016.
Nowlin, Bill. *Mr. Red Sox: The Johnny Pesky Story.* Cambridge, MA: Rounder Books, 2004.
———, ed. *Pumpsie and Progress: The Red Sox, Race and Redemption.* Burlington, MA: Rounder Books, 2010.
Nowlin, Bill, and Dan Desrochers, eds. *The 1967 Impossible Dream Red Sox: "Pandemonium on the Field."* Burlington, MA: Rounder Books, 2007.
Nowlin, Bill, and Jim Prime. *The Boston Red Sox World Series Encyclopedia.* Burlington, MA: Rounder Books, 2008.
Okrent, Daniel, and Harris Lewine. *The Ultimate Baseball Book.* Boston: Houghton Mifflin, 1988.
Okrent, Daniel, and Steve Wulf. *Baseball Anecdotes.* New York: Harper & Row, 1989.
Pearlstein, Rick. *Nixonland: The Rise of a President and the Fracturing of America.* New York: Scribner, 2008.
Peary, Danny. Ed. *We Played the Game: Memories of Baseball's Greatest Era by Brooks Robinson, Tim McCarver, Harmon Killebrew, Don Newcombe, Lew Burdette, Jim "Mudcat" Grant, Johnny Antonelli, Ralph Kiner, Bob Turley, Vic Power, and Fifty-five More Legends of the Majors.* New York: Black Dog & Leventhal Publishers, 1994.
Peterson, Richard, ed. *The St. Louis Baseball Reader.* Columbia: University of Missouri Press, 2006.
Petrocelli, Rico, and Chaz Scoggins. *Rico Petrocelli's Tales from the Impossible Dream Red Sox.* Champaign, IL: Sports Publishing, 2007.

Pluto, Terry. *Our Tribe: A Baseball Memoir*. New York: Simon and Schuster, 1999.
Prime, Jim, and Bill Nowlin. *More Tales from the Red Sox Dugout: Yarns from the Sox*. Champaign, IL: Sports Publishing LLC, 2002.
Pritchard, David, and Alan Lysaght. *The Beatles: An Oral History*. New York: Hyperion, 1998.
Reedy, George. *Lyndon Johnson Johnson: A Memoir*. New York: Andrews and McMeel, 1982.
Reichler, Joe. *Baseball's Great Moments*. New York: Crown, 1974.
———, ed. *The Game and the Glory*. Englewood Cliffs, NJ: Prentice-Hall, 1976.
Remnick, David. *King of the World: Muhammad Ali and the Rise of an American Hero*. New York: Random House, 1998.
Ritter, Lawrence S. *The Glory of Their Times: The Story of the Early Days of Baseball Told by the Men Who Played It*. New York: HarperPerennial, 1992.
Roberts, Randy, ed. *The Rock, The Curse and The Hub: A Random History of Boston Sports*. Cambridge, MA: Harvard University Press, 2005.
Robinson, Jackie, as told to Alfred Duckett. *I Never Have It Made: An Autobiography*. Hopewell, NJ: Ecco Press, 1995.
Robinson, Ray, ed. *Baseball Stars of 1969*. New York: Pyramid Books, 1969.
Rosenfeld, Harvey. *Roger Maris: A Title to Fame*. Fargo, ND: Prairie House, 1991.
———. *Still a Legend: The Story of Roger Maris*. Lincoln, NE: iUniverse, 2002.
Ross, Alan. *The Red Sox Century: Voices and Memories from Fenway Park*. Nashville, TN: Cumberland House Publishing, 2004.
Rossi, John P. *The National Game: Baseball and American Culture*. Chicago: Ivan R. Dee, 2000.
Rubin, Robert. *Tony Conigliaro: Up from Despair*. New York: G.P. Putnam's Sons, 1971.
Rust, Art, Jr. *"Get That Nigger Off the Field!": A Sparkling, Informal History of the Black Man in Baseball*. New York: Delacorte Press, 1976.
Rygelski, James, and Robert L. Tiemann. *10 Rings: Stories of St. Louis Cardinals World Championships*. St. Louis, MO: Reedy Press, 2011.
Scheinin, Richard. *Field of Screams: The Dark Underside of America's National Pastime*. New York: W.W. Norton, 1994.
Schoendienst, Red, with Rob Rains. *Red: A Baseball Life*. Champaign, IL: Sports Publishing, 1998.
Shaughnessy, Dan. *The Curse of the Bambino*. New York: Dutton, 1990.
———. *Reversing the Curse: Inside the 2004 Boston Red Sox*. Boston: Houghton Mifflin Harcourt, 2005.
Sinibaldi, Raymond. *1967 Red Sox: The Impossible Ream Season*. Charleston, SC: Arcadia Publishing, 2014.
Smiley, Tavis, with David Ritz. *Death of a King: The Real Story of Dr. Martin Luther King's Jr.'s Final Year*. Boston: Back Bay Books, 2014.
Smith, Curt. *America's Dizzy Dean*. St. Louis, MO: Bethany Press, 1978.
Smith, John Matthew. *The Sons of Westwood: John Wooden, UCLA, and the Dynasty That Changed College Basketball*. Urbana: University of Illinois Press, 2013.
Sneddon, Rob. *The Phantom Punch: The Story Behind Boxing's Most Controversial Bout*. Camden, ME: Down East Books, 2016.

Snyder, John. *Cardinals Journal: Year by Year and Day by Day with the St. Louis Cardinals since 1882*. Cincinnati, OH: Clerisy Press, 2010.
———. *Red Sox Journal: Year by Year and Day by Day with the Boston Red Sox since 1901*. Cincinnati, OH: Emmis Books, 2006.
Stewart, Wayne. *Stan the Man: The Life and Times of Stan Musial*. Chicago: Triumph Books, 2014.
Stahl, John Harry, and Bill Nowlin. *Drama and Pride in the Gateway City: The 1964 St. Louis Cardinals*. Lincoln: University of Nebraska Press, 2013.
Stout, Glenn, ed. *Impossible Dreams: A Red Sox Collection*. Boston: Houghton Mifflin, 2003.
Stout, Glen, and Richard A. Johnson. *The Cubs: The Complete Story of Chicago Cubs Baseball*. Boston: Houghton Mifflin, 2007.
———. *The Dodgers: 120 Years of Dodgers Baseball*. Boston: Houghton Mifflin, 2004.
———. *Red Sox Century: 100 Hundred Years of Red Sox Baseball*. Boston: Houghton Mifflin, 2000.
———. *Yankees Century: 100 Years of New York Yankees Baseball*. Boston: Houghton Mifflin, 2002.
Sullivan, George. *The Picture History of the Boston Red Sox*. New York: Bobbs-Merrill Company, 1980.
Swandson, Krister. *Baseball's Power Shift: How the Players Union, the Fans, and the Media Changed American Sports Culture*. Lincoln: University of Nebraska Press, 2016.
Tan, Cecilia, and Bill Nowlin. *The 50 Greatest Red Sox Games*. Hoboken, NJ: Wiley, 2006.
Testa, Judith. *Sal Maglie: Baseball's Demon Barber*. DeKalb: Northern Illinois University Press, 2007.
Thomas, Joan M. *Baseball's First Lady: Helen Hathaway Robison Britton and the St. Louis Cardinals*. St. Louis, MO: Reedy Press, 2010.
Turner, Steve. *Beatles '66: The Revolutionary Year*. New York: Ecco Press, 2016.
Tygiel, Jules. *Baseball's Great Experiment: Jackie Robinson and His Legacy*. New York: Vintage Books, 1983.
———. *The Jackie Robinson Reader: Perspectives On an American Hero*. New York: Dutton, 1997.
Veeck, Bill, and Ed Linn. *Veeck-As in Wreck: The Autobiography of Bill Veeck*. New York: Bantam Books, 1962.]
Vescey, George. *Baseball: A History of America's Favorite Game*. New York: Modern Library, 2008.
———. *Stan Musial: An American Life*. New York: Ballantine Books and ESPN Books, 2011.
Vincent, Fay. *It's What Inside the Lines That Counts: Baseball Stars of the 1970s and 1980s Talk About the Game They Loved*. New York: Simon and Schuster, 2010.
Walton, Ed. *This Date in Red Sox History: A Day by Day Listing of Events in the History of the Boston American League Baseball Team*. New York: A Scarborough Book, 1978.
Ward, Geoffrey C., and Ken Burns. *Baseball: An Illustrated History*. New York: Alfred A. Knopf, 1994.

Wendell, Tim. *Summer of '68: The Season That Changed Baseball—and America—Forever.* Boston: Da Capo Press, 2012.

Westcott, Rich. *Diamond Greats: Profiles and Interviews with 65 of Baseball's History Makers.* Westport, CT: Meckir Books, 1988.

Whalen, Thomas J. *Dynasty's End: Bill Russell and the 1968–69 World Champion Boston Celtics.* Boston: Northeastern University Press, 2004.

———. *When the Red Sox Ruled: Baseball's First Dynasty, 1912–1918.* Chicago: Ivan R. Dee, 2011.

White, Bill, with Gordon Dillow. *Uppity: My Untold Story about the Games People Play.* New York: Grand Central Publishing, 2011.

Williams, Dick, and Bill Plaschke. *No More Mr. Nice Guy: A Life of Hardball.* San Diego, CA: Harcourt Brace Jovanovich Publisher, 1990.

Williams, Ted, with John Underwood. *My Turn at Bat: The Story of My Life.* New York: Simon and Schuster, 1988.

Yastrzemski, Carl. *Yaz.* New York: Rugged Land, 2007.

Yastrzemski, Carl, and Gerald Eskenazi. *Yaz: Baseball, The Wall and Me.* New York: Doubleday, 1990.

Yastrzemski, Carl, with Al Hirshberg. *Yaz.* New York: Viking Press, 1968.

## Baseball Hall of Fame Player and Inductee Clipping Files

Nelson Briles
Lou Brock
Orlando Cepeda
Tony Conigliaro
Curt Flood
Bob Gibson
Ken "Hawk" Harrelson
Elston Howard
Jim Lonborg
Roger Maris
Tim McCarver
Rico Petrocelli
Red Schoendienst
George Scott
Dick Williams
Carl Yastrzemski
Tom Yawkey

## Newspapers and Periodicals

*Beverly Times*
*Black Sports*
*Boston Daily Record*
*Boston Globe*
*Boston Herald*
*Boston Herald-American*
*Boston Herald-Traveler*
*Boston Post*
*Boston Record-American*
*Boston Red Sox Official Programs and Scorecards*
*Cardinals Gameday Magazine*
*Chicago Tribune*
*Christian Science Monitor*
*Collier's*
*Inside Sports*
*Life*
*Look*
*Milwaukee Journal*
*The National Pastime*
*The National Sports Daily*
*Newsday*
*Newsweek*
*New Yorker*

*New York Daily News*
*New York Times*
*Parade*
*Philadelphia Evening Bulletin*
*Pittsburgh Post–Gazette*
*Pittsburgh Press*
*Pro Sports*
*Reach Baseball Guide*
*Salem Evening News*
*San Francisco Chronicle*
*San Francisco Examiner*
*Saturday Evening Post*
*The Sporting News*
*Sport*
*Sports All Stars: Baseball 1962*
*Sports Illustrated*
*Sports Today*
*St. Louis Globe-Democrat*
*St. Louis Post-Dispatch*
*USA Today*

## Websites

www.baseball-almanac.com
www.baseball-reference.com
www.baseballhall.org
www.bostonbaseballhistory.com
www.deadspin.com
www.espn.com
www.usgennet.org
www.hardballtimes.com
www.thisgreatgame.com
www.sabr.org
www.salon.com
www.sfgate.com
www.stltoday.com
sports.yahoo.com

## Interviews

Gary Bell
Steve Buckley
Jim Lonborg
Tim McCarver
William McSweeny
Rico Petrocelli
Gary Waslewski

**Author's Note:** Portions of this book have been repurposed from my earlier works: *Dynasty's End: Bill Russell and the 1968–69 World Champion Boston Celtics* (Boston: Northeastern University Press, 2004), *When the Red Sox Ruled: Baseball's First Dynasty 1912–1918* (Chicago: Ivan R. Dee, 2011), and *JFK and His Enemies: A Portrait of Power* (Lanham, MD: Rowman & Littlefield, 2014). I have also chosen to use material from autobiographical sources in first-person quotation form.

# Index

Note: Page numbers for figures are italicized.